MAKE YOUR **WORKPLACE**
GREAT

MAKE YOUR WORKPLACE GREAT

THE 7 KEYS TO AN EMOTIONALLY INTELLIGENT ORGANIZATION

STEVEN J. STEIN, PH.D.

BICENTENNIAL
1807
WILEY
2007
BICENTENNIAL

John Wiley & Sons Canada, Ltd.

National Library of Canada Cataloguing in Publication Data
Stein, Steven J., 1950-
    Make your workplace great : the 7 keys to an emotionally intelligent organization / Steven J. Stein.

Includes index.
ISBN-13: 978-0-470-83830-3

    1. Psychology, Industrial. 2. Emotional intelligence.
3. Success in business — Psychological aspects. 4. Personnel management. I. Title.

HD31.S84 2006   158.7   C2006-906371-0

Production Credits
Cover design: Mike Chan
Interior text design: Tegan Wallace
Wiley Bicentennial Logo: Richard J. Pacifico
Printer: Friesens

John Wiley & Sons Canada, Ltd.
6045 Freemont Blvd.
Mississauga, Ontario
L5R 4J3

Printed in Canada

1 2 3 4 5 FP 11 10 09 08 07

This book is dedicated to the memory of my father,

Morris Abraham Stein,

and my brother,

Dr. Howard B. Stein.

CONTENTS

Part Two: What to Measure and How to Fix It   **81**

ACKNOWLEDGMENTS

Getting a book like this out on time requires the help and coordination of a number of people. First I want to thank everyone at MHS because they make it possible for me to spend time on projects like this.

Specific people who were involved in data collection, item refinement, data analysis, and many other aspects of development of the BOEI included Dr. Gill Sitarenios, Dr. Peter Papadogiannis, Tammy Kostecki-Dillon, Dr. Rich Handley, and Deena Logan. Others involved in the project included Melany Eli, Maria-Luisa Randazzo, Tania Georgescu, Jeanette Bartosik, Karen Lyncook, Gail Ogden, Dr. Jodi Schwartz, Rick Walrond, Noel Demello, and Alex Pinski.

A special thanks to Wendy Wilson who not only contributed to the development of the BOEI but reviewed this manuscript and pointed out many ways to improve it. Cheryl McClelland, HR Director at MHS, reviewed portions of this book from an HR person's perspective to ensure that as a psychologist I didn't get too far removed from the realities of human resources. My assistant, Francesca Dipasquale, helped manage events around me so I could get the writing done. Also thanks to my daughter, Lauren Stein, who read through chapters proofreading for grammatical errors.

I want to thank Don Loney at Wiley for encouraging me to write this book and gently reminding me to finish it. Nicole Langlois helped with all the detailed editing ensuring consistency along the way. Also, thanks to the great team at Wiley for the support both before and after the finished product.

Finally, thanks to my wife and partner, Rodeen, for living through all the trials and tribulations of my need to make deadlines.

Introduction

Dramatic changes have been underway in workplaces throughout the world, yet few companies have fully grasped their significance and implications. This book focuses on the new workforce that drives organizations and provides you—the executive, manager, or team leader—with a new definition of the high-performing workplace. I use data based on our company's—Multi-Health System's—surveys and assessments of thousands of employees and leaders from a variety of organizations located in different parts of the world.

My goal is to guide today's and tomorrow's leaders in leveraging these factors not only to make workplaces more productive, but to make them a source of pride and joy in the lives of the people who work there. Too often our workplaces are stress factories with huge and unnecessary losses of productivity. We need to stop and look at how important work is in people's lives. By paying more attention to the emotional aspects of the workplace, we can make the work experience much more meaningful. The organizations that get this right are the ones that will compete successfully in the global workplace.

Through a combination of our own cutting-edge research, independent studies and reports, opinions of various leaders and experts, and my own personal experiences, I have identified seven key factors that will help create the successful organization. I present examples of how these key factors can be implemented in the workplace. You don't have to be a senior manager to initiate the implementation of many of these initiatives. In fact, most senior managers are distracted by other issues and may not have the time and resources to be aware of, let alone initiate, these kinds of human resource changes. If you can get support from your senior manager (by lending her or him this book, or others like it), then you can get the process started in your workplace. What's important is that everyone can gain from constructive changes.

I started working on this topic area after a personal experience with a business associate some years ago. My day job is CEO of an innovative, fast-growing test publishing company. We have approximately one hundred people working in our organization. We often welcome visitors from various organizations around the world who come to see our facility. Two things are noticed by practically everyone who comes to visit our offices. First, visitors rarely leave our offices without commenting on the photographs that decorate the walls of our building (photos that I've taken on my various travels). Second, something is always said about how friendly, enthusiastic, and helpful our people are.

Following one of these visits I drove our guest, who was president of a large U.S.–based publishing company, to the airport. We had just completed negotiating a significant distribution agreement that had taken more than two years to close. Over this time period, he had carefully reviewed our company from a number of different perspectives.

"Your people seem to be really enthused," he remarked, as I crawled along with the rest of the rush-hour traffic.

"Yes, we have really good people," I said, almost reflexively. Having heard this comment so often, it almost seemed routine. Somehow I had the naïve view that working people in all companies were happy, friendly and loved to talk to visitors about what they do. At the time I hadn't yet visited many other organizations. My response was really no more than making casual conversation.

"So, are you getting some kind of government funding or grant?" he asked.

Suddenly, he got my attention. "What do you mean?"

"Well, you have so many cultural minorities; it looks like they're from all different countries. You must have some government program to support that?" he continued.

A bit shocked, and taken by surprise, as I've never really thought of our staff as culturally unique, I replied, "No, for every position we hire the best person we can find. We test everyone before they're hired."

For the first time I started to think that maybe we were different from many other companies. We always believed that people were our most important asset, but so does everybody else. Could there actually be something that differentiated our organization from many others? From then on I thought it would be a good idea to pay more attention to other workplaces. I was especially interested in what differentiated the great workplaces (at least in my opinion) from those that were mediocre, or even worse, in decline.

What is a great workplace?

Is it a place with well-stocked cappuccino machines, afternoon foosball, and goofy Thursdays? There are many ways you could define "great"—increased revenues each year, soaring profits, clobbering the competition, most fun place to work, producing the coolest products, having an unbeatable brand, attracting the top talent, paying the highest salaries, doling out the greatest benefits, or re-engineering the most convoluted organizational chart.

We've spent years studying the impact of emotional intelligence on human performance. I've even documented (with co-author Howard Book) how emotional intelligence significantly impacts your behavior at work and at home. In our book, *The EQ Edge: Emotional Intelligence and Your Success,*[1] we present numerous examples of jobs that are significantly impacted by a person's emotional intelligence: lawyers, collection agents, real estate salespeople, reality TV show contestants, and many others.

The question now becomes, how do we take what we've started to learn about individual performance and apply it to the organization? Could there in fact be an organizational emotional intelligence? What would happen if we were able to select the right people for the organization, put them in the right job (or in the right seat on the bus, as Jim Collins, author of *Good to Great,*[2] puts it), and fine-tune the corporate culture for optimum performance?

Could the whole be greater than the sum of its parts? In other words, will the right combination of people and culture produce something that's really great? And, if so, what are the keys to unlocking that culture? By finding out what's really important in organizations, we can focus on things that matter and stop wasting time on those that don't—such as fancy cappuccino machines.

What defines an emotionally intelligent workplace?

Let's start by defining what an emotionally intelligent workplace looks like. Organizational emotional intelligence involves people's feelings and thoughts about the work they do, their co-workers, supervisor, top leadership, the organization itself, and their impact on the world around them.

My definition of organizational emotional intelligence is: *An organization's ability to successfully and efficiently cope with change and accomplish its goals, while being responsible and sensitive to its people, customers, suppliers, networks, and society.*

Together with the people at MHS I've spent several years of research fine-tuning the definition, creating survey items that measure the key factors, testing the items in organizations, refining the factors based on the results, and so on. The result of our work to date has led to identifying seven key factors of the emotionally intelligent organization. The instrument resulting from this work is the Benchmark of Organizational Emotional Intelligence or BOEI.[3]

The seven keys are:

Key #1: Hire capable people who love the work they do and show them how they contribute to the bigger picture.

Job Happiness: It's more than the employee just being satisfied with his or her job. Organizations must better understand what connects people to their work. First, you need to hire the right people. Second, you have to ensure the right person is doing the right job. Now there are new approaches to getting the right fit. While job interviews and tests for interest, aptitude, and personality are traditional ways of matching people to jobs, we will explore emotional skills as part of the new formula. Finally, people need to see the bigger picture—how they contribute not only to the organization, but to their community, society, or the world.

Key #2: Compensate people fairly.

Compensation: It's not just what workers get for their work; it's how fairly they feel they're being treated. Feelings of fairness override how much people get paid. I've seen teenage professional athletes who scoffed at their first contract—more than $600,000 for a season of playing hockey. Compare that to the man in his forties I met cleaning litter at a Disney park. He told me how much he loved his job, even though his pay was only slightly more than minimum wage.

Organizations need a clear, fair, and well-articulated compensation system. People want to know that they've been dealt with in a personal and just way.

Key #3: Don't overwork (or underwork) people.

Work/Life Stress Management: No, not just the employee's—the organization's. Organizations can benefit from paying attention to proper work-life balance in their people. Manageable workloads can be done with much better quality than overloading people with more than they can handle. While we assume everyone can multi-task without limits, there are optimum amounts of work that people can process well. Just as important—don't give people too little work because they'll get bored.

Key #4: Build strong teams with shared purpose and viable goals.

Organizational Cohesiveness: Work has become too complex for the "lone wolf" approach. An organization needs to foster strong interpersonal relationships among its people. While it's easy to sit back and say, "These are adults, let them figure out how to work together," this approach won't maximize performance. You need the right people working together in teams with common goals and a purpose. The right mix of strengths, weaknesses, skills and abilities in people together with concrete outcomes for performance will lead to success.

Key #5: Make sure managers can manage.

Supervisory Leadership: What does it take to be a good supervisor? Many organizations have not grasped the fact that more people leave their jobs because they have not received the proper support and leadership from their manager than any other reason. After all we've supposedly learned about managing, companies still promote top performers—whether in technical or sales positions—into management positions, whether or not they're the right people, and with little or no preparation.

Being a great salesperson does not predict how well you will manage five other salespeople. Likewise for engineers, computer programmers, shop-floor workers, financial analysts, technical writers, accountants, marketers, and so many other occupations. Managing people requires specific sets of skills.

First, you need to select the right people to manage. It's not for everyone. Often your best salesperson is better off—and should remain—as a top salesperson. The challenge is to creatively avoid the seduction of moving her or him "up the corporate ladder" into management.

Second, once you've identified potential managers, you need to train them in management. Managers require specific sets of skills. These include the ability to read people well, understand what motivates them, and communicate clearly—knowing how and when to deliver good news as well as bad news. Providing appropriate feedback requires managers to be more of a coach or mentor and less authoritarian or critical. Managing also requires numerous administrative skills such as organization and time-management abilities.

Key #6: Treat people with respect and leverage their unique talents.

Diversity and Anger Management: Smart companies use diversity to leverage their products and services while at the same time gauge the underlying mood of their people. Diversity-friendly workplaces can be very productive. People who are open to differences learn more from others. People from different cultures bring different views and opportunities to the table when solving problems. Also, in this global economy, they give you better perspectives on what it takes for you to be successful in other parts of the world.

Organizations must be vigilant for signs of racial and gender tension, foster an accepting climate, and have the tools to defuse anger before it worsens into violence. If you're lucky, anger seeping into an organization can be like a slow leak in a tire, or a fuse on a stick of dynamite if you're not. Bad moods permeate the organization and sabotage mental energy and work outputs. You would be amazed at how creative some people are at sabotaging the workplace.

Key #7: Be proactively responsive by doing the right things to win the hearts and minds of your people.

Organizational Responsiveness: An organization that is responsive to its people builds the company's brand. What do employees feel and think about the organization they work for? In order to win the hearts and minds of its people, organizations must offer training, encourage innovation, nurture optimism, promote honesty and integrity, demonstrate courage to make changes and adapt, and provide support in meeting needs and gaining trust.

The Right Stuff—the Right Culture

While all of these keys are important, some will contribute more to organizational success than others. For example, compensating people fairly will help ensure loyalty or at least prevent some talented people from leaving. However, paying people excessive amounts of money will not motivate them to new heights or performance for any sustained period of time.

On the other hand, organizational responsiveness goes a long way towards motivating people's performance. A responsive organization builds trust among its people. Being responsive means showing you care by providing things that matter at a higher level. These include opportunities for training and advancement, providing an optimistic environment, embracing innovation, demonstrating integrity and honesty from the top down, showing the courage to make changes in the organization when needed, and being supportive of people.

Throughout this book I will introduce you to some of the key findings I've learned about the changing workplace and the role leaders can play in maximizing their workforce. With the current rate of globalization, it is no longer a luxury to have a high-performing workplace. While the war for talent is heavily engaged, the next battlefront will be maximizing productivity from all that high-priced talent. You can fill an organization with all the highly intelligent and educated people you want. But without the right culture and discipline, your chances of success are slim.

The information and prescriptions presented in this book are useful for anyone working within an organization. As workplaces democratize, everyone can have some responsibility for bringing forth good ideas that maximize productivity and a positive work environment. Use this book as a gauge to see how your workplace measures up to the seven keys. If you are a leader, this book should stimulate you to think about the kinds of changes you might want in your organization. If you are an employee, this book may help you decide if your workplace is ready for change or whether it's time to look around for an organization more responsive to your needs.

PART 1 | Why Our World—and the Work We Do—Will Never Be the Same Again

CHAPTER 1

Changes in Society and Their Impact on Work

"It's not your father's workplace anymore."

When Work Works, Family and Work Institute

Juggling our lives to find the perfect balance between work and personal time is the ongoing preoccupation of most working adults today. We just don't seem to have enough hours to get everything done, or even to feel that we're close to completing many of our major tasks. Feeling stressed seems to be a way of life. Why is it that with all the increased automation in our lives we seem to have less free time than ever before?

Over a number of years, researchers at When Work Works—a project of the Family and Work Institute, a non-profit organization funded by IBM, the Alfred Sloan Foundation, Johnson & Johnson, and others (http://familiesandwork.org/3w/)—have been looking at the changing nature of society and work. Using surveys of thousands of organizations and working adults, and by studying best-practice companies, they have arrived at a number of interesting conclusions that are summarized here.[1]

Our Changing Economy

Our economy has significantly evolved from the days of the Industrial Revolution. In the so-called old days, jobs were more clearly defined. People got paid for what they produced. Work centered much more on the making and selling of products. Work hours, while extended for factory workers and laborers, especially in the early 1900s, were also more clearly defined than they are today. Work was separate from home life. The goal of the labor movement was to move towards a nine-to-five workday.

Today's workplace is primarily knowledge- and service-based. We work in a much more abstract world; fewer of us continue to be makers of things. Dealing with intangibles presents its own set of issues. For example, it has become harder to gauge the quality of our work, or how satisfied our customer or client is.

The markets we serve have changed as well. The economy is now global. A rebel uprising in Nigeria can affect the price we pay to put gas in our car the very same week. The rules affecting prices and services are influenced by practices and events that occur thousands of miles away. This adds both complexity and volume to work that was once fairly straightforward.

The world is much faster paced. We live in a 24/7 environment. You can make purchases or pay bills in the middle of the night while sitting in your pajamas in your bedroom. For those who provide products or services, the bar has risen in terms of customer expectations for both quality and speed. People are getting used to more customized service, and word spreads quickly if you fail to deliver.

Our Changing Workforce

Along with the economy, our workforce has changed significantly. In the United States, Canada, and most of Europe, we have a dynamic multicultural population. Along with the influx of different cultures comes the need for managers to know how to manage people who bring to the table different workplace experiences and expectations. New practices have had to be learned in order to be inclusive.

The number of male and female workers in the workforce today is almost equal. This growing equality has impacted the workplace in many ways, not the least of which includes the organization's need to plan around maternity leaves.

Today's workforce is older than in previous generations as baby boomers have moved up the ranks. Approximately 56% of U.S. workers today are 40 years of age or older, compared to 38% in 1977. Succession planning takes on a new level of importance as experienced managers begin to leave the workforce.

Not Your Father's Workplace

Times have changed dramatically at work. Fewer fathers are the sole income earner than ever before—33% today compared to 51% a mere 25 years ago (in the United States). The "job for life" has been replaced by growing job mobility and job insecurity. Employees no longer work from nine-to-five. Work hours are longer and the workweek has been extended.

Technologies blur the distinction between work and home. With the advent of cell phones, pagers, and BlackBerries, work has pushed its way into the home and into family time, whether it's dinnertime or a child's school concert. We held the belief in the 1960s that technology would decrease our work time to give us more leisure time; instead, we have created more technology that actually increases the amount and duration of our work. So much for the four-day workweek.

A new vernacular has been coined to describe our current predicament, such as "time famine," illustrating the ongoing thirst for more personal time. In a survey undertaken by the When Work Works project, 67% of employed parents reported that they felt they did not spend enough time with their children. When asked whether they had enough time for themselves, 55% said they did not.[2]

The Company's Role in the Changing Realities

Organizations have only started to learn that they have to adapt to the new realities. In looking at best-practice companies, several themes emerge. The first is that job autonomy is a significant factor. People are becoming much more responsible for the way in which they accomplish their tasks, assignments, and goals. Supervision will be replaced by coaching. New forms of accountability will be being implemented to ensure that people are productive.

Management and supervision are taking on new forms. We've been moving away from the more paternalistic attitude that we must supervise, monitor, and control employees. Micro-managing is out and goal-setting is in. It's now about coaching. Moving employees towards success on the job is the new focus of best-practice leaders. Once we've hired the right people, we have to give them the support and space needed to get the job done.

The importance of creating learning environments has been well established. At one time, you would hire someone for the accounting department, give them a desk and calculator, and tell them to get to work. The workplace has become so complex that everyone, whether working in the warehouse or the boardroom, has to keep up with changing technologies—be they computers, phones, or pagers, or the newly converged all-in-one devices.

I remember being on a business trip out of the country during the early days of email. I became frantic when I realized I was not able to retrieve my email from my computer. It turned out that someone in the IT department had innocently changed the password system before informing everyone of the change. Sometimes even small changes in technology require awareness and training for everyone in the organization.

The superior employees will gravitate towards those organizations that keep them up-to-date in their fields and provide opportunities to advance their knowledge and their careers. But it's not enough for those employees to learn all the newly automated office procedures; you now also have to be a specialist in your field of work. You're not just a shipper anymore: you may need to understand export and customs procedures, taxes, tariffs, and duties, online tracking of packages, instant online comparison shopping of couriers and carriers, efficient and environmentally friendly packaging, and so on. Companies need to make their people not only feel like specialists, but equip them with the knowledge and tools to be on the leading edge of whatever they do.

The bottom line, though, is flexibility. Flexibility in the workplace is no longer an option, but rather the new necessity. The most valued component of flexibility is time. Employees require workplaces that provide for time exchange that make maximum use of their work-life hours.

A Balancing Act

One of the critical areas (which will be described in detail in Chapter 9) is work-life stress management. We have learned about a number of practices, some rather simple, that distinguish organizations that excel in this area.

High-performing organizations start out by ensuring that people have the basic necessities to do their jobs. This includes both material factors, such as a proper workspace and environment, as well as providing and supporting knowledge factors relevant to their job and performance. People are given realistic deadlines (often negotiated) in which to complete their tasks.

The organization will ensure that workloads are balanced among employees. Workloads are perceived as fair based on criteria that fit within the organization. As much as possible, the organization strives to have predictable workloads. This presumes no major changes in workloads, work schedules, or responsibilities.

Well-functioning organizations make a conscious effort to ensure people have time for their family and personal life. It has been known for some time now that creating workaholics does not lead to the best-quality work. It actually contributes to burning people out—usually your best people. Unfortunately, many organizations are known to encourage their most productive employees to work over evenings and weekends. It was often assumed to be a rite of passage to the next level of the organization. Working long hours has often been seen as a sign of loyalty to the company as well as motivation for success. Today's employees are different. Loyalty and motivation are now more a result of how the organization treats them—how much the organization cares about its people and how honest the organization is with them.

The organization must demonstrate, through concrete and visible action, that it cares about its people and their families. The following case example illustrates this point.

In a small manufacturing company, Alan, who worked in shipping, had a stepson who was involved in a serious car accident. After emergency care, his stepson was placed in long-term intensive care. It was pretty clear that he required an extended stay in intensive care and the amount of time off Alan needed to visit his stepson was well beyond the normal company policy, but the company went out of its way to ensure that Alan could spend as much time as possible at the hospital without worrying about the work time missed.

By relieving Alan of the additional burden of work pressure, at the cost of missed time from work, the company won significant loyalty, gratitude, and trust over the long term. Most return-on-investment equations fail to take these human factors into account.

The cost of forcing an overly stressed employee, whose mind is elsewhere, to continue working would most likely be reflected in their performance both in the short term and over time. The cost of errors in shipments, wrong products being sent out, and tardiness can be calculated. But there is a steeper price to pay for an employee who believes his company doesn't care about him or her.

What is the cost of an employee who starts to resent every additional demand made on his or her time? Is it possible he or she would end up wasting far more time at work in the long run than the time that would have been taken for compassionate reasons? What about other employees who see how their fellow worker is treated by the company? What message do you send to them? After all, they may be in similar circumstances some day. In fact, these costs can be far more expensive than the original request.

In this case Alan was truly grateful to the company for giving him the time. When he returned he voluntarily put in extra time to make up for the time missed. Alan shared a sense of responsibility for the organization and for its mission. Of course his passion for the company was not solely based on this single incident. The company had, by its overall responsiveness to its employees, built up a bank account of goodwill, of which this was just one example.

The way in which organizations deal with these challenges—large and small—are instrumental to their future survival in the increasingly competitive and global environment.

What's happened to motivation?

Natasha looked very busy at her desk. She seemed so deep in concentration at her computer that Amir, her co-worker, thought twice about interrupting her for advice on a task he needed help with for a major project.

"Natasha, excuse me," he said with hesitation.

"Yeah, what is it, Amir?" she asked without even looking over.

"I need some help with this project, I was wondering if you had some time?" he said.

"I guess so, but I have to finish getting this purse on eBay. I've been trying to get a used Louis Vuitton for weeks. Come back in an hour," she said, somewhat annoyed.

Look at these findings on workplace activity, as reported by journalist Amy Harmon in *The New York Times*:

> Workers with Web access typically spend five to ten hours per week to send personal e-mail or search for information not specifically related to their jobs. ... Popular entertainment sites, such as ESPN's Sport Zone, where visitors can check sport scores, and the Sony Corporation's, where they can play *Jeopardy*, sustain heavy traffic during the work day. As everything from CDs to cars go on sale over the Web, some employees are also spending more time shopping on-line.[3]

According to a survey carried out by America Online entitled "Internet Use Tops Workplace Time-Wasting Tasks," the "unproductive tasks in the workplace, from Web surfing to water cooler chit-chat, is costing companies $759 billion annually."[4]

In addition, the research reported:

> In a survey of 10,000 employees, the average worker admits to frittering away 2.09 hours per day, not counting lunch. The number one way they waste time at work is personal Internet use (e.g., email, IM, online polls, interactive games, message boards, chat rooms, etc.). Personal Internet use was cited by 44 percent of respondents as their primary time-wasting activity at work. Socializing with co-workers was the second most popular form of wasting time at work (23 percent of respondents). Conducting personal business, "spacing out," running errands, and making personal phone calls were other popular time-wasting activities in the workplace.[5]

One of the most frequent questions I hear from CEOs is, "How do I motivate my people?" It's almost as if they are looking for some big carrot they can hang in front of their workers (or a boot they can suspend from behind).

The study of work motivation, job satisfaction, and their relationship to performance and worker efficiency has been well documented throughout the 20th century. The nature of worker motivation, like the other work issues previously discussed in this chapter, has changed dramatically over the century.

In fact, one of the main reasons companies have used organizational surveys has been to gauge employee motivation. Employee motivation has been studied since the beginning of industrial/organizational psychology.[6] Since the early 1900s there have been dozens of theories developed to explain what makes people willing to exert effort towards the goals of the organization.[7] We will briefly look at how these theories have changed over time.

Motivational Theories

Motivational theories can be broken into two types: needs theories and process theories. Needs theories "describe the types of needs that must be met in order to motivate individuals," while process theories "help managers understand processes they might use to motivate employees."[8]

One of the most widely known needs theories was developed by psychologist Abraham Maslow. He posited that people have needs that drive them to perform. In his system, these needs are referred to as a hierarchy of needs. In order to meet their needs for food, shelter, positive self-esteem, or even higher values of self-actualization, people will work. It is through their work they help accomplish these personal goals.

Dozens of work motivators have been identified and studied within the needs framework. These include the effects of offering good wages, improving working conditions, promising job security, changing the nature of the work, and providing greater variety of work.

Other programs have looked at the importance of raising an employee's status in their workgroup, encouraging them to feel "in" on what's going on, improving relations with supervisors and associates, and providing more freedom or less supervision, greater recognition for work done, and more opportunities to show initiative. Still other studies have gauged the impact of providing opportunities for advancement, winning personal loyalty, utilizing tactful discipline, implementing better grievance procedures, helping with personal problems, and enhancing the organization's ability to provide visible results of work accomplished.

Process theories, on the other hand, focus on methods or procedures that can be implemented to motivate employees. These theories tend to focus on people's commitment to setting and achieving goals within the organization relative to how well they feel they can accomplish them. By giving employees control over their work, this research supports the idea that people are committed to achieving these goals.

So then, *what is work motivation*? Is it something from within the person, or does it come from setting up the right environment around the person? One theory says it includes both. A comprehensive definition that reflects the history of research and theory on this subject that is often quoted by leading industrial organizational psychologists was developed by Craig Pinder. He defines motivation in the workplace as "a set of energetic forces that originate both within as well as beyond an individual's being, to initiate work related behavior, and to determine its form, direction, intensity, and duration."[9]

This definition is both psychological—looking at the direction, energization, and regulation of behavior—and takes into account the work environment, such as characteristics of the job itself, or the working conditions. According to this theory, these factors create the force that is necessary for motivation.

In order to really understand and predict motivation, we need to know the specific goal a person is motivated towards. The amount of energy expended will depend on how difficult that goal is to reach. How long a person sticks with it will depend on how much the person believes he or she can actually reach the goal. That is, how confident the person is. Psychologists refer to this as "self-efficacy"—similar to self-confidence. People high in self-efficacy are more confident and therefore not afraid to try harder to reach their goal.

How can an organization increase inborn/intrinsic motivation?

There have been a number of prescriptions for increasing people's intrinsic motivation. Here is a nine-point plan:

1. *Give people ongoing feedback.* Let them know how they are doing, where they are performing well and where there is room for improvement. This can be done in brief conversations or on a more formal basis.

2. *Provide opportunities for growth and development.* People need to know there are available avenues for them to improve themselves by learning more or upgrading their skills.

3. *Offer flexible schedules.* Time is an important commodity for people today. By giving people the opportunity to juggle their time around critical personal or family events and responsibilities, you will increase their work motivation.

4. *Emphasize personal accountability.* Self-management is highly motivating. Most people will work much harder for their own sense of accomplishment than they will because "the boss told me to do it."

5. *Provide an open, trusting environment.* Fear and mistrust are negative motivators. They keep people on their toes, but do not produce the best work. Having an open and trusting environment encourages more creative approaches to solving problems and supports healthier teamwork.

6. *Involve everyone in decision making.* No one today likes being told what to do. By involving workers in decisions that involve them, you are much more likely to get buy-in for your initiatives. You may even get some creative input along the way. People at the front lines may know about certain impacts of decisions that executives may not be aware of.

7. *Ask employees what motivates them.* You may be surprised how small changes in job design or reporting systems may be very motivating to some people. You won't really know what people want unless you ask them.

8. *Celebrate employee and company success.* All too often we ignore or forget about accomplishments. It's important to stop and recognize successes, whether individual, team, or organizational. Let everybody see that hard work is recognized and worth carrying out.

9. *Offer interesting work assignments.* It can be quite exciting for someone to receive a special assignment. It could be working on a new initiative, a special project, or with an important client. When a company doesn't have a lot of room for vertical growth into management positions, special assignments can be used as an opportunity to stretch an employee's skills. It takes them out of the daily grind and provides new challenges. Also, it's helpful if rewards are tied into performance.[10]

The Key to Motivating Different Generational Groups

Of course, any discussion of motivation today must take into account the generational differences. There have been many discussions of these demographic shifts, but we'll review them here briefly. Linda Duxbury, a professor at the Sprott School of Business at Carleton University in Ottawa, Canada, has surveyed thousands of working people to better understand these differences.[11]

The first group, the "Veterans," is the group of workers that were born just before or just after the Second World War. Their values and working styles were heavily shaped by the stories they heard from their parents of hardships that included the stock market crash and Great Depression that followed, and rationing during the war. Descriptors of the work values of these people include loyal, dependable, persistent, hard-working, and authoritarian. The "Veterans" value wisdom more than technical knowledge.

"Baby Boomers" are the second group of workers. You qualify if you were born between 1947 and 1964. Their values were shaped by events that included economic prosperity, the birth control pill, the Vietnam War, and rock and roll. As workers, this cohort tends to be workaholic, accepting of stress, desirous of titles, admiring of symbols and the trappings of material wealth. They tend to demand the respect and loyalty of their subordinates.

The "Baby Bust" generation, also known as "Generation X," was born between 1961 and 1974. The Gen Xers grew up with economic recessions, an anti-child society, AIDS, personal computers, the wake of the boomers, government cutbacks, and rap music. At work, they tend to work within the system, sacrifice personal life to get ahead, are goal oriented, prefer close supervision, and like to be recognized for achievement.

Finally, the "Echo Boomers," also known as Nexus, Generation Y, or Millenniums, have arrived. This cohort was born between 1975 and 1990. They are only 42% of the size of the Boomers in population. Their values were shaped by information technology, a child-focused society, violence, terrorism, and, last but not least, "gangsta rap"—a more violent stream of the previous group's rap music. At work, they tend to prefer independence; they seek challenges and variety, distrust authority, like to continue developing their skills, aren't particularly loyal, and believe in work-life balance—mostly the "life" part. They like a fun and communal workplace.

Are there universal workplace motivators?

The real challenge for organizations is identifying a set of workplace motivating circumstances that apply to workers across the generational divides. Are there important factors that cut across these different groups? Can organizations find the right balance of pay, teamwork, learning opportunities, etc., that will motivate all workers?

Among the critics of the demographic approach to motivation are David Sirota and his colleagues. They also conducted a large survey sample of several thousand workers and provide the following three criticisms to most work motivation theories:

1. Most demographic approaches simplify workplace motivation by focusing on just *one* aspiration as the *central* motivator (and explanation) of employee morale and performance at the expense of other workplace factors. For example, Gen Xers are often described as "slackers" who rarely, if ever, receive enough recognition for their accomplishments.

2. They claim that most people are frustrated with trying to achieve that aspiration ("the sky is falling") and by trying to solve that single frustration, all the problems will be solved. So, if employers would only provide these Gen Xers with lots of love and attention they would become highly motivated and productive.

3. Uncovering the frustration leads to the discovery of a "new generation" of workers.[12]

In their view, there are three universal factors that all working people want today, regardless of age, gender, culture, or any other factor. These are:

Equity: To be treated justly in relation to the basic conditions of employment.

Achievement: To take pride in one's accomplishments by doing things that matter and doing them well; to receive recognition for one's accomplishments; to take pride in the organization's accomplishments.

Camaraderie: To have warm, interesting, and cooperative relations with others in the workplace.[13]

In this book I will also be presenting data that my company has collected from a large sample of working people. As well, I will supplement these findings with research from others and well-grounded observations made by experienced people in the field. It is only through careful research and analysis of data that we can make sense of what is really happening in the workplace. In this way we can learn about what motivates employees and go beyond armchair quarterbacking.

In the next chapter we will see how what keeps CEOs up at night is related to their skills at leading the organization.

CHAPTER 2

What Keeps CEOs Up at Night?

"I find it rather easy to portray a businessman. Being bland, rather cruel and incompetent comes naturally to me."

John Cleese

"So much of what we call management consists in making it difficult for people to work."

Peter Drucker

"Good leaders make people feel that they're at the very heart of things, not at the periphery. Everyone feels that he or she makes a difference to the success of the organization. When that happens people feel centered and that gives their work meaning."

Warren Bennis

What does it take to run an organization today?

"There just aren't any good people around," Brian complains. "The younger people have no work ethic and the experienced ones care more about salary, bonus and fringe benefits than about what the job is." Brian is the CEO of a 200-employee manufacturing firm. He's among the CEOs who have told me about one of the biggest problems business leaders face today—the search for good talent.

Nigel, the CEO of a very specialized and fast-growing software firm, talks about how he attracts the best talent. "We really want to hire the youngest, brightest minds we can find. We know the people we want like toys, but they haven't built up the equity to get them yet. So we offer new employees a lease on a BMW 300 series as a signing bonus."

"But what if they don't last the term of the lease?" I innocently ask.

"That's okay. We have so many leases that the dealership works with us in transferring them," he replies without hesitation.

While I thought that kind of thinking went out with the dot-com craze, it seems that some CEOs will still go to almost any length to find the people they need. Unfortunately, there's a lot more attention paid to attracting warm bodies than to attracting the right bodies. And probably even less attention paid to retaining the best people.

As a member of the Innovators Alliance (IA), a Canadian CEO organization for leaders of fast-growing companies, I carried out a survey of the membership to try to ascertain what issues keep these CEOs up at night. Obviously, this is just one group of leaders, but we'll soon see how they compare to corporate leaders elsewhere in the world.

The IA was initiated by the government of Ontario, for CEOs of fast-growing companies. What's the definition of a fast-growing company? In order for a CEO to be a member, their company must show a minimum cumulative revenue growth rate of 35% over three years. They need to generate a minimum of $2 million (Cdn) or more in annual revenue, employ between 10 and 500 people, and maintain an Ontario-based head office. The sample membership surveyed in my study included 76 members: 61 men and 15 women.

These CEOs represent a number of different industries, including manufacturing, business services, marketing, software development, and computer sales/service. The group also includes professional services, organizational consulting, publishing, communications, retail, internet, property development, and financial services.

As part of the study, I wanted to see if there was any connection between a CEO's personal characteristics and how confident they felt about dealing with their business challenges. Along with the survey, I asked them to complete an emotional intelligence inventory. They all completed the Emotional Quotient Inventory (EQ-i®), the world's most widely used and best validated measure of emotional intelligence.[1] The results were surprising in terms of what keeps these CEOs up at night.

What are the biggest challenges facing today's business leaders?

What challenges these leaders the most? Perhaps it's the need for capital to feed their fast-growing companies? Or maybe the changing pace of technology makes it hard for them to keep up?

Well, neither of these is correct. You can find the answer in the graph in Figure 2-1. As you can see, their biggest challenge is hiring the right people. The least challenging issue is dealing with changes in technology.

How do we explain this? Well, many of these companies are technology oriented; it's easy to see why changing technology presents the least challenge for them. In fact, many of these leaders see changing technology as an opportunity. However, hiring people is pretty foreign territory for many entrepreneurs, as well as for many leaders in large corporations.

In addition to making the right hires, managing growth and managing people were the next biggest challenges. These issues all relate to driving the culture of the organization. The ability to manage a growing organization and its people requires skills beyond accounting, marketing, sales, customer service, engineering, or other technical areas. At an individual level you have to understand yourself and those around you. A completely different set of skills, such as emotional self-awareness, empathy, and stress tolerance, becomes important. Managing the culture requires yet another set of skills that includes reality testing and interpersonal relationships.

Dealing with changing business systems and processes as the company grows requires a high level of technical expertise or at least a good infrastructure with the right people in the organization managing the accounting and other operational issues. But even when making operational changes, people are involved. More often than not, insufficient attention is paid to the "people" side of the issues.

Who manages the people in these organizations? There may be levels of managers, or even a human resource person. The resources available, of course, depend on the size of the company. The leader, however, always has an impact on how people and systems are dealt with.

How do emotional and social intelligence relate to real-world business challenges?

In our study, we wanted to look at whether there was any relationship between the CEO's emotional and social intelligence and the areas that challenged him or her the most—or, alternatively, between the leader's emotional intelligence and the areas of confidence.

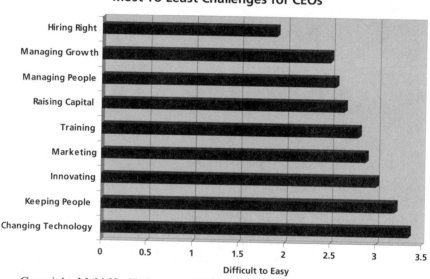

Figure 2.1
Most To Least Challenges for CEOs

Copyright: Multi-Health Systems (2005)

What are the relationships, if any, between the emotional and social intelligence of a CEO and the difficulties experienced by specific business challenges? For example, do CEOs with good people skills find it easier to hire people? After all, hiring is often done by human resources people, who are known for their interpersonal skills. (These and other questions related to emotional intelligence and business challenges will be dealt with in the remainder of this chapter.)

By emotional and social intelligence, which will be explained in more detail in Chapter 4, we refer to a set of skills that enables us to make our way in a complex world. These are the personal, social, and survival aspects of overall intelligence, the elusive common sense and sensitivity that are essential to effective daily functioning.

Overall Emotional and Social Intelligence

We looked at the total emotional and social intelligence scores of our CEOs; that is, the combination of all the emotional and social intelligence factors. Higher emotional and social intelligence are related to two challenge areas: the leader's confidence in keeping people and their perceived ability to manage the growth of their company.

Keeping people and managing growth are enduring challenges. High emotional intelligence ensures the leader has the skill set and energy to confidently deal with these aspects of running the business. The rest of this chapter deals with specific emotional and social intelligence skills.

Hiring People

Does having people skills help a CEO with hiring? Well, according to our study, apparently not. It turns out that only one emotional skill was related to a CEO's confidence in selecting people—flexibility. Leaders who are more adaptable find that hiring the right people comes easier. One of the advantages of being flexible is that it allows you to look beyond a fixed notion of who should get the job. It also opens you up to hiring people who are different from yourself.

Too often we surround ourselves with people who are similar to us. Selecting people with different skills, strengths, interests, and opinions can be good for the organization. However, we do want people who share the organization's core values and attitudes. Shared values—such as customer focus, integrity, doing quality work and loyalty—are the glue that keeps the organization functioning well.

But being different in other areas—ways of problem solving, past experience, personal strengths, and skills—makes the organization stronger. Being flexible allows you to separate your own strengths and weaknesses from those of the candidate and lets you be more objective in selecting what you really need—not just what you like.

In an article that focuses on managing in the new millennium, Patricia Buhler recommends:

> While the tendency is to hire similar types of people, the manager who is helping to build a high-performance organization will hire a heterogeneous workforce. This manager fights the temptation to hire everyone who is just alike. Instead, hiring those with complementary skills enables the unit to be more creative and accomplish more.
>
> An effective team is heterogeneous in nature. That is, the team is comprised of members who have a variety of broad-based skills. This ultimately enhances the team's task performance and improves its decision-making ability.[2]

Managing People

A recent report from the United Kingdom audited the process of managing people in 150 county councils throughout the country. One of the findings parallels a trend occurring throughout the world. Managers have become more directly responsible for managing their people: "People management is not just a responsibility for personnel officers; it is the responsibility of managers at all levels in an organisation."[3]

What emotional skills are related to how well a leader feels he or she manages people? Is this an area where interpersonal skills are important? Well, apparently not. The two most important skills we found in our study are self-actualization and impulse control.

People high in self-actualization love what they do. They've found the fit between what they enjoy and what they do best. They are often role models for their employees. They genuinely love their work and it shows. Employees can sense when their leaders are authentic. CEOs who fake their passion or simply go through the motions of doing their job are pretty transparent to everyone around them. These are the leaders who tell their employees they're working when they're off to the golf course for the afternoon. The reality is they're not fooling anyone.

Having good impulse control is essential for managing others. In previous studies with leaders, we found that low impulse control was a major cause for derailment. Just think of the boss who flies off the handle at the slightest annoyance. Not being able to control your temper or blurting out hurtful things to others without thinking weakens relationships and makes you less effective as a leader. So it was interesting to find here that managing impulses makes it easier to manage others.

Managing people was also seen to be easier for leaders who scored higher in reality testing. Being able to see things as they are, as opposed to how one wishes them to be, or fears they are, relates to how well our leaders feel they manage others. By being realistic, they are better able to help others set realistic work goals and expectations.

Self-regard also relates to managing others. In our studies we consistently find that knowing your strengths and weaknesses and having the right amount of confidence is essential for successful leadership. Leaders who are good at accepting their own weaknesses are better at providing constructive criticism or feedback to their direct reports.

For these leaders, their confidence in managing others also relates to their personal happiness. Happy leaders are in a better frame of mind to lead and manage. By being happy they are motivating to others. Just think of the last time you got excited by going to work in a company directed by a sad or depressing leader.

Finally, we found that a leader's ability to tolerate stress relates to their people management. Leaders who can deal well with stress and keep calm have an easier time of managing others. Employees don't work well when they live in fear of their supervisor's anger. People do their best work when they can focus on the task at hand. Fear not only distracts, but creates anxiety—not a good combination for being productive. Employees want to work for people who can manage their stress and not those who fly off the handle at life's minor irritations.

I must admit, it was surprising to find that it wasn't the leader's interpersonal skills, but rather a cluster of skills that includes self-actualization, impulse control, reality testing, self-regard, happiness and stress tolerance, that makes it easier for these CEOs to manage people.

Keeping People

Retaining good people is often cited as a major issue for companies today. According to a broad-based survey of human resource professionals throughout the United Kingdom: "Staff retention and talent management will be the top HR issues facing UK businesses for the rest of 2006. A survey of 250 HR professionals, by HR consultancy RightCoutts, reveals that 41% cite the retention of key staff as their organisation's most critical issue this year."[4]

You might expect that the same skills our CEOs used for managing people would be the best ones for keeping people in the organization. However, life's never that simple. While we found some overlap, there were also some important differences.

This time, we would be correct to guess that interpersonal relationship skills was one of the most important factors related to retaining staff. Leaders who have good relationships with their staff are more likely to keep them. Building social and emotional bonds with employees makes them feel better about their leaders and the workplace.

Another important skill related to staff retention is self-regard. As we found with people management, the leader's confidence and self-knowledge help with retaining people. High self-regard leaders (who know their strengths and weaknesses) project the kind of confidence (and *humility*) that is more likely to make people want to stay with the organization.

Flexibility, the skill that helps leaders with hiring, also appears to be related to keeping good people. In today's world, being a rigid leader neither inspires nor attracts people. On the other hand, by being too flexible a leader appears to stand for nothing and have no backbone. By showing the right amount of flexibility, leaders demonstrate they can be reasonable, listen to other points of view, and not be bound by rules and regulations. A leader who is seen as flexible maintains the bonds that keep people engaged more easily.

Happiness, which was related to confidence in managing people, is also associated with keeping people. People are less likely to want to stay in an organization that projects a mood of sadness, pessimism, anger, or other unpleasant emotions. It's the leader who sets the tone for the organization. People are energized when working around others who are happy. They tend to be sapped or demoralized when surrounded by gloom and doom. Leaders, good or bad, radiate their emotions throughout the organization.

We found leader optimism also related to retention. After all, who wants to stay in an organization with leaders who are pessimistic about the future? Pessimistic leaders get people thinking about updating their resumes and keeping them ready in the top drawer.

Stress tolerance and self-actualization are both important for retention. Leaders who manage stress well and are excited about their work contribute to staff retention. Once again, these emotional tones help create the environment that is conducive to productive work.

Training

Training has become another one of the more significant challenges for organizations around the world. In a 2003 study funded by the New Zealand Department of Labour's Future of Work Research Fund it was reported that "in-house training is very common. The survey of Business New Zealand's membership found that 90 percent of responding firms currently provide some form of training to employees."[5] (However, these results should be treated cautiously since job orientation was included as training in this survey.) The challenge here is to provide meaningful training that results in learning that goes beyond basic job orientation.

In our research it was interesting, and not unexpected, to find relationships between leaders' emotional intelligence and the desire to train their people. The most significant aspects of emotional intelligence concern happiness and self-actualization. This makes a great deal of sense because people who are self-actualized believe in continuing to better themselves (and often others as well). They strive for self-improvement and they want others in the organization to do so as well, often through learning.

What does leader happiness have to do with training staff? I must admit, this finding puzzled us as well. It may be that happy leaders want to see their employees happy and successful—which to them also means well trained. After all, these leaders are smart enough to see the connection between organizational success and the continued development and training of their people.

Leaders confident in training are also more assertive. That means these CEOs are good at expressing their thoughts, feelings and beliefs in a constructive way. These leaders can effectively communicate the importance of training in their organizations.

Good interpersonal relationship skills are related to success with training as well. Leaders who maintain good relationships with their staff are more aware of what their needs are. Using the various skills described here, they act on these needs and implement training initiatives as necessary.

High self-regard also relates to training. Having high self-regard means you have an awareness of your own strengths and weaknesses. Being aware of your own weaknesses helps you be more sensitive to the weaknesses or deficits in others. This, in turn, can play a role in supporting others in recognizing their training needs.

The CEOs higher in reality testing were also more confident about training in their organization. These leaders have a more honest view of where their people are and where they need to be.

Finally, flexibility and optimism were significant factors here as well. Optimistic leaders, always looking for solutions, know that a knowledgeable organization can be a better performing organization. Flexibility allows one to see the various options available and comfortably choose which road to follow.

Managing Growth

The next issue, managing growth of the organization, is seen as less of a challenge by leaders who are flexible, optimistic, and good problem-solvers. Dealing with growth requires flexibility. As the organizational needs change, the expectations and the demands of the leader must also adapt. In our studies of the Young Presidents' Organization (YPO), Young Entrepreneurs' Organization (YEO), and other leader groups, we've found that the ability to adapt to change—both within and outside the organization—is critical. I would go so far as to say that *adaptability* is the signature strength of today's leaders.

Yesterday's Leaders

If we look back at leaders of the past, we'll see that *consistency* was a signature characteristic. When yesterday's CEO made a decision, that decision was defended by everyone in the organization from top to bottom, even when contradicted by the data.

Taken to the extreme, leaders were expected to go down with the ship. The ability to "stick with it" and ride the tide was important for leaders who were ego-driven. That is, they feared *looking* bad as much as they feared doing bad. Changing your mind (or altering course) was perceived as an unbearable weakness. It was the kiss of death upon which the leader would lose respect and no longer be able to face his workers.

Who epitomizes this type of leadership? An example can be found by looking at one of the icons of corporate leadership during the first half of the 20th century—Henry Ford. Being steadfast and staying the course were significant characteristics in Ford's early success. However, there came a time when flexibility, willingness to change, and listening to others would be the right thing to do for the company.

Here is Lee Iacocca's view on Ford, from his seminal article in *Time* magazine: "The problem was that for too long they [Ford] worked on only one model. *Although people told him to diversify, Henry Ford had developed tunnel vision. He basically started saying 'to hell with the customer' who can have any color as long as it's black.* He didn't bring out a new design until the Model A in '27, and by then GM was gaining."[6] (emphasis added)

Getting stuck at that time gave Ford's biggest competitor, General Motors, the break it needed to capture significant market share. It was Ford's son who stepped in and finally insisted on bringing out new models needed for the continued survival of the company.

The other key aspect of this leadership style is that these leaders were driven by the past. They looked at the past to guide their future. What seemed to work before should continue to work again. This, of course, supports the need to be consistent.

Today's Leaders

On the other hand, let's look at how one of the 20th century's icons of corporate success—Bill Gates—faced a changing business landscape. I remember attending a presentation given by Gates in Toronto sometime during the early 1990s (along with about 2,000 others). At the time Gates talked about how Microsoft spent several million dollars looking at the potential of the internet. He concluded that the best commercial use would be for video-on-demand, and that the bandwidths required would be insufficient until the year 2010. As a result, Microsoft chose to take a pass on the internet.

The following quote is taken from another speech Bill Gates gave around the same time: "Bandwidth is a big issue. Unfortunately it's not like microprocessors where every year you're going to see exponential improvements...*But to make this happen will take something like 20 years*. And the main reason is to get these high-speed connections to be pervasive, particularly getting them into homes around the world, will take a long time."[7] (emphasis added)

Then something happened that changed everything. Silicon Valley veteran Jim Clark got together with a recent University of Illinois computer science graduate named Marc Andreson. In Clark's kitchen they created a small company with a plan to harvest the little-known World Wide Web. They called their enterprise Netscape. As soon as their little company went public, it changed the landscape of initial public offerings — it also changed the world as we knew it.

What was Bill Gates' reaction to this? After all, he was already one of the richest human beings on the planet. Would he stick with his decision to pass on the internet? Or would he risk publicly changing his mind? Would he base his decision on what others would think of him? Was he concerned about his ego? Come on, do you really think Bill Gates would make that kind of decision based on what people would think of him?

Gates turned his multi-billion-dollar organization around, practically on a dime, and went flat out after the internet. Microsoft Explorer was developed and eventually became the world's most widely used web browser. As documented in *Time* magazine: "The World Wide Web emerged in 1994, making browsers necessary, and Netscape was founded that same year. Sun Microsystems developed Java, the Internet programming language. Gates hung back. It wasn't until 1996 that Microsoft finally, according to Gates himself, 'embraced the internet wholeheartedly.'"[8]

Bill Gates, like many of today's successful leaders, is driven by the future and its opportunities, not by the past or his ego. Learning from the past is valuable, but preserving it can waste energy. Worrying about looking good, being consistent, or keeping the status quo were yesterday's virtues, but today's kiss of death.

Our CEOs who were high in flexibility, optimism, and problem-solving found it easier to manage growth. All of these qualities can be found in our Bill Gates example above. Once Gates saw the opportunity of the Internet, he showed flexibility by changing his position and optimism by believing that it was the right way to go for the future.

Problem-solving was important in planning and implementing the strategy to follow. A significant effort requiring the redeployment of people and resources had to be put into place. One can only imagine the number of obstacles that had to be overcome along the way.

There's another signature characteristic that I believe will define tomorrow's leader. But I'll get to that shortly.

Changing Technology

Changes in technology were less challenging for leaders who were high in flexibility and stress tolerance. It goes without saying that managing change requires flexibility. But it probably should be said that change can be stressful and the ability to manage stress is equally important for these leaders. This was reinforced by an article in the Canadian newspaper the *Globe and Mail*, which focused on managing change in the technology industry:

> Issues of change management can be most difficult for executives in the high-technology field, where employee loyalty to certain tools and ways of thinking can be very strong. But CEOs in virtually all industries must find ways to steer in new directions without alienating the work force. While the process can be painful, the alternative is to risk becoming an industry laggard.[9]

The article goes on to point out the importance of the emotional components of change. Quoting Connie Freeman, managing partner of MICA Consulting Partners:

> "While executives are usually proficient at analyzing numbers tied to big changes, they often don't fully appreciate the emotional impact those changes can have," Ms. Freeman says. "There's no such thing as a change that doesn't have an emotional component. It's about the degree to which the emotional component overrides the intellectual component."[10]

Other Business Challenges

Finally, the remaining business challenges showed no significant relationships with the emotional intelligence of our CEOs. These challenges include raising capital, marketing challenges, and managing innovation. Suffice it to say, other factors may play a more prominent role in dealing with these issues.

What about CEOs in different parts of the world?

Another, larger survey looking at what preoccupies CEOs today was carried out by the Conference Board and Accenture. That survey included 500 CEOs from across North America, Europe, and Asia. Among the findings in their summary they reported the following, "And, what is keeping American CEOs up at night? Shortages of key skills—especially in information technology."[11] Similar to our study's findings, hiring the right people is a major challenge for these business leaders.

The number-two concern among CEOs in Europe is "competing for talent." This also parallels our finding that "people issues" are the most difficult—whether it's finding, selecting, or keeping the best talent. Another key concern is flexibility and speed also impacting on the people within the organization: "Increasing flexibility and speed has become a top management concern. For CEOs in Europe, it has been the top management challenge for the past two years, and it's on the rise in North America and Japan."[12]

The Technology Fast 500 Asia Pacific 2004 CEO survey carried out by Deloitte also reached some similar conclusions. They surveyed 500 public and private technology, media, and telecommunications companies based in the Asia Pacific region. These CEOs were asked what their biggest operational challenges are in managing growth.

By far their biggest challenge, rated first by 34% of CEOs, is "finding, hiring, and retaining qualified employees." Number two, rated by 17%, is "keeping up with rapid market change."[13]

A more recent global survey of CEOs by Deloitte came out with similar findings. The 2006 Global Survey of CEOs in the Deloitte Fast 500 included technology, media, and telecommunications companies. One of their conclusions was: "As predicted in last year's report, the biggest obstacle to future growth will likely be finding people with the requisite skills. Hiring and retaining quality employees has always been an important operational challenge, but now the importance is growing to unprecedented levels."[14]

Also notable was the following: "In this year's survey, companies cited 'high quality employees' as the factor that most contributed to their spectacular growth."[15]

The top personal concerns of these CEOs reinforce our contention that leadership will continue to be a challenge for companies worldwide: "For CEOs of fast-growing companies, 'developing leaders and delegating responsibility' is the top personal priority. Quality people—the leaders of the future—are in increasingly short supply, and the technology sector is feeling more and more exposed as competition for the brightest and most agile minds intensifies."[16]

What about tomorrow's leaders?

I have spoken to many groups of CEOs about our research on emotional intelligence and leadership. After presenting the idea of signature characteristics of leaders, using the Henry Ford and Bill Gates examples given earlier, I typically ask a question. I ask them what they think the signature characteristic of tomorrow's leader will be.

I get some pretty interesting answers. They include things like being a global thinker, master strategist, emotionally intelligent (I think they add that to humor me), financial wizard, multi-lingual, futurist, business analyst, technological wizard, having high integrity, and even being "motherly." I think they enjoy the challenge of guessing, because sometimes I can't get them to stop throwing out answers. However, with all those interesting suggestions, they never seem to be able to guess my answer.

In our studies of leadership and emotional intelligence over the years, I have begun to notice a trend. One of the characteristics gaining in importance has been social responsibility. This factor has been unexpectedly associated with some of the best leaders we've seen. Most of the good leaders we see today are assertive, have good self-regard, are optimistic, tolerate stress well, and show flexibility. But the presence of *social responsibility* has been an unexpected finding.

The socially responsible leader puts her or his people first. This leader genuinely cares about the well-being of the people in the organization. This leader is also committed to the community and those less fortunate in the world. Actions speak louder than words with these leaders. They "walk the talk." We've noticed that socially responsible leaders get higher ratings from staff, tend to have better staff retention, and get more people engaged throughout the organization.

Where do we look for examples of this kind of leadership? There were very few at one time, but the numbers are slowly growing. Perhaps one of the first companies that had social responsibility built into its business plan from its inception was The Body Shop. Started in England by Anita Roddick in 1976, the company has continued to promote social causes:

> The Company's campaigns against human rights abuses, in favor
> of animal and environmental protection and its commitment to
> challenge the stereotypes of beauty perpetuated by the cosmetics

industry, have won the support of generations of consumers. The company continues to lead the way for businesses to use their voice for social and environmental change.[17]

Another leader, one who redefined his company into a socially responsible organization, is Jeffrey Swartz, CEO of Timberland. A number of years ago, while presenting at a conference in Hyannis, I had the opportunity to hear Swartz speak. The ostensible topic of his session was staff retention. What he really spoke about was being socially responsible.

He described himself as the "rich kid" grandson of Nathan Swartz, shoemaker and founder of Timberland. The success of the company came about after Nathan invented the waterproof boot. Nathan's son Sidney Swartz eventually took over and grew the company. Then his son Jeffrey ran the business. Jeffrey told the story of his transformation to social consciousness when he was called upon to personally help with a charitable cause. Somewhat reluctantly, he helped out—but the experience changed him.

As a result of his involvement, and the personal connection from helping others, he suddenly embraced the concept of social responsibility with zeal. Social responsibility became a signature characteristic of the entire organization due to his personal commitment and drive. While there are numerous helping activities at Timberland, this quote from its website gives you an example of the company's commitment:

> During the '90s, bold ideas like the Path of Service™ program began. It gives Timberland employees 40 hours of paid time off to serve in their communities. ...Jeffrey Swartz stepped up to grow the company his grandfather started and the brand his father built by turning Timberland into a 21st century example for socially responsible corporations around the world.[18]

Oh, yes, and did I mention the reason I went to hear him speak was about staff retention? Well, the moral of his story was that retention went up significantly, even with semi-skilled workers who sew the clothes and make the boots, as a result of the company's commitment to being socially responsible. We'll come back to this topic in Chapter 13 on Organizational Responsiveness.

Rather than being driven by the past or the future, these leaders are driven more by what could be. They look at the possibilities of what would make the world a better place. They are guided to a greater degree by their conscience and how their business can make real changes in the world.

Most CEOs see the light pretty quickly after I present these examples. I believe we are heading into a major corporate transformation in this direction—post–Enron, WorldCom, and Tyco. It's just one of a number of examples of how a responsive organization can win the hearts and minds of working people.

CHAPTER 3 | What Do We *Really* Know About Job Satisfaction and Productivity?

"Real success is finding your lifework in the work that you love."

David McCullough

"It does not seem to be true that work necessarily needs to be unpleasant. It may always have to be hard, or at least harder than doing nothing at all. But there is ample evidence that work can be enjoyable, and that indeed, it is often the most enjoyable part of life."

Mihaly Csikszentmihalyi, *Flow: The Psychology of Optimal Experience*, 1990

"There is a vast world of work out there in this country, where at least 111 million people are employed in this country alone—many of whom are bored out of their minds. All day long. Not for nothing is their motto TGIF—'Thank God It's Friday.' They live for the weekends, when they can go do what they really want to do."

Richard Nelson Bolles, *What Color Is Your Parachute?*, 1970

"Pleasure in the job puts perfection in the work."

Aristotle

One day in 1927, factory workers at the Western Electric Hawthorne Plant in Cicero, Illinois, took part in an unusual experiment. Without any fanfare they went about their everyday jobs on the shop floor, assembling telephone relays. It's unlikely that the workers, their managers, or even the researchers involved could have predicted the impact of their efforts.

The number of relays assembled per shift had been counted over the previous weeks. When the workers arrived for their shift that day, the lighting surrounding their work area had been noticeably brightened. The researchers, perched quietly nearby, watched carefully as the plant employees went about their usual routine. The results were remarkable. Productivity increased dramatically with the new lighting arrangement. However, the increased productivity didn't last very long. Production rates eventually slowed and returned to their norm. Nevertheless, for the researchers, this was the beginning of a six-year journey exploring the relationship between the workplace and productivity.

Once the workers' rate of putting together relays returned to the baseline level, the next intervention was implemented. This time researchers dimmed the lighting throughout the assembly area. Again, they watched as the relays were assembled. To their surprise, production rates went up once again. But alas, after running its course, the rate eventually returned to its normal tempo for a second time.

The interventions continued, with changes made to other aspects of the workplace: more breaks, longer breaks, then fewer breaks, and finally shorter breaks. Changes were also made to the way employees were paid for their work, looking at the effects of piecework.

The project leader, Elton Mayo of the Harvard Business School, documented his work in a book called *The Human Problems of an Industrialised Civilisation*. Mayo and his associates, Fritz J. Roethlisberger and William J. Dickson, started out by looking at how employees were affected by the physical and environmental influences of the workplace (e.g., brightness of lights, humidity). Then they moved on to study the impact of the psychological aspects of work (e.g., breaks, group pressure, working hours, managerial leadership).

Elton Mayo concluded that the employees were more productive as a result of being closely watched by the researchers. Their work rate improved due to the special attention they received. This is the most widely accepted interpretation of what became known as the "Hawthorne Effect."

Mayo's ideas have had a lasting influence on our understanding of worker-employer relationships: the collection of data at work, better understanding of labor-management relations, and learning from the informal interaction among factory employees. The Hawthorne studies dramatically impacted the next 50 years of industrial-organizational psychology, guiding the focus on how management, worker satisfaction, and other workplace activities affect performance.

But while the Hawthorne studies brought attention and even fame to the study of industrial organizational psychology, they also brought their share of dissent.

Some people challenged Mayo's explanation of what happened at Hawthorne. For example, H. McIlvaine Parsons, writing in _Science_ magazine, believed the effect was due to a combination of rest periods between the changes, learning what went on during the experiment and feedback that the workers received from seeing changes in their performance.[1]

Debates about the results continued for decades, as a 1998 article in the _New York Times_ illustrates: "Take the 'Hawthorne Effect,' which is much embraced in social psychology. ... The workers, or so the story goes, produced more because they saw themselves as special, participants in an experiment, and their inter-relationships improved.

"Sounds very compelling. 'The results of the experiment, or rather the human relations interpretation offered by the researchers who summarized the results, soon became gospel for introductory textbooks in both psychology and management science,' said Dr. Lee Ross, a psychology professor at Stanford University."[2]

Differences in interpretation aside, there were many lessons learned from the Hawthorne studies. But one of the most important contributions seems to have gotten lost in the debate. It has to do with _why_ the project was carried out in the first place. Mayo wanted to validate his belief that working conditions were important. If people could feel better about their jobs, they would be more productive. He was interested in "how management can make workers perform differently because they _feel_ differently."[3] (emphasis added)

In the late 1950s, interest in the study of job satisfaction suddenly declined, most likely due to an article published in 1955 by psychologists Arthur Brayfield and Walter Crockett. They wrote a critical review of the work in this area. Using the few scientific studies that were available at the time, they concluded that there was "minimal or no relationship"[4] between job satisfaction and performance.

The job satisfaction-productivity connection came alive again in the late 1960s. But alas, it declined once more in the 1980s. Over the years, interest in this area has come and gone. In fact, some critics have referred to job satisfaction as a fad, not worthy of research and of negligible importance.[5]

The connection between job satisfaction and job performance has often been referred to as the Holy Grail of industrial-organizational psychology. There have been significant changes in the way researchers have approached this topic over the years. One of the lasting outcomes of this work has been its focus on humanizing the workplace. Shift workers, who were once treated as cogs in a wheel, were now being seen as people who had thoughts, feelings, and desires. It was just the beginning of an understanding that treating workers as people might benefit both the organization and its employees.

Current Views of Job Satisfaction and Work Performance

A recent article by psychology professor Timothy Judge and his colleagues reviewed more than 60 years of research on the job satisfaction-performance connection. In their effort to make sense of this area, their analysis included 312 workplace samples and studies related to 54,417 workers.[6]

According to Judge, the relationship between job satisfaction and performance can be quite complicated. It's not simply a matter of making someone happy at work and watching their performance soar. There's a feedback loop that has to be taken into account. When you are happy with your job, you perform better, which then makes you feel good, which then feeds back into more good performance. On the other hand, you can start out happy, perform well, then not be recognized for your performance, or be poorly paid. The likelihood in this scenario is that your productivity will suffer.

There are important "mediating" factors that strengthen or weaken the relationship between job happiness and performance. These include things like the amount and perceived fairness of your pay, how well recognized you are for your work, and your own sense of accomplishment. Each of us weighs these factors differently. Some people only work hard for a lot of money, others prefer job security, and still others work hardest when they are passionate about what they do. These factors play out differently depending on the person and the job.

How strong is the link between job satisfaction and performance? In the analysis by Judge and his colleagues, they found differences between simple jobs (such as those done by laborers) and complex jobs (such as those done by scientist-engineers). They concluded that job satisfaction accounts for about 9% of performance for simple and medium-complexity jobs. So if you work in a fast-food restaurant, it's likely that about 9% of your performance will be due to how much you like your job. Because these jobs are fairly repetitive and often supervised, job satisfaction may not be the main driver for high performance. That's why other incentives are needed to keep people engaged in these sorts of jobs.

On the other hand, for complex jobs, such as scientist-engineers or architects, job satisfaction drives about 25% of performance. When a scientist-engineer solves a complex problem or invents a new process, that in itself can be highly rewarding. The thrill of successfully overcoming a difficult challenge is exciting for people doing highly complex work. I've been told in confidence by several highly skilled (and highly paid) specialists that they loved their work so much they would continue doing it even if they were paid half as much.

When all different types of jobs are lumped together, Judge concludes that job satisfaction drives slightly less than 10% of performance. That leaves about 90% of performance that can be influenced by other factors. But more about that later.

Ten percent of productivity can still be a big bump on a company's bottom line. So let's explore some of the factors that mediate between job satisfaction and increased productivity.

Personality and Job Performance

Mary is an in-house corporate attorney. She used to work at a law firm, but the pressure of constantly increasing her billable hours while trying to bring in new business was just too much. She loved law, and wanted to work where she could focus on what she was trained to do—law—and not on sales and marketing. So she left the big-name firm for a small but growing software company.

At the law firm she mainly interacted with lawyers. It was easy socializing with like-minded people who shared many common traits. In her new job she works with a variety of different people. In the course of a day she'll encounter programmers, accountants, marketing and sales people, customer service representatives and a number of others who work at the software company.

Mary is diligent about her work. Her responsibilities include all the company's software licensing agreements. The documents she deals with need to be properly organized, reviewed, and executed. One day she realized that she probably works just as hard now as she did in her previous job, but with far less pressure. Her work is intense and the workflow has been steady. In fact, she has been constantly busy, regardless of whether company sales were up or down.

After a lunch meeting with a group of other managers, she realized that the salespeople in the company operated quite differently than she did. For one thing, they showed much more variability in how hard they worked. When sales were up, they relaxed and took it easy. But when sales dropped and there was talk of cutbacks, they suddenly woke up and went into action. All the sales reps would run off and work non-stop until the sales got back on track. It puzzled her why they didn't just work hard all the time.

Each of us has our own way of approaching the world. Our personality influences our style of interacting with others. Some people are more extroverted while others tend towards introversion. There are those of us who are conscientious and others who prefer to be more laissez-faire. In our example, Mary is high on the conscientiousness scale. She loves her work and pays attention to the details. Getting it done right and as soon as possible are priorities for her.

Her colleagues in sales, however, are less driven by the nature of their work. They don't spend their extra time reading up on the latest sales techniques the way Mary keeps up with the law review journals. Mary's colleagues in sales are more driven by outside forces. In this case, they are motivated by fear of losing income or their jobs.

The sales reps could choose any time they wanted to go out and close sales. If they were more conscientious, they'd wake up in the morning driven to hunt for sales. While Mary meticulously deals with all the details in her work, the salespeople pay less attention to their paperwork or the details of their follow-up calls. It's not that they're bad people or that they lack talent. Their personality styles are different.

Traits such as conscientiousness play an important role in mediating the job satisfaction-productivity connection. As another example of this, people like Mary pay less attention to their work environment and focus more on the work itself. The salespeople in our story are much more attuned to the workplace issues around them and less concerned with the art of selling. They are influenced much more by their compensation packages, company perks, and other external factors.

The more conscientious you are, the harder you work, regardless of the job conditions. When the work environment worsens, people who are less conscientious are more likely to withdraw from their work, reducing their productivity. So when you initiate workplace changes, you can expect it to have a much greater impact on your less conscientious employees. The more conscientious they are, the less of a difference it will make in their work output.

Self-Identity and Job Performance

Dr. Brown is an endodontist.

That's probably as much as he would want you to know about him. And, if some well-known statistics are true in his case, that should tell you everything you need to know about him. For example, you know he's well educated, has a profession, not just a dentist but a specialist, drives a nice car, has a nice house, lives in a nice neighborhood, plays golf, takes nice vacations, has a good health plan, works in a fancy office, and has great teeth. You may even know more than he wants you to know. For example, it's likely that he's had an affair with his dental assistant and he's soon to be or already is divorced.

Does Dr. Brown like his job? Chances are good that he loves his job. He probably reads dental magazines on the beach while he's on vacation. I don't even have to be a psychologist to know all of this.

Some people believe their job is central to their lives. It's how they identify and define themselves and others. "I'm a doctor," or "You're a plumber"—that just about says it all. What else is there to know? Well, how does that relate to job satisfaction?

Job satisfaction increases performance for people who define themselves by their occupation. Because their identity is so wrapped up in what they do, bad performance is not an option. They love their job and do their best because that's how they define themselves. In fact, it can be quite devastating for these people if, for some reason, they perform badly at work (or get caught or accused of poor performance). It becomes a very personal blow to their self-esteem.

On the other end of the spectrum there are people who treat their work as a means to an end. They take jobs just to earn the money they need to live on. Job satisfaction does little to motivate these people. They are mainly motivated by money and will easily switch from one job to the next for a few dollars more in pay.

Job Autonomy and Job Performance

Marilyn loved her job as a human resource coordinator. She was a self-starter. She never had to be prodded or reminded to do any of her tasks. She was proud of her work and she knew her job inside out. Marilyn was used to working on her own. Her supervisor checked in periodically to see how things were going. Quality checks were built into her job, so if anything went wrong it was flagged.

When Bill, the new director of human resources, came on the scene, things suddenly changed. Bill was a perfectionist and liked to micro-manage people. He wanted to review everything Marilyn did. He felt that in order for him to be on top of his job he needed to be familiar with what everyone in his department was doing. After all, as Marilyn's supervisor, he was responsible for any mistakes she made. It didn't really matter that she had performed her job flawlessly for ten years with little direct supervision.

Within a few weeks of Bill's arrival, Marilyn started having stomach cramps. A couple of weeks later she began getting headaches in the afternoons. She saw her doctor, who couldn't find anything physically wrong with her. She told him everything was fine at work.

Her health continued to get worse. The stress was building up. She missed more and more time from work. This was especially troubling because before Bill arrived Marilyn had rarely missed a day of work. The quality of her work suffered as well. Now there were mistakes being made on staff employment records. Marilyn was shocked when they were pointed out to her. This only led to a further deterioration of her work. As things got worse, Bill's determination to supervise her work only increased.

Bill helps illustrate another important link in the job satisfaction-performance connection. When someone is responsible for their own accomplishments, they become more satisfied and perform better. Job autonomy directly influences performance. People who believe they have more control over their work not only feel better about their work, but they do a better job.

There are still managers unwilling to give up control to their employees. For some, it is a fear of letting go. Others worry about all the mistakes their employees will make if they are not carefully watched. Yet if you've properly selected your people (more about that in Chapter 5), trained them, and set expectations (with transparent feedback), performance should soar.

Everybody in the organization should have clear goals with measurable results. A well-developed orientation and training program should be in place. As part of the training program there should be feedback, even if only informal, from every participant in order to improve the process.

If an employee has had good training and clear performance goals (which are achievable), and continues to show poor results, then it's likely you've hired the wrong person for the job. If you want a job to be done well, then you need put the right people in place.

Keeping people in the organization who continually fail to meet reasonably set goals is bad for everyone. It's bad for the person who keeps failing at his or her job. It's bad for others in the organization to see someone continually rewarded for failing. When that happens, people start to rethink their own efforts and goals. Finally, it's bad for the organization as a whole once it's seen as having lowered its standards. Performance levels start dropping throughout the organization.

One of the best-performing companies in the technology world today is Google. In a feature article in *Fast Company* magazine by Keith Hammonds, Google is described the following way: "Its performance is the envy of executives and engineers around the world ... For techno-evangelists, Google is a marvel of Web brilliance ... For Wall Street, it may be the IPO that changes everything (again) ... But Google is also a case study in savvy management—a company filled with cutting-edge ideas, rigorous accountability, and relentless attention to detail ... a company from which every company can learn."[7]

One of the lessons learned from Google's formula for success is that great people can manage themselves. First, they invest the time needed to hire the right people: "Google spends more time on hiring than on anything else. It knows this because, like any bunch of obsessive engineers, it keeps track. It says that it gets 1,500 resumes a day from wannabe Googlers. Between screening, interviewing, and assessing, it invested 87 Google people-hours in each of the 300 or so people that it hired in 2002."[8]

Taking risks is highly valued at Google. That makes it even more challenging to put people in charge of themselves. Hammonds describes the risk of putting people in charge of their own work and how Google manages that risk:

The challenge is negotiating the tension between risk and caution. When (Wayne) Rosing started at Google in 2001, "we had management in engineering. And the structure was tending to tell people, 'No, you can't do that.' So Google got rid of the managers. Now most engineers work in teams of three, with project leadership rotating among team members. If something isn't right, even if it's in a product that has already gone public, teams fix it without asking anyone.

"For a while," Rosing says, "I had 160 direct reports. No managers. It worked because the teams knew what they had to do. That set a cultural bit in people's heads: You are the boss. Don't wait to take the hill. Don't wait to be managed."[9]

What happens when your idea fails at Google?

And if you fail, fine. On to the next idea. "There's faith here in the ability of smart, well-motivated people to do the right thing," Rosing says. "Anything that gets in the way of that is evil."[10]

It can't be stressed enough how important it is to have the right people in place. People with the right emotional and social skills are better at managing themselves as well as managing others. There is a danger in just hiring a group of smart people, throwing them together, and hoping for success. By selecting for and nurturing skills such as emotional self-awareness, independence, interpersonal relationships, assertiveness, and empathy, you increase your chances of putting together people who can function well.

Success and Job Satisfaction

Joe was top salesperson for a large sportswear manufacturer. He won the platinum award five years in a row. Now at the end of the first quarter he was already leading the other sales reps by a good margin. He had all the winning characteristics. He was outgoing, assertive, confident, made people feel at ease, knew how to listen, and was always ready to help someone out.

People often asked Joe why he was so successful. There are probably a number of factors involved, such as finding the right prospects, knowing your product, understanding what your customer wants and needs, knowing the marketplace, and getting the customer what he wants when he wants it.

But there's one other factor that helps maintain the success: as the old saying goes, nothing breeds success like success. In the job satisfaction-performance equation, the road goes both ways. While satisfaction (high or low) affects performance, performance (high or low) also affects satisfaction. So not only does job satisfaction drive better work performance, but better work performance then increases work satisfaction. That's what feeds a success-driven culture.

A dramatic example of success breeding success was reported in the *Kalamazoo Gazette*. Kalamazoo Central High School in Michigan was not doing a good job with its minority students. The school, unlike the population as a whole, is approximately 50% African-American. A program was implemented that focused on creating a culture of success for a subset of African-American girls. Teachers, parents, and coaches all worked to foster an environment of excellence. As a result of this program, the number of African-American girls graduating from the school increased 50% between 2001 and 2006—from 39 to 60, even though the enrollment rate stayed the same.

But the program didn't just increase the graduation rate, it succeeded in creating a far-reaching culture of success for these students. As the *Gazette* reported:

Erin McCormick is going to Harvard with plans to be a scientist, Cassie Dickerson is headed to Ohio State with an eye on veterinary school, and Sierra Calvin is going to the University of Michigan with hopes of becoming a psychiatrist.[11]

Just by reading their stories it becomes clear that these students will be the top picks for the college of their choice, and following that, most likely their organization of choice. How did the students themselves describe their experience in the program? The *Gazette*:

"It's all about attitude and about how the people around you look at education," Robinson said.

[Sierra] Calvin agreed, saying teachers are more than willing to help students who want to learn.

"If you show a teacher that you want to make something of your-self, they'll help you, they'll push you," she said. "I've had some great instructors here. I feel like K-C definitely has been a great place to learn."

"Being around girls that are driven makes you even more driven," Calvin said. "It definitely helps."[12]

What mood are you in? Emotion, Performance, and Job Satisfaction

One of the emerging topics in the study of work performance is the interrela-tionship of mood, emotion and performance. A lot of research has looked at how mood affects performance. Now researchers are starting to look at how performance affects mood.

According to Judge and his associates: "[A]lthough there is a great deal of research on the effect of mood on performance, it surprises us that the research on the effects of performance on mood is lacking. Most individuals would rather do something well than poorly, and thus doing something well is likely to elevate mood. Mood, in turn, is related to job satisfaction."[13]

It seems obvious that being successful puts you in a better mood. In a business magazine article, Melanie Johnson observes:

> Just as it would seem obvious that a person's mood would have an impact on their job performance, the reverse is also true. A per-son's work or job performance can greatly affect their mood, health and sense of well-being.
>
> As humans, we have the unique ability to experience a wide variety of emotions and moods. When moods become intensely negative, they may interfere with our work and personal lives.[14]

Purdue University psychologist Howard Weiss, quoted in *USA Today*, promoted the importance of studying people's moods at work. He believes that most satisfaction surveys are too general to really get at worker morale; they're more of a snapshot of where things are at. Instead, he advocates look-ing at people's day-to-day moods:

Weiss, who studies job satisfaction, says daily events drive the emotional states of employees and thus affect their behavior and overall job satisfaction. While an unhappy employee can be productive and may decide for other reasons not to quit the job, his or her attitude may negatively impact fellow workers, customers, or clients. [According to Weiss,] "Actually, workplaces are more like emotional cauldrons, with daily circumstances influencing employee feelings and job performance."

In fact, daily turmoil may be the most important factor affecting job satisfaction. He suggests supervisors be "events managers," controlling to whatever extent possible the events that affect employees. For example, a boss yelling at workers may start a chain reaction of irritation as berated employees interact with others throughout the day. "It's particularly important to keep the number of negative events down, in order to minimize negative emotional states." Research shows that the negative effects of negative emotions affect job performance more than do the positive effects of positive emotions.[15]

Cynthia Fisher, an Australian psychologist, has followed up on Weiss's work and advocates redefining job satisfaction. She believes in separating the mood or feelings part from the thinking or attitudes part.

Fisher studied the actual moods and thoughts of working people over time and came to a number of interesting conclusions. One hundred and twenty-four workers from 65 different companies had their moods continually monitored over a two-week period. They wore special watches with an alarm that went off five times per day. Each time it went off, they completed surveys about how they were feeling at that time. These mood measures were then related to their overall job satisfaction.

You might think nothing of those everyday feelings of joy and irritation you experience going about your work. Fisher found that those moods, along with any positive and negative emotions, were all directly related to your overall job satisfaction. In fact, they account for somewhere between 5% and 25% of how satisfied you are with your job, depending on how work satisfaction was measured.

She also found that positive and negative emotions operate differently in how they affect overall job satisfaction. For positive emotions, the percentage of time you feel good is more important than the intensity of the emotions. So one "feel-good party" at the end of the month isn't likely to make up for a lot of small stresses or hassles throughout the week. It's better to try and keep the mood positive as many times as possible throughout the course of each day.

Negative emotions, on the other hand, are more closely related to stress, strain, and burnout. Ongoing negative feelings at work increase distraction, disengagement, and can lead to absenteeism. Negative moods at work increase employee dissatisfaction. Dissatisfied workers tend to withdraw more. This can be through staff turnover, absences, illness, or just plain tuning out at work.

Fisher has suggestions on how managers can better manage these emotions: "[E]mployers should concentrate on providing a work environment free of minor irritations and hassles which tip the balance towards more frequent, if mild, negative effect. ... They might also build in small frequent positive reinforcements or 'uplifts,' perhaps through job design and informal reward systems, rather than relying on more intense but less frequent positive emotions created by formal rewards, promotions, or public celebrations, in order to enhance job attitudes."[16]

While there are many things employees can do to improve their moods, there are also interventions that employers can make to improve the work environment. These will be discussed in the coming chapters.

CHAPTER 4

Emotional Intelligence and Organizational Culture: A New Relationship

"Many people think that if they were only in some other place, or had some other job, they would be happy. Well, that is doubtful. So get as much happiness out of what you are doing as you can and don't put off being happy until some future date."

Dale Carnegie

"What we need to do is learn to work in the system, by which I mean that everybody, every team, every platform, every division, every component is there not for individual competitive profit or recognition, but for contribution to the system as a whole on a win-win basis."

W. Edwards Deming

"Never continue in a job you don't enjoy. If you're happy in what you're doing, you'll like yourself, you'll have inner peace. And if you have that, along with physical health, you will have had more success than you could possibly have imagined."

Johnny Carson

"To find out what one is fitted to do, and to secure an opportunity to do it, is the key to happiness."

John Dewey

"The future may be made up of many factors but where it truly lies is in the hearts and minds of men. Your dedication should not be confined for your own gain, but unleashes your passion for our beloved country as well as for the integrity and humanity of mankind."

Li-Ka-Shing, East Asia's richest man and philanthropist

What is emotional intelligence?

It was worse than the usual morning rush hour. Anita, a senior manager at a biotechnology firm, was stuck in traffic and about to be late for an important meeting. As she finally entered a free stretch of highway, a swerving Corvette cut her off, just missing the front right corner of her car.

"Damn you!" she screamed out her window at the driver, now several car lengths ahead.

When she finally arrived at her office, with the meeting already in process, she threw her coat on her chair and swung around to get to the board room.

"Anita, coff –?" offered Maria, her assistant.

"Not now. Out of my way!" Anita barked as she leaped out the door.

This was the third time in two days Anita was rude to Maria. Maria, who prided herself on being extremely competent and conscientious, was alarmed by Anita's behavior.

Maria's interpretation of the situation played out in the self-talk in her head. "She must really hate me. Why else would she be so rude to me? I know I'm not good enough to be working here. I should start looking for work somewhere else where I'll fit in better. I really can't measure up to Anita's standards."

Was there any objective evidence to support Maria's interpretation of what was going on? Could there be any alternative explanations? Anita actually thought Maria was the best, most efficient assistant she'd ever had. She just didn't bother spending the extra few minutes it would take to: 1) manage her emotions once she got to the office, and 2) pay attention to managing Maria's expectations, feelings, and understanding of the situation.

Anita was a Harvard Business School graduate. She stood in the top third of her class. She was an excellent strategist, able to take complex business problems and find concrete, manageable solutions. But somehow, she was unable to calm herself down for just a few critical moments. She couldn't take the focus off her own anger long enough to think about the effects her behavior might have on her assistant.

Later on she would wonder, in disbelief, "How could something so small and inconsequential cause someone so competent to leave for another job? This is so disruptive; the last thing I need right now is to spend my time trying to find another assistant." Of course, it wasn't one incident, but numerous displays of lack of concern that had built up. The real question, of course, is why didn't Anita have the wherewithal to realize the effect she was having on the most important person to her in the workplace? This can be characterized as a lack of emotional intelligence.

What is individual emotional intelligence?

Ever since the release in 1995 of Daniel Goleman's bestselling book *Emotional Intelligence: Why It Can Matter More Than IQ*,[1] the term has become part of our everyday language. Prior to 1995, only a handful of researchers had even heard the phrase. Now, it seems to be everywhere. In 1997, when we released the world's first test of emotional intelligence (the Emotional Quotient Inventory or EQ-i®),[2] one of the most frequently asked questions on the topic was whether or not this was just another fad, like reengineering, total quality management, management by objective, quality circles, and others long forgotten.

The answer then and now is quite simple. As long as two conditions exist in the world, emotional intelligence will be important. *The first is that there are human beings. The second is that they interact with one another.*

In fact, emotional intelligence was important even before the second condition. When our ancestors lived in caves they were hunters. Every once in a while, when man encountered a larger, stronger, carnivorous animal, emotional intelligence meant the difference between eating and being eaten for dinner. It was the successful navigation of the "flight or fight" response that determined whether he would survive. This was an early example of managing emotions.

When was emotional intelligence identified?

Charles Darwin, in his work on evolution and survival, documented the importance of emotions as a signaling system. The angry look on a wolf's face serves as a signal that the hunter could ignore at his peril. Once again, this is where the "flight or fight" response kicks in. This, according to Darwin, led to our survival as humans. The lower, more primitive areas of the brain mediate this response—the same parts that control our emotional responses today—the limbic system and the hippocampus.

These emotional parts of the brain influence the way our higher, more advanced areas— the neocortex—function. So while we are making complex decisions, interacting with people, solving problems, and so on, the lower parts of the brain are still active—playing a role in how effectively we carry out various tasks. Emotions impact our decisions, our reaction to things and to people. Some of us are more aware of our emotions than others. Some of us have better control over our emotions. We get along with people better, we manage stress better, we are more optimistic about our future. *If you don't think these qualities matter at work and in life, you may be missing out on something pretty important.*

Definitions of emotional intelligence

There are two leading models of emotional intelligence. The first was developed by Yale University professor Peter Salovey (currently dean of Yale College) and University of New Hampshire professor John (Jack) Mayer, the psychologists who coined the term "emotional intelligence."[3]

They defined the term as "the ability to perceive emotions, to access and generate emotions so as to assist thought, to understand emotions and emotional meanings, and to reflectively regulate emotions in ways that promote emotional and intellectual growth." In other words, it's a set of skills that enables us to make our way in a complex world—the personal, social, and survival aspects of overall intelligence, the elusive ability to be sensitive to and manage our emotions in everyday life.

They developed what is referred to as an "ability model" of emotional intelligence. This model views emotional intelligence in a similar way that psychologists define cognitive intelligence (IQ). Like cognitive intelligence, emotional intelligence consists of specific abilities, but instead of solving arithmetical equations or putting together puzzles we recognize emotions in people's faces or understand the best way to manage someone else's emotions.

Along with their psychologist colleague David Caruso, Salovey and May-er developed a test to measure these emotional abilities.[4] The test, called the MSCEIT™ (Maye–Salovey–Caruso Emotional Intelligence Test), has been used in hundreds of research studies worldwide in order to help us understand the ways in which emotional intelligence affects our lives.

A second model, by psychologist Reuven Bar-On, who coined the term EQ (for emotional quotient)—to parallel the more commonly known IQ—was developed in the late 1980s and early 1990s.[5] He defined emotional intelligence as "an array of non-cognitive (emotional and social) capabilities, competencies and skills that influence one's ability to succeed in coping with environmental demands and pressures."[6]

The Bar-On model of emotional and social intelligence includes five general areas:

Intra-Personal – your ability to be aware of, manage, and express your emotions;

Inter-Personal – your ability to initiate and maintain relationships with others, your "people skills";

Adaptability – your ability to be flexible, solve problems, and be realistic;

Stress Management – your ability to tolerate stress and control impulses; and

General Mood – your happiness and optimism.

These five areas break down into 15 specific factors. Identifying, measuring, and validating these factors are the result of more than 20 years of research on emotional and social intelligence in more than 30 different countries. The factors are:

The Bar-On EQ-i Scales and What They Assess

EQ-i Scales	The EI competency assessed by each scale
Intra-personal	
Self-regard	*Ability to respect and accept one's strengths and weaknesses.*
Emotional Self-awareness	*Ability to be aware of and understand one's feelings and behaviors and their impact on others.*
Assertiveness	*Ability to express feelings, beliefs and thoughts in a non-destructive way.*
Independence	*Ability to be self-directed and free of emotional dependency on others.*
Self-actualization	*Ability to set personal goals and realize one's potential.*
Inter-personal	
Empathy	*Ability to be aware of, understand and appreciate the feelings of others.*
Social Responsibility	*Ability to demonstrate oneself as a cooperative, contributing member of one's social group.*
Interpersonal Relationship	*Ability to establish and maintain mutually satisfying relationships with others.*
Stress Management	
Stress Tolerance	*Ability to effectively withstand adverse events and constructively cope.*
Impulse Control	*Ability to resist or delay an impulse, drive or temptation to act.*
Adaptability	
Reality testing	*Ability to accurately assess the correspondence between what is experienced and what objectively exists.*
Flexibility	*Ability to adapt and adjust one's feeling, thinking, and behavior to change.*
Problem-solving	*Ability to solve problems of a personal and interpersonal nature.*
General Mood	
Optimism	*Ability to be positive and look at the brighter side of life.*
Happiness	*Ability to feel satisfied with oneself, others and life in general.*

Definitions presented with permission of Multi-Health Systems. Slightly modified from R. Bar-On, Bar-On Emotional Quotient Inventory Manual, Toronto: Multi-Health Systems: 1997.

Bar-On developed the world's first scientific and standardized test of emotional intelligence to be statistically standardized. Called the Bar-On Emotional Quotient Inventory (EQ-i®), it has subsequently tested the emotional intelligence of more individuals than any other scientifically developed test—more than 500,000 people worldwide.

While experts may disagree on the precise meaning of emotional intelligence, it's important to remember that this is a relatively new area of study. The first scientific paper on emotional intelligence was only published in 1989. Cognitive intelligence (IQ) has been with us for over 100 years and we still have no agreement on the definition of intelligence.

However, there is consensus on the basic principles behind what we refer to as emotional intelligence. It's widely agreed that it involves the ability to understand and manage emotions. Broadly speaking, emotional intelligence addresses the emotional, social, and survivor dimensions of intelligence. These are often more important for daily functioning than the more cognitive or intellectual aspects of intelligence. Emotional intelligence is concerned with understanding oneself and others, relating to people, and adapting to and coping with the immediate surroundings.

In my book (with co-author Howard Book) *The EQ Edge: Emotional Intelligence and Your Success*,[7] we presented the case for the importance of emotional intelligence both at work and at home. Dozens of studies were presented making the case that emotional and social intelligence are key factors, beyond IQ and personality, in successfully navigating your way through work and personal endeavors. Also of importance is the finding that emotional and social skills, unlike your IQ, can be improved with the right interventions.

What is organizational emotional intelligence?

Work on emotional and social intelligence has now extended into organizations. If individual emotional and social intelligence can make a person more successful, is the same true of the culture of an organization?

Leaders of successful organizations recognize that their employees are their key assets and that by developing their people there will be benefits to the bottom line. By understanding employee needs, wants, and perceptions, the organization can identify and capitalize on its strengths. Areas of weakness can also be determined and targeted for action as needed. Increasingly, organizations are recognizing that the key to maximizing their competitive position in the market requires paying attention to the satisfaction, motivation, and goals of its employees.

An organization is more than the sum of its parts. The satisfaction, motivation, and goals of each individual in the organization add up to be much greater. It is this collective that plays a key role in maximizing the organization's competitive position. Being able to measure and understand the nature of the organization's emotional and social intelligence is a first step to helping the organization reach its full potential.

In fact, Howard Book has described the impact of the emotionally intelligent organization:

> Organizations that lack Emotional Intelligence (EI) are at risk of failing to attain their strategic goals. Their style and culture inhibit spontaneity, prize only routine, don't tolerate errors, devalue diverse views, stifle criticism of superiors or encourage secrecy and retribution.
>
> The Emotionally Intelligent Organization (EIO), on the other hand, promotes a culture in which openness and transparency are the norm, and respectful assertiveness is commonplace. It also encourages diversity, tolerates constructive disagreement, and values contained flexibility and multi-directional communication.[8]

Corporate Culture

In the early 1980s, Terry Deal and Allan Kennedy, in their bestselling book *Corporate Cultures*, made the very convincing case that every organization has a culture. They cited *Webster's* definition of culture: "the integrated pattern of human behavior that includes thought, speech, action, and artifacts and depends on man's capacity for learning and transmitting knowledge to succeeding generations."[9]

A more informal definition, provided by Marvin Bowler, former managing director of McKinsey & Company, and applied to business was "the way we do things around here."[10]

Every organization does indeed have a culture. Companies, which are social enterprises, encompass tribal habits, well-defined cultural roles for individuals and various strategies for determining inclusion, reinforcing identity, and adapting to change. Deal and Kennedy argued against early concepts of "reengineering" the organization—Japanese management, cost curves, econometric models, and so on—as solutions for making businesses more productive. Instead, they stressed the need to re-learn old lessons about "how culture ties people together and gives meaning to their everyday lives."[11]

Historical examples of strong builders of culture in organizations were people such as Thomas Watson at IBM, Harley Procter at Procter & Gamble, and General Robert Wood Johnson of Johnson & Johnson. The culture in most of these cases could be boiled down to a paramount belief, or a "superordinate goal." For example, at IBM, "IBM means service"; at General Electric, "Progress is our most important product"; and at DuPont, "Better things for better living through chemistry."

While these were effective aspirations in their time, today's mission has to be more "emotive" in order to motivate people. People are looking for greater meaning in their missions today. There should be a purpose that demonstrates how you and your organization make the world a better place.

The relationship between the organizational culture and a variety of corporate benchmarks has been widely studied over the years since Deal and Kennedy's book. One interesting study looked at the role of culture—or organizational climate—in a completely different culture, that of mainland China. Zhang Zhen, Ma Li, and Ma Wenjing surveyed 148 organizations throughout mainland China. Even in this diverse culture they found that non-bureaucratic, supportive, and communicative climates were the best predictors of employee engagement or involvement in the organization.[12]

Merging Culture and Emotional Intelligence

Leslie works in what she describes as a young, laid-back advertising firm. She is friends with her colleagues, spends a lot of her leisure time with them, and describes how her bosses are cool about forwarding email jokes and sharing funny websites. Everyone gathers around Leslie's computer to laugh over the latest download—it's all part of the creative and hip atmosphere.

But Leslie is at work from 9:30 in the morning to 8:30 almost every night. When her friend Alice picks Leslie up at the firm at 5:30 p.m.—Leslie's official end of the day—for a weekend away, Leslie feels guilty about leaving so early.

She says everyone else is still at the office, and thinks she is letting her manager down. Alice doesn't share Leslie's guilt because she is rarely pressured to stay late at her records management job. Her co-workers and supervisor do the occasional lunch, but it's usually kept at the professional level. It would be unheard-of in Alice's more conservative workplace for anyone to make a show of checking personal emails or surfing the web. Alice can't help but think that if Leslie's workplace was a little more focused, her friend would get her job done during work hours and wouldn't feel obligated to work evenings.

In our research we have been looking at how culture fits together with what could be described as an "emotionally intelligent" workplace. Organizational emotional intelligence involves people's feelings and thoughts about the work they do, their co-workers, supervisor, top leadership, the organization itself, and their impact on the world around them.

I've stated previously that my definition of the emotionally intelligent organization is "an organization's ability to successfully and efficiently cope with change and accomplish its goals, while being responsible and sensitive to its people, customers, suppliers, networks, and society."

So, while the people at Leslie's workplace strive to create a "fun" place, they sacrifice efficiency and personal time in the process. By overstaying the amount of time people need to spend at work, the organization is not being responsible and sensitive to its people.

Organizational emotional intelligence combines what are often referred to as *strategic* and *tactical* elements. At the tactical level of the organization we look at the transactions that go on within the workplace. These include day-to-day operations such as the way managers manage their people—the rewards and punishments used to get compliance with the written and unwritten rules. It also includes people's individual needs and values, the job-skills match, motivation, and teamwork.

The strategic component can be understood at the transformational level. These come from the organization's mission and strategy, its leadership and the overall organizational culture. These transformational factors drive the change and growth of the organization and affect the behaviors that are designed to change or transform individuals.

In Leslie's workplace, the strategic aspects of the organization would have to be looked at for any significant change to take place. Creative workplaces are often seen as more loose and carefree than regular workplaces and there are ways in which this atmosphere can work. However, if it's at the expense of productivity it may not be in the long-term interest of the organization. As well, the toll taken by overworking employees can be costly in terms of burning out or losing good talent.

The organization itself reflects a culture that is larger than the sum of its parts. This culture can be positive, negative, or neutral in terms of its ability to emotionally bond with people. The organization must be seen as a place that is fair to its people, optimistic in its outlook, courageous in dealing with challenge, and as a learning environment where there is opportunity for people to grow. When people feel stifled in these areas, motivation and performance suffer. On the other hand, organizations that encourage these values are well on the way to winning the hearts and minds of their people.

What impact does emotional intelligence have on the organization?

A person's feelings about the work they do affects the way they carry out their job. People who are bored at work, for example, are less likely to be efficient than those who are energized and excited about what they do. People who feel they have accomplished nothing at the end of the day are going to be less motivated than those who have successfully completed what they set out to do.

Working with other people that you get along with enhances work outcomes. If a team is dysfunctional, or if people do not get along, there is likely to be anger, aggression, subversion, or other bad feelings that interfere with productivity. If, on the other hand, co-workers or team members feel positively about each other and support each other, there will be more cooperative behavior. This enhances problem solving, coping with stressful situations, and other areas that make the work environment stimulating.

A manager's skill in supervising others significantly impacts the work of direct reports. When a supervisor poorly manages employees by not caring about them, giving inadequate feedback, or making unrealistic demands, this demoralizes people and negatively impacts their performance. When people feel they are being managed badly, regardless of the reality of the situation, they are less likely to be positive about their work.

When employees feel they have the attention of their supervisor, their concerns are listened to, and their ideas are considered, they are more likely to be motivated and contribute significantly to the organization. Studies have found that the number-one reason people leave organizations is because of their boss or supervisor.

The top leadership impacts an organization through its guidance, direction, and even more importantly its responsiveness both to its people and the outside world. Leaders steer the organizational ship through calm and rough seas to its destination. People need to understand the mission or destination of the ship. They need to know that resources are being adequately and efficiently used, they are going in the right direction, that leaders are competent in their decision making and have the best interests of the organization as a whole as a guiding principle.

When people have these assurances about their leadership and know where they fit into the overall plan, they feel better about their contribution to the whole organization. When leaders are found to be uncaring, self-centered, uncommunicative, arrogant, or lacking in integrity, the organization is deflated and work motivation suffers. A leader with the right values and ability to communicate them throughout the organization will inspire people to their best performance.

Only recently has the importance of emotions in the workplace been accepted. One of the ways in which an organization emotionally bonds to its people is by serving an overall purpose that is greater than the organization itself and its leaders. Being part of a group that has, as a major part of its purpose, the betterment of the community or society at large is a powerful motivator. We will be looking at the growing importance of corporate social responsibility in galvanizing an organization's people.

CHAPTER 5

Selecting the Right People: Round Pegs in Round Holes

"Never hire or promote in your own image. It is foolish to replicate your strength and idiotic to replicate your weakness. It is essential to employ, trust, and reward those whose perspective, ability, and judgment are radically different from yours. It is also rare, for it requires uncommon humility, tolerance, and wisdom."

Dee W. Hock, *Fast Company*

"If you hire only those people you understand, the company will never get people better than you are. Always remember that you often find outstanding people among those you don't particularly like."

Soichiro Honda

"When you hire people that are smarter than you are, you prove you are smarter than they are."

R. H. Grant

"You're only as good as the people you hire."

Ray Kroc (founder of the McDonald's Corporation in 1955)

"First-rate people hire first-rate people; second-rate people hire third-rate people."

Leo Rosten

Greg sat fidgeting in his chair, not quite looking at the interviewer.

"So, you were near the top of your class at Cornell?" asked Bronson.

"Yeah, I was third. Probably could have been first, but I had the flu the day I wrote my marketing exam," Greg answered.

"That's pretty impressive. Your work project looked pretty good. Were you part of a team for that?"

"Well, I was, but some of the others slacked off, so I probably did 70 percent of the work myself," Greg proudly answered.

"Really, you came up with most of the interventions on your own?" Bronson queried, quite impressed.

"Yes, it was pretty easy. I can see through a problem pretty quickly. Then I just plow through with a solution," he responded.

"Well, did you get to work as a team?"

"We started to, but like I said, there were some slackers. I don't have much patience for people who don't get it. You know what I mean?" Greg responded.

Yes, Bronson did—but then again, he didn't. He was so impressed with Greg's credentials he failed to pay attention to the warning signs. Bronson knew, even before the interview, that he wanted to hire Greg. After all, near the top of his class at Cornell, superb references from his professors, a star athlete, and his resume looked terrific.

Surprisingly, Bronson wasn't new in human resources. He had hired enough people to know that the second biggest reason why people left the company was because they couldn't get along with co-workers. The biggest reason, of course, was that they had problems with their manager. Not being able to work successfully in a team was a pretty accurate predictor of failure in the organization. But, like many other human resource professionals and managers I've seen, Bronson gets bowled over by what looks, on paper at least, like star material.

Selecting the Right People

Corporations and organizations around the world are realizing the significance their people contribute to bottom-line operational performance. The term "human capital profiling" has become popular in emphasizing this trend. All but the most archaic of organizations have come to appreciate that people are the bricks and mortar of today's enterprises. The ability to select the right bricks, shape and place them with just the right amount of mortar, and ensure they stick together (work as a team) is today's greatest business challenge. Organizations ready for the future already recognize this, while those who don't will be as abundant as dinosaurs.

One of the most important steps in developing today's high-performance workplace is ensuring you select the right people for the right jobs. Jim Collins, in his acclaimed book *Good to Great*, referred to selection as getting the right people on the bus, and then the right people in the right seats.[1] One of the best and most objective ways of selecting people is through proper job profiling and testing. Organizations have saved millions of dollars and increased job retention rates using emotional intelligence–based job profiling. In this chapter I will describe the remarkable impact this profiling has had on US Air Force recruiters.

How do you go about selecting "the right person" for "the right job?" There's no simple answer to this question. First, you need to find people who are capable, at a technical or ability level, to carry out the job. But, probably more importantly, you need to go beyond these skills. This means not only the people with the right technical skills, but also the right attitude, the right emotional skills, and the right fit with the organizational culture.

Having a person with the right technical skills for a job is pretty much a given. We start our search by looking at the quality of the person's basic skills for the job—engineering, accounting, programming, sales, technical support, marketing, or whatever. Once we've satisfied this area, we usually want someone with the right attitude: they want to work, they are reliable, honest, and willing to learn.

Are job interviews fair?

Unfortunately, interviews (whether informal, unstructured or behavioral) are the most frequently relied upon selection method. And while interviews can be useful for getting a feel for the person, they are usually unreliable in terms of predicting performance. Many applicants, especially salespeople, are great at selling themselves in interviews.

One of the biggest problems with selecting people on the basis of job interviews is that interviewers are heavily influenced by irrelevant factors or biases. Factors that have nothing to do with future job performance influence the interviewer. These could include the person's dress, whether they have an accent, the way they react to certain questions, and so forth.

Worst of all, interviewers are biased by demographic variables such as race, gender, and age. As soon as the candidate enters the room, the interviewer becomes aware of and is influenced by the color of the candidate's skin, whether the person is male or female, and if they are young or old. Research has looked into these effects in real-life job selection situations. They even have a name for this phenomenon, which is "social identity theory." According to this theory, interviewers prefer to select people who are similar to themselves in race, age, and gender.

One study by Lynn McFarland and her colleagues looked at structured interviews (which are supposed to be unbiased) with 1,334 police candidates. Structured interviews are set up so that each candidate will get the exact same questions during the interview. This reduces the possibility of anyone being asked anything that would be considered unfair or biased. However, McFarland found that answers given by candidates were scored differently based on the race of the interviewer, which led to unfair decision making.[2]

In another study, Caren Goldberg also found significant differences in how well job candidates were rated on their interviews based on their race. These differences were most pronounced when the job interviewers were Caucasian recruiters. The bias affected not only the overall interview assessment, but the offer decisions as well. In addition, her study found significant biases due to gender. One of the more interesting aspects of the gender effect was that males more often preferred attractive females.[3]

Can you trust resumes?

Resumes have been found to be useful for assessing job candidates as well, but not to be completely reliable. Studies have found high levels of fabrication on resumes and job applications. In an article that appeared in the Society for Human Resource Management (SHRM) magazine called "The Truth About Lies," the following item was reported: "People lie on their resumes. They lie on job applications. And they generally get away with it—despite HR's best efforts to derail the dishonest.

"Although no one knows the exact proportion of job seekers who enhance their personal work histories, estimates range from 40 percent to 70 percent."[4]

The authors, Joey George and Kent Marett, carried out a study to see if interviewers could catch applicants who fabricated information about themselves. When interviewers were not forewarned that job candidates might offer specious information, they were able to detect 2% of false information afterwards. On the other hand, those interviewers who were warned in advance about potential dishonesty were able to identify only 15% of lies afterwards. So, even while being vigilant about candidates who might falsify personal information, interviewers accepted 85% of fabricated information.

How trustworthy are job references?

Contacting previous employers for work references is part of most job selection processes. But, once again, this is a practice that is not taken too seriously by some professional job recruiters. It's usually the last piece of the selection puzzle that gets carried out in order to "rule out" a candidate if something negative comes up. Most former employers are reluctant to give honest (especially when negative) references for fear of potential litigation. According to a business "toolkit" designed to protect employers from using unlawful selection procedures, employers who provide employment references may find themselves being sued for defamation (a claim that the references are false and damaging to their reputations and, therefore, defamatory) or claims that personal information has been disclosed without consent.

"Given the potential lawsuit risks, many employers have adopted a policy of giving out no references at all or of giving out only basic employment data such as dates of employment, job titles, and wage rates."[5]

What about using testing to screen applicants?

Perhaps the fairest, most reliable method of screening candidates is through objective assessment tools—psychological tests. While there are hundreds of assessment tools available today, it's important to select those that have met professional standards and have been validated for screening job applicants.

In most cases a professional who is trained in and qualified to use these tests should be the person responsible for the process. They will be aware of any limitations of the tests and will know how to use them properly—that is, in a legally defensible way.

There are widely accepted standards for tests. These standards detail the appropriate development and use of these instruments. The best tests require professionals who have been trained in how to use and interpret them. The standards are available through the American Psychological Association.[6] Information on employment testing is also available through the Society of Industrial Organizational Psychology (SIOP).[7]

There are a number of advantages to validated selection tests. First, these tests are color blind to the person taking the test. Properly developed tests have gone through extensive evaluation to rule out any adverse impact due to the race or disability of the candidate.

Second, when gender is used in a test, good tests, validated on thousands of men and women, factor any gender differences into the scoring. In some jurisdictions, however, it is not legally acceptable to ask a candidate their age or gender. Third, if allowable, age can be factored into the scoring algorithms as well, making the test fair across the lifespan.

Additionally, assessments must be shown to be relevant to the job. Often, the assessment has already been used to profile the key factors important for the job under consideration. In my work, for example, one of the specialty services provided is called "star performer" profiling. It is not that uncommon to profile the best or "star" performers in a job as well as groups of average or poor performers. However, using emotional intelligence as the basis of this profiling is a new and exciting approach to selection. It is now possible to differentiate key emotional and social factors that characterize the high performers. These can be used for selecting new employees. Or, when a good candidate comes along, but is lower in one of the key areas, training can be provided as part of the orientation process.

What kinds of tests should be used?

For many years psychologists and employment consultants have relied on traditional measures of cognitive ability or intellectual quotient (IQ) and personality to help select the right people for various jobs and careers. Yet, after more than 100 years of IQ testing, there remains some debate about its success in predicting performance in the workplace. The most optimistic data, after adjustments, shows that IQ can predict up to only 20% of success at work. Other, more realistic data, comes in at 5% to 10% of work success.[8]

It's a lot easier to teach a person specific work skills than it is to teach him or her how to have the right attitude towards work, supervisors, fellow workers or the organization. For example, take someone who has a negative attitude towards authority. Regardless of how smart, technically proficient, or well educated they are, that person can be disruptive to the organization. Not only are they likely to perform poorly, but they will be a bad influence on others. Like a virus, these people can infect the corporate culture.

I've been in numerous meetings with groups of CEOs who have agonized over one particular person in their organization who was so good at their job, or, more accurately, potentially good, but with a cost. "My top salesperson is just too good to do without," or, "This one customer service person is the only one who really knows how to deal with people on the phone," except that they disrupt and destroy relationships within the organization.

In many of these cases you find high staff turnover, employee conflict, and general disruption around these prima donnas. The cost of having them in the organization tends to far outweigh any benefits delivered through their "can't live without" performance. High-maintenance employees are rarely team players and are disruptive to the organizational culture.

Personality tests may be helpful in the selection process, especially if they have been well validated. However, in our work we have been focusing on the use of emotional intelligence testing. These tests identify key emotional skills that relate to success in the workplace and they have had a major impact on many organizations that we and others have worked with. Factors that have long been regarded as important, but never objectively measured, have been identified, defined, and can now be benchmarked. These include areas such as emotional self-awareness, empathy, social responsibility, problem solving, stress tolerance, optimism, and others.

Measuring Emotional Intelligence

While there are many types of tests—intelligence, personality, ability, interest, and so on—I will limit our discussion here to the area of emotional intelligence testing. There are two widely accepted and well-researched tests of emotional intelligence used in organizations for selection and development. These are the Emotional Quotient Inventory (EQ-i®) by Reuven Bar-On[9] and the Mayer, Salovey, Caruso Emotional Intelligence Test (MSCEIT) by John Mayer, Peter Salovey, and David Caruso.[10]

Some information about the models behind these tests have been presented in Chapter 4: Emotional Intelligence and Organizational Culture. To reiterate, emotional intelligence, according to the model and measure developed by Bar-On, includes five general areas:

Intra-Personal – your ability to be aware of and control your emotions;

Inter-Personal – your ability to get along with others, your "people skills";

Adaptability – your ability to be flexible, solve problems and be realistic;

Stress Management – your ability to tolerate stress and control impulses; and

General Mood – your happiness and optimism.

The reality is that emotional intelligence is still in its infancy, and measures of emotional intelligence are not yet widely used in selecting employees. It is being used by a number of very smart organizations who have experienced great success after trying it out, examples of which will be presented here. Emotional intelligence represents an important aspect of the job–person–organization fit, rarely taken into account—the *emotional* fitness for the job.

Case Study: Selecting Recruiters for the US Air Force

The US Air Force was experiencing a high turnover rate in its recruiters—close to 50% per year. The financial cost of this turnover rate was substantial. Being a recruiter in the military is very similar to being a salesperson in civilian life. In fact, military recruiters are often referred to as salespeople. The cost of selecting, training, and relocating a recruiter is quite high. Having that person not work out in his or her position increases that cost considerably. Not only is there a high price associated with the training program they must go through, but the person often has to relocate his or her family and set up a new home, sometimes hundreds or even thousands of miles away. The human cost doesn't always factor into the financial one.

Major Rich Handley knew there must be a more effective way to select Air Force recruiters than the traditional practice. He learned about emotional intelligence and recognized that it included variables that might be useful in the selection of salespeople. He wanted to know more about the Bar-On EQ-i and how it might apply to selecting recruiters.

Working together, we tested all of the US Air Force recruiters throughout the world with the EQ-i—1,171 recruiters in total. The idea was to see if we could find a relationship between their emotional intelligence test scores and their performance in the field. One of the complexities organizational psychologists often have in their research is determining how to measure work success.

One of the most common ways of measuring work success has been through the reports of managers. Another option is to ask the person himself or herself how well he or she is performing. Of course, there is always the risk that the person will tell you they are doing very well, when, in fact, they are not. On the other hand, when someone says they are doing poorly, the chances are pretty good that they are. In our study, as one of the measures, we asked recruiters how well they thought they were doing on the job.

In any job it's important to have a benchmark of performance and a goal for success. In this case, each person has a recruitment quota. The quota serves as a bottom line of performance. These quotas were created to take into account the region in which the recruiter worked. In some cases, recruiters may have felt their quota was unfair, especially if they were new to the job. They may have thought they would need more time to adjust to the job prior to reaching the quota. For that reason, we decided to use measures of both perceived success as well as actual success.

We plugged all the data—their EQ-i scores, perceived success, and actual percent of quota reached—into a statistical formula (called logistical regression). We looked at other variables as well, including geographic region, years of experience, age, marital status, marital satisfaction, and so on.

Analyzing the data, we were able to account for 45% of the recruiter's self-report of success. This is higher than most previous studies using cognitive intelligence to predict work success.

We then looked at actual performance quotas. Many of the same factors led to the prediction of success. While the percentage accounted for by EQ was slightly less, the following factors were found to be most important: assertiveness, social responsibility, interpersonal relationships, happiness, empathy, and problem solving.

Using the data, we profiled their "star performers"; that is, the best-performing recruiters in the Air Force.

A computer-administered version of the EQ-i was developed that instantly matched any new candidates against the star performers' profiles. Applicants were classified as a good match, fair match, or not a match. As well, the report includes specific areas that should be developed before considering the candidate for the position.

The Air Force provided an opportunity for candidates to improve in the areas that were low, but regarded as necessary for job success. They developed specific training programs that covered the targeted areas for success, such as empathy training. After all, why put a candidate in a job where you know that they are likely to fail without the requisite skill set? Neither the candidate nor the organization benefits from this type of failure. The emotional skills identified as important are also included as part of recruiter training.

Of course, many other factors are taken into account in addition to the testing. There are work histories, references, interviews with candidates and their spouses, detailed presentations of the nature of the job, ensuring the candidate's motivation to make the change, etc. In addition to, and following the self-report EQ-i, the selection officer administers a semi-structured EQ-i interview. This serves as a backup and helps confirm or double-check the findings of the inventory. The results of the interview are keyed into the computer and a report combining the self-report inventory and the interview is generated. In addition, there is a 360-degree (or multi-rater) version of the EQ-i completed by supervisor, subordinates, and spouse.

The results of this project with the Air Force were an increased retention rate of 92% in the first year. In terms of cost this resulted in $2.7 million (US) saved the first year alone. These savings have continued for several years now.[11]

There were also significant benefits on the human side. Unnecessary relocation and disruption in people's lives was reduced, and morale increased from having more people succeed at work and fewer failures. We even found that marital relationship satisfaction increased with success at work. Finally, successful candidates were able to make their quotas and work fewer hours than the unsuccessful recruiters.

Emotional intelligence continues to be an increasingly important contributing factor in the workplace. Organizations harnessing the power of their people are the ones who happily and productively survive the future in the global workplace.

Case Study: Selecting Wireless Phone Salespeople

In a project we carried out for a large national electronics chain in the United States, we were asked to help in the selection of wireless phone salespeople. These people would be stationed in the retail stores and would represent not just one but several different carrier phone plans, all available through the outlet.

It was very important that these people have an adequate level of cognitive intelligence, or IQ, since they would be responsible for knowing the details of a number of complicated wireless plans for each of the carriers. The selection and training, which was carried out by an outside sales service organization, was carefully monitored. Tracking of the success of candidates on the job was carried out in real-time as all sales were instantly electronically documented and transmitted to the head office.

Candidates who were unsuccessful in sales were usually let go within two weeks. A ratio of sales per hour was instantly calculated for each sales associate. We tested the cognitive intelligence and emotional intelligence of highly successful "star performers" as well as average and low-performing associates. We then came up with a statistically based formula that could predict well beyond traditional methods whether the candidate would be successful.

Some of the factors that predicted success in this case were obvious, such as assertiveness. In order to sell phones to strangers, you need to be assertive enough to approach them, engage them in conversation, and close the sale. On the other hand, there were several factors that were less obvious and worked in a negative capacity. These included emotional self-awareness.

Our successful candidates scored *lower* in emotional self-awareness than our unsuccessful candidates. After reviewing this in more detail we eventually realized that too much self-awareness can be detrimental to salespeople who spend their day doing cold calls. The high frequency of rejection would make it difficult to continue working if you were overly sensitive to your feelings. You need to have a pretty thick skin to succeed.[12]

A side benefit of these findings was that it made it easier for us to conduct our testing nationally over the internet. Ordinarily, tests such as this are carefully proctored to ensure the individual is not cheating. Even live proctors, however, can't always prevent candidates from using creative cheating tactics. How could we test thousands of applicants online and reduce the effects of faking or cheating?

In most cases job candidates cheat by making themselves look good—or score high on tests. So you could cheat by indicating (falsely) that you are a very assertive person. Of course, this would work against you once you were hired, since you would find yourself in a job position where it would be difficult to succeed if you were not truly assertive. Fortunately, all the items are not obvious as to what they measure, so it would not be easy to cheat on some of the assertiveness items.

Chances are, if you were cheating to get hired, you would rate yourself as high on the other areas of emotional and social intelligence as well. You would have no way of knowing that we actually selected people who scored lower on emotional self-awareness and several other factors. So, unless you knew our formula for successfully selling wireless phones, it would be highly unlikely that you could fake the right profile used in our selection.

How Emotional Intelligence Can Separate the Wheat from the Chaff

Over the past 10 years or so we've been carrying out the "star performer" analysis in a number of occupational groups in different organizations. We see the star performer as someone who really excels at his or her job, both individually and as a team player.

We've looked at salespeople, engineers, teachers, CEOs, fighter pilots, physicians, NHL hockey players, nurses, human resource professionals, consultants, reporters, politicians, lawyers, and dozens of other groups of working people.

Not every organization goes to the effort of carrying out "star performer" analyses. There are still benefits of using emotional intelligence as part of the selection process, along with other tools, when selecting key positions on a smaller scale.

When selecting an employee, we get back to our basic questions. What are the most important characteristics to look for when hiring this person? Are technical skills more important than "soft" skills? What if you have three candidates who are equally competent technically? Which one should you hire?

While there is no single formula that covers hiring the best person among all the groups we looked at, one characteristic turned up the most frequently among successful hires. Specific and unique elements of emotional intelligence were found to separate high performers from the average performers in practically every occupational group we examined. It's almost like baking a cake, with a specific set of ingredients required for each type of work.

Finding People Who Are Self-Actualized

The one factor that most frequently came up in our selection formula was something called self-actualization. This concept, made famous by the psychologist Abraham Maslow, was something he identified long ago in his study of high-achieving individuals. Maslow carefully studied the history and backgrounds of famous people such as Albert Einstein, Abraham Lincoln, Thomas Jefferson, Mahatma Gandhi, Eleanor Roosevelt, Benedict Spinoza, and others. One of the features they all shared was this multifaceted characteristic.

One feature of self-actualization is the way that you look at life goals. People who score high in this factor feel that the ends don't necessarily justify the means, and that the means could be ends in themselves. For these people, the means—the journey—is often more important than the ends. They discover what they love in life and work hard to attain more of it. This quality can be found in many Olympic athletes who put in countless numbers of hours to reach their dreams. One of the greatest hockey players of all time, Wayne Gretzky, was asked upon his retirement why he was such a great player. He could only talk about how much he loved every aspect of the game. He admitted he would have played just as hard without his multimillion-dollar salary.

Another aspect of self-actualized people is their concern and caring for people and society. These people have a strong desire to do good things for others. They are compassionate towards those in need. They want others around them to succeed in whatever they do. They are the best of team players.

Hire the Best

What does this all mean when hiring? You should strive to hire the best person you can for every position available. That doesn't mean you should look for the best person in the world, but the best person for the position. That holds for whether you're looking for a salesperson, shipping clerk, service technician, financial officer, or CEO. You want people who really love the kind of work they are applying for. If you're hiring a graphic artist, find out what each candidate has done beyond his or her basic training. Have they voluntarily taken specialized training, do they attend conferences on design, do they subscribe to design magazines? What signs do they give you that they really love graphic design?

How do you find out which "emotional" and "social" qualities to look for in a position? Well, the ideal way is to profile the positions you have with a standardized emotional intelligence measure such as the EQ-i. Examine the differences between your high- and low-performing people in each position. Then you can select your new hires using the information you have learned. Of course, this approach works best in organizations with numerous people in each position.

What about smaller companies? Well, you can still use a scaled-down version of this approach without testing large numbers of people. Look at each position you are hiring for. Try to determine who the best people were that you had in those positions. Think about what personal qualities your high per- formers had that made them stand out. When interviewing candidates, com- pile a shortlist of questions that try to get at the extent to which they may have those qualities. Use questions that determine how the person handled actual situations in the past that would be opportunities to demonstrate the quality. For example, if you want to see how empathic a customer service candidate is, you may want to ask, "Can you give me an example of how you showed an angry customer you cared about her problem?"

In my previous book, *The EQ Edge* (with Howard Book), there is a sec- tion which presents the top five emotional skills that separate high performers from the rest in many different occupational groups. While there may be spe- cific differences between top salespeople or engineers in different organiza- tion, there are some overall similarities that can be useful.[13]

By targeting the right qualities, you can make better hiring decisions. Evaluating emotional and social skills goes beyond the standard procedures of reviewing resumes, getting references, conducting interviews, and checking out technical skills. While these all have their place, having an organization with emotionally smart people gives you that extra edge in tough times as well as in good times.

Perhaps if Bronson, in our example at the beginning of the chapter, had profiled the emotional and social skills that were important for the position, it would have saved him time in interviewing candidates. He may have spent his time focusing on and confirming that he was selecting a new employee based on qualities that were known to be important for success on the job. He would have been less likely to be distracted by other qualities, such as overly high cognitive intelligence, that may not be as relevant. And, of course, the reten- tion rate for the organization would have been improved.

PART 2

What to Measure and How to Fix It

CHAPTER 6

Taking the Organization's Temperature

"It is much more difficult to measure nonperformance than performance."

Harold S. Geneen

"How you measure the performance of your managers directly affects the way they act."

Gustave Flaubert

Murray was puzzled. He knew things weren't going well but he just couldn't put his finger on the problem. Sales were down, two of his key department level managers had left the company, and his middle management team seemed disengaged. The company had always been a highly motivated, fast-growing organization.

After a two-hour meeting with Alice, an outside management consultant, Murray was hopeful that she could find a solution. They agreed that she would speak to each of the senior managers individually. Interviews were scheduled with the heads of sales and marketing, financial services, research and development, production, and human resources.

Alice uncovered lots of small issues going on, but nothing that seemed big enough to disrupt the flow of the company. There was no dominant theme that she could isolate and begin to work with. At this point one option would be to pull all the senior managers together and see if she could facilitate them through the problem.

Another option was to start meeting with supervisors the next level down—the department heads—and get their perspectives. While Alice saw this as possibly helpful, it would be time-consuming for her and costly to the client. Also, she thought it would be better, if she did approach this group, to have specific issues of concern identified in advance. That would make the meetings more efficient than merely exploring issues in a general way.

Some consultants might start intervening early on based on a gut feeling of what was happening. It's not uncommon to try one intervention, see how it feels, and then maybe try another one. This could be pretty hit-and-miss, and hopefully there wouldn't be much damage caused along the way. For example, you could start looking at reporting relationships and see if there could be any realignment. Perhaps there were system inefficiencies that could be fixed.

Fortunately, Alice had a better idea. At this point she realized that the most effective way to proceed would be to survey the entire organization. It would be like taking the organization's temperature, in the same way the doctor takes a patient's temperature while conducting an examination before prescribing treatment.

Following the survey, Alice was able to provide Murray and the senior team with a more accurate picture of what was going on in the organization. She pointed out that the middle-management group was scoring lower than both senior management and the line staff in a number of areas. When the specific factors were examined, it became even clearer that these managers were unhappy. In addition, the results from the line staff also indicated there were problems at the department supervisor level.

Some of the middle managers felt they had been passed over when two senior managers were hired from outside the company. As well, they had difficulty dealing with the demands from the senior managers, whom they felt were still too new to fully understand the industry.

Another issue was the difficulty they had balancing their own workload while trying to manage their direct reports. A number of managers had only recently been promoted to management, with little or no training in managing others.

Murray was as surprised as he was relieved. None of the middle managers had approached the senior managers about these issues. He wondered how long these symptoms would have continued if the survey had not brought these problems to light. Armed with this new knowledge, Murray felt confident that his company was on the right track to positive change.

Why survey employees?

As we see in our example, Alice was able to get information from the survey that was used to feed into the business strategy of the organization. Along with the issues of the middle managers, she uncovered other concerns related to the top leadership and the way the organization responded to challenges. Many employees felt the top leadership lacked the courage to make changes in the organization when necessary. By waiting too long to adapt to external threats, momentum was often lost. These challenges included updating products, getting new products ready for market, and adjusting ineffective marketing programs.

Organizational surveys have been used since the 1930s, around the time of the previously described Hawthorne studies. The nature of these surveys has changed over time. In the 1940s, surveys were designed mainly to measure employee morale. It was a way of determining how motivated workers were. It was hoped that these surveys would also be useful in preventing unionization of the workforce.

In the 1960s, the purpose of surveys changed somewhat with more of a focus on measuring job satisfaction. The intention of the survey was to improve productivity. Prevailing thought suggested that a satisfied worker was a more productive worker. The surveys were largely used to measure how satisfied employees were.

Then, in the 1980s, surveys were used to predict job turnover, reduce absenteeism, and decrease stress among workers. The surveys became more attitude oriented, asking what employees thought about various programs being implemented in addition to other aspects of the workplace.

Surveys today are commonly used to help determine if the company is properly focused on its strategic objectives. It's one thing for the senior managers to have a plan, sign off on it, and commit to executing it. However, if key objectives don't reach the very people charged with carrying them forward, the plan will have difficulty succeeding. Surveys today are also broader in scope. They look at aspects of the individual jobs, the team, managers, and top leadership.

There have been numerous reports on how surveys of staff have led to dramatic effects on an organization's bottom line. Examples include both profit and non-profit organizations. Decatur Memorial Hospital described the importance of surveying their employees:

> Keys to financial success? Let's see—there's staying on top of operating margin, days cash on hand, net days in accounts receivable. And organizational culture? At first glance, focusing on culture may not seem like a top priority for the typical bottom-line-focused CFO. Yet clearly there's more to improving margin than simply monitoring standard financial measures. Most successful senior financial executives recognize it's also important to understand the factors that drive those metrics. This discovery of the "how" part of the equation is where the importance of culture comes in.
>
> The shared values, goals, and practices that characterize a company or corporation can have a significant effect on productivity, quality of service, and employee and customer satisfaction. At Decatur Memorial Hospital in Decatur, Ill., leadership recently undertook an initiative to better understand this important dynamic, and the resulting improvements have been notable.[1]

Organizational psychologists A. Catherine Higgs and Steven Ashworth believe that the surveys of tomorrow will increase their focus on business strategy even more.[2] In addition, they will be key components of measuring an organization's readiness for change. Change will be integral to any organization of the future. The more adaptable a company is, the more successful it will be in making transitions. Surveys help pinpoint where the workplace needs to be focused in order to make the needed changes flow smoothly.

A recent article by Charlotte Garvey in *HR Magazine* described this trend:

More companies are breathing life into their employee survey results. Rather than letting results sit lifeless on an HR executive's bookshelf, organizations are using survey data to create dynamic tools that spur action plans and interactive, ongoing dialogue between company leaders and employees. Companies are moving away from the idea that an employee survey is a one-shot event that elicits general feedback. Instead, they are developing surveys that query progress on key organizational goals and tie results data to business plans.[3]

Future surveys will focus even more on teams, customers, organizational structures, and networks. Previously, surveys have focused primarily on the individual employee and how he or she rated their job and the organization.

How have survey methods changed?

The ways in which surveys are administered to employees has changed over the years as well. Originally, surveys were conducted by way of interviews with each individual employee. Then paper and pencil questionnaires became more common and cost efficient.

Now there's increased use of computers, email, and online administration of surveys. These newer processes have changed the nature of the data collected. Surveys can now be more tailored to specific groups, departments, and individuals. As well, it's much easier to add in specific questions each time the survey is carried out. Rather than waiting weeks or even months for the results, they are now tabulated as quickly as they come in.

As surveys have transitioned into new formats, such as online administration, there have been changes to the way employees respond to the surveys as well. In a controlled study comparing an organization's use of paper-and-pencil and an internet-based survey, employees tended to give higher ratings on the internet: "Participants in the present study who completed the survey instrument online rated items more positively than those who took it via paper, indicating that method had a significant effect on responses to survey items."[4]

It may be that employees find it easier and less frustrating to get through an online survey than a paper one. My own studies have found that people finish online surveys faster and report feeling better about the organization as a whole with automated as opposed to paper-and-pencil surveys. They actually rate the organization as more modern and up-to-date. I generally recommend employees complete organizational surveys online.

Using the Survey as a Process for Change

Surveys are no longer a static, one-time event. In fact, they have become the beginning of an ongoing dialogue and change process. As Garvey goes on to describe the process:

> That end game varies from company to company. But the basic process involves analysis of the data (often by a consultant), communication of the data to various levels of the organization, development of action plans to address key issues identified through the survey, and then action plan execution and follow-up. Experts emphasize that good action plans must be built with data that is "actionable," meaning information that focuses on issues over which a manager has some control.[5]

The benefits of surveys are understood by executives who have used them before:

> Option One CEO Bob Dubrish, who helped develop the survey, says he was motivated to launch it after he saw a similar survey work well at another company. In addition, when he met with employees at various branches of his company, they repeatedly cited the company culture as a top reason for staying. Dubrish says he and HR vice president Kristiina Hintgen, SPHR, decided it would be important to measure that sense of engagement. "Any time you measure something, you get better at it," Dubrish notes.[6]

In order to successfully carry out an organizational survey, you need to get support from the top of the organization. Garvey reported:

> At both Intuit and Option One, one of the key ingredients of success has been active CEO support. Olivia Smith, workplace assessment program manager at Intuit, says CEO Steve Bennett does not

regard the survey process as an HR-only function. "He understands that's how you run your business."[7]

Measuring Organizational Emotional Intelligence

Just as a person's emotional intelligence has been found to be important in individual performance, organizational emotional intelligence or how groups of people feel about the organization drives organizational performance. In this case the whole is greater than the sum of its parts.

Emotional intelligence has been identified as an important part of a person's ability to successfully contribute to an organization's success. While there are several definitions of individual emotional intelligence, they all share themes that include awareness of one's emotions, the ability to express those emotions appropriately, the ability to recognize emotions in others, the understanding of emotions and the ability to manage one's own and other's emotions. Measures of individual emotional intelligence can also include factors such as interpersonal skills, adaptability, stress management, and general mood.

A number of characteristics related to emotional intelligence and found to be important in creating a productive work environment have been identified and studied. I've defined the emotional intelligence of an organization as follows: *An organization's ability to successfully and efficiently cope with change and accomplish its goals, while being responsible and sensitive to its people, customers, suppliers, networks, and society.*

Together with the people at MHS, I developed a survey called the Benchmark of Organizational Emotional Intelligence (BOEI) to measure the level of emotional intelligence in an organization as a whole, as well as among its departments, teams, or divisions.[8]

The BOEI assessment comprises factors that range from workplace necessities to company ideals. These areas were developed based on our definition of organizational emotional intelligence, reviews of the research literature on organizational surveys, pilot study data collection with early versions of the BOEI, and ongoing statistical analysis to ensure the BOEI is a valid and reliable measure.

The scales and subscales were selected as areas that impact directly on employee motivation and organizational performance. The survey was designed to give organizations and their departments a clear picture of what and where the high and low points are. The BOEI assessment indicates which weaknesses should be targeted and which strengths should be maximized for the best results. The areas of the BOEI were also chosen because of their amenability for improvement through organizational and individual development.

The seven areas we found to be essential in meeting these goals are:

- Job Happiness
- Compensation
- Work/Life Stress Management
- Organizational Cohesiveness
- Supervisory Leadership
- Diversity and Anger Management
- Organizational Responsiveness.

These break into 14 more specific factors that are graphed for the overall organization as well as its parts. Different departments, divisions, or work groups can be compared as well as the different levels of staff, from senior management to front line.

The BOEI assessment combines formalized facets of emotional intelligence with traditional aspects of industrial/organizational (I/O) psychology. We've already discussed some of the history of organizational surveys and the content areas usually addressed. It should be clear at this point how the principles of motivation, job satisfaction, and related factors support and complement the factors of emotional intelligence.

Using the BOEI

In order to move our definitions from theory to practice, we needed to find a way to measure them. There are hundreds of theories on what makes organizations great or how you can motivate people, but there is still a great need to validate the theories.

The BOEI is the first scientifically developed measure of the emotional intelligence of an organization or group. It was developed through surveying thousands of people working in a variety of organizations (in countries as diverse as the USA, Canada, Sweden, England, South Africa, Cyprus, and India) that include financial services, government, military, engineering, publishing, information technology, dot-com, insurance, college, healthcare providers, and manufacturing. Through this process we were able to confirm the existence of a specific group of factors that contribute to the emotional intelligence of the organization.

The BOEI survey contains 143 items and takes 30 to 45 minutes to complete. One unique feature of it is that each individual in the organization gets his or her own personal feedback report that compares their individual results to the overall organization. This enables the employee to determine to what degree he or she "fits" within the organization and how their feelings and thoughts compare to others in the organization. When a person deviates from the rest of the group there are several options. Sometimes this leads to re-evaluating his or her feelings and thoughts about the organization, or it may lead to creating proactive change in the organization. For others, it serves as a wake-up call to begin to find work elsewhere.

In order to arrive at these factors, the BOEI underwent two major stages of development. In the first stage, several areas were identified and rationally defined based on the belief that a) these factors were emotional and motivational aspects of employees at work, and b) these factors were related to job performance. Numerous items were created to measure each of these constructs.

The research identified seven key factors that play a key role in organizational emotional intelligence. Figure 6:1 illustrates these components. Some of them are more basic and include concrete issues such as having the right resources to do the job and satisfaction with pay and benefits, while others are less tangible, such as teamwork, courage, and how the organization deals with change.

Figure 6.1: The BOEI Model and 7 Factors

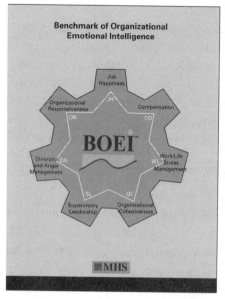

Reprinted with permission of MHS (2006)

The BOEI scales and subscales are presented in Figure 6:1. The descriptions of these factors follow:

Table 6:1
BOEI Factor Structure

Scales	Subscales
Job Happiness	
Compensation	Pay Benefits
Work/Life Stress Management	Stability Stress Management Work/Life Balance
Organizational Cohesiveness	Co-worker Relationships Teamwork

Continued

Supervisory Leadership	
Diversity and Anger Management	Diversity Climate Gender/Racial Acceptance Anger Management
Organizational Responsiveness	Training and Innovation Optimism and Integrity Courage and Adaptability Top Management Leadership
Positive Impression	
Negative Impression	
Total BOEI	

Reprinted with permission of Multi-Health Systems (2006). www.mhs.com

Job Happiness

This factor measures the degree to which people are challenged and fulfilled by their job. It includes job satisfaction, enthusiasm, and enjoyment of the workplace. It also looks at whether people feel there are opportunities for career advancement.

In any organization you want people doing work they like. The more people feel challenged and fulfilled by their work, the more productive they are likely to be. Whether it's designing graphics, collecting late payments, or selling television sets, people who like what they do will undoubtedly do it better.

People should also be challenged at work. Even simple or repetitive tasks can be made more challenging by setting daily goals, or having friendly competitions. In fact, people should be acknowledged, or even rewarded for work well done.

Compensation

This factor measures the degree to which people are satisfied with their basic pay, bonuses, commissions, vacations, and benefits, and the degree to which they perceive wages to be fair in the organization. There is often a tradeoff between pay and job security, and the focus here is on the amount and fairness of pay. It also looks at whether there are perceived opportunities to increase earnings.

The Compensation factor actually has two separate parts. These are Pay and Benefits:

Pay

Statements about pay focus on people's satisfaction with their pay and the degree to which they believe remuneration keeps them committed to the organization. Feelings about the opportunity for growth in the organization, fairness of assignment of pay increases, and openness of the organization in sharing financial information are explored.

Organizations tend to fall into one of three categories in this area. First, there are workplaces where employees are highly paid. The tradeoff is often low job security. You may be a highly paid salesperson, but if you miss your quota for a month or two, you may lose your job. Second, there are organizations known for paying low wages. Yet these same organizations can be known for their high job security (no one gets laid off, even during recessions) and their pleasant, calm work environment. Third, there are companies that deliberately fall in the middle in pay scales, but offer opportunities for participation in the company's success through profit sharing or generous bonuses.

Benefits

The degree to which benefits are perceived to be comprehensive, flexible, and competitive are evaluated here. This area also taps the significance of benefits in employee retention.

Work/Life Stress Management

The degree to which the workplace is stable, people are managing stress, and feel their work and home life is balanced is assessed in this section. There are three subfactors: Stability, Stress Management, and Work/Life Balance.

Stability

This looks at the degree to which the nature and amount of work has remained consistent over the past six months. Changes include increases or decreases in workload over the previous six months. The degree to which these changes impact negatively on productivity is tapped.

Stress Management

The degree to which specific work stressors are not a major factor in getting the job done is evaluated here. Its important to look at whether there are adequate resources available and any negative impacts of changes in the organization.

Work/Life Balance

Does the nature or amount of work one does interfere with home and social activities? That is explored here, along with the unpredictability of the work itself.

Organizational Cohesiveness

This factor measures the ability of co-workers to get along and work teams to be cohesive. It contains two subfactors: Co-worker Relationships and Teamwork.

Co-worker Relationships

The degree to which people get along well with each other, trust each other, are comfortable working both independently and together, and prevent letting personal feelings interfere with work relationships is measured here. Are people aware of and sensitive to the feelings of others they work with?

Work should be a friendly place. Getting support from and being able to rely on the people you work with makes work more productive. When people actually care about each other, they're more willing to help when needed.

Teamwork

It's important to gauge the degree to which people who work together as a team work well together. Trust, morale, complementary skills, group pride, ability to communicate, and productivity are all keys to successful teamwork.

In high-functioning companies, there are identifiable teams where people work together. They get along with, trust, and depend on their teammates. They are comfortable sharing with and relying on their designated peers.

Team members may even socialize together. Politics have no place in effective teams. People genuinely want each other to succeed.

In well-functioning organizations, there are team goals as well as team rewards. In order to deal with individuals that may not be carrying their weight in a team, individual goals must be met before one can share in the team's rewards.

Supervisory Leadership

This factor evaluates the effectiveness of supervisors as seen by the people they supervise. It includes the ability to share information, involvement in decision-making, coaching, providing feedback, mediating conflicts, trustworthiness and confidence, self-awareness, and general satisfaction with immediate supervisors.

Most people who leave their jobs really leave their supervisor, not their job. Poor supervision has been cited as the number-one reason people quit their jobs. Providing proper supervision can go a long way towards building a loyal and dedicated team.

An effective supervisor ensures everyone knows what their job is and why they are there. She or he keeps people informed about changes and events and acts like a coach or mentor to direct reports.

A good supervisor wants to see everyone succeed and will do what is needed to help make that happen. By being honest and demonstrating integrity a manager gains the trust and support of staff.

This factor measures the degree to which employees have confidence in and respect for their immediate supervisor.

Diversity and Anger Management

This factor measures the degree to which the organization is open to employee diversity and the organization's effectiveness in managing employee anger and frustration. It contains three subfactors: Diversity Climate, Gender/Racial Acceptance, and Anger Management.

Diversity Climate

The degree to which people are treated fairly, regardless of age, race, gender, physical limitation, or disability in the organization is assessed here.

Gender/Racial Acceptance

This measures the degree to which people are not harassed or discriminated against due to race or gender.

Anger Management

This area looks at the degree to which conflicts have been successfully managed over the previous six months. It includes verbal and physical aggression as well as subtle attempts at getting even with others or the organization.

Organizational Responsiveness

This factor measures the degree to which the organization meets the needs of its people through offering training, encouraging innovation, and demonstrating optimism, honesty, and integrity. It also explores how well the organization deals with difficult issues, solves problems, and takes appropriate risks. The amount of support top management provides in meeting employee needs and gaining their trust is evaluated as well.

There are four subfactors: Training and Innovation, Optimism and Integrity, Courage and Adaptability, and Top Management Leadership.

Training and Innovation

This measures the degree to which training and innovation are seen as valued by the organization. It includes the individualization of training as well as the availability of a clear career path program within the organization.

How up-to-date are people about their jobs? Does the organization value time and expense paid to learn? Companies that want to stay ahead financially will budget time and resources to train their people throughout the organization. Whether it's information technology, graphic arts, customer service, financial management, project management, or logistics and shipping, if the organization falls behind current practice in any of its key areas, the whole organization can suffer.

Optimism and Integrity

This measures the degree to which employees view the organization as optimistic and honest in terms of what it stands for. The openness of the organization's goals and the alignment of people and resources to attain these goals are included. It also measures the degree to which the organization listens to its customers or clients and is socially and environmentally conscious.

What does it really mean for an organization to be optimistic? Do we just wear rose-colored glasses and plow on with our daily drudge? Not if you really want to be an optimistic organization. Optimism is not just believing that the world will be great. Optimism has to do with the way in which you deal with obstacles. It's an approach to dealing with difficult situations. It's strategic. Organizations that are truly optimistic look for challenges and relish overcoming those challenges.

Courage and Adaptability

The degree to which the organization handles challenges head-on is evaluated here. It includes the ability to confront difficult issues, solve problems systematically, make decisions efficiently, act on its decisions, and address mistakes when they occur. It also includes taking appropriate risks and organizational flexibility.

How does the organization deal with change? Is it regarded as a nuisance and a cost that has to be tolerated? Or do people in the organization embrace change? Do they get excited over new technology, newer and more efficient ways of doing their jobs? Do people spend significant amounts of time looking for new ways to do things? Organizations that move towards the future and stay just ahead of the curve stand to be tomorrow's winners. Unfortunately, companies that resist change will struggle to survive.

Being courageous means not being afraid to take risks or confront challenges. Organizations high in this area do not hide or bury their heads in the sand when difficulties emerge. They manage to plan a course of action and execute it without hesitation. Courageous organizations admit when they are wrong, address mistakes, and quickly implement change.

Top Management Leadership

This measures the degree to which people see top management as supportive of their ideas and initiatives and earning their trust and confidence. It also includes the degree to which the top leadership offers a clear vision to the organization.

Organizations perform better when employees believe in their leadership. Leaders need to be credible, effective, and show integrity. Also, leaders need to be seen and heard throughout the organization in a supporting way.

Positive Impression

One of the problems in many surveys is that people can be overly positive about their organization. They indiscriminately rate everything high, regardless of the reality of the current situation.

The BOEI takes overly positive and perhaps unrealistic ratings into account with a specific scale. This scale measures the degree to which people give a general positive view of their organization.

Negative Impression

In the same way that some people are overly positive, there are others who are overly negative about their organization. This scale measures the degree to which people have an overly negative view of the organization.

Total BOEI

When all the items from these areas are responded to, an overall BOEI score is produced as well. The total score and all the factors are compared against our database of organizations.

So what difference can measuring the organization make?

The BOEI has been used by a number of organizational consultants to guide their understanding and intervention with for-profit and non-profit workplaces. One consultant, Marcia Hughes of Collaborative Growth, finds the BOEI extremely useful in bringing together a great deal of information for her clients.

For example, in one large organization she ran several different summary reports over the course of five months. In this organization she found a number of common responses from employees across different departments with regards to global human resource issues. There were common concerns about the prospects for job advancement, training, and the adequacy of benefits. There were also differences in results across departments, which provided information on where strong team relationships existed, strong relationships with supervising managers, and strong relationships with both. The reports also shed light on those departments in which these relationships were poor.

The department heads and division leader were then able to focus on the places where there were strengths in order to better understand what worked.

They analyzed those areas that presented challenges. Their best results occurred when they could take the strategies learned where teams and leaders worked well and introduce those strategies into the more challenged areas.[9]

In Murray's case, at the beginning of this chapter, the general results of the survey were shared throughout the organization, department by department. The meetings then focused on each specific department and how its results compared to the company overall. Alice got precisely the kind of feedback she was looking for. It helped her develop a clear intervention plan based on the needs of the organization.

In this case, the plan involved implementing a customized management-training program for the middle management group. There were specific aspects of their role they were uncomfortable with. They were also provided with coaching to ensure they consolidated the learning and were able to practice the skills. Through this process, the managers learned to better understand their own strengths and weaknesses. They saw how their personal style of interacting worked for them in some instances, but against them in others.

There were also some concerns about compensation that had to be addressed. The company's benefit package wasn't flexible enough to meet their needs. There were specific adjustments that were made to the package. While the cost of these changes was minimal, the increased flexibility made a big difference in the lives of these managers.

The same survey was re-administered a year later. There was a dramatic difference in the ratings of the middle-management group. As well, their direct reports reported higher satisfaction with management. The company performance had improved in a number of other benchmarks as well.

Measuring the organizational culture cannot be done in a vacuum. It is assumed by everyone that giving their thoughts and feelings will lead to something or somewhere. There is an implied action. The beginning of this action is the feedback that all participants receive.

Hopefully, the next chapters will help you prepare for the rest of the journey. We will look at the seven key success factors in greater detail and how each affects organizational wellbeing. In the last chapter, I'll show how you can facilitate all these factors.

CHAPTER 7

Job Happiness: Don't Worry, Be Happy

"If we agree that the bottom line of life is happiness, not success, then it makes perfect sense to say that it is the journey that counts, not reaching the destination."

Mihaly Csikszentmihalyi

"What is it that you like doing? If you don't like it, get out of it, because you'll be lousy at it. You don't have to stay with a job for the rest of your life, because if you don't like it, you'll never be successful in it."

Lee Iacocca

"If you want to be successful in a particular field of endeavor, I think perseverance is one of the key qualities. It's very important that you find something that you care about, that you have a deep passion for, because you're going to have to devote a lot of your life to it."

George Lucas

"The true measure of a career is to be able to be content, even proud, that you succeeded through your own endeavors without leaving a trail of casualties in your wake."

Alan Greenspan

Key #1: Hire capable people who love the work they do and show them how they contribute to the bigger picture.

Mary is a real "people person." She loves to talk with others and she especially loves talking on the phone. When she started her job as a customer service representative in a medium-size plumbing supply company, she was very excited about getting paid to do what she loved best. She would be talking all day long to customers.

However, her work didn't quite turn out the way she expected. While speaking to customers was important, there were other parts of the job that were equally, or even more, important. For example, when customers had complaints, Mary had to find their file in the computer system, record the nature of the problem, and then go about solving it.

Sometimes the customer problems were quite involved and the solutions were time-consuming. It could involve looking up a number of different orders, finding out who took the order, getting support from the manufacturer, following up with the shipping department, getting authorizations for returns, and other tasks that always took longer than she expected.

As if that wasn't enough, Mary was very carefully supervised in her job. Her phone calls were often monitored by her supervisor, and any decision she made regarding a customer complaint had to be checked and signed off by a supervisor. Often the supervisors weren't available so the sign-offs were delayed, and customers called Mary more than once or twice to complain about the length of time it was taking to fix their problem.

Because of the constant pressures (from both customers and management), she was unable to plan or organize how her time was spent throughout the day. The phone would start to ring from the moment she started her shift in the morning and the customer chase would begin once again. She was always several days behind in fixing problems and new ones were added daily. The stress was starting to get to Mary. She spoke to her supervisor several times, even offering suggestions on how things could be improved. She was told that the other customer service reps were doing fine and *they* weren't complaining.

Of course, Mary knew that most of them were fairly new, due to the high turnover rate, and were not yet confident enough to speak up. In fact, the whole department had turned over several times since Mary started; she was considered a veteran. Her frustration at work began to seep into her home life. When she got home she was exhausted and moody. She no longer participated in weeknight activities she enjoyed such as going to movies, bowling, and dancing. She now had difficulty falling asleep.

There are many managers who would see Mary as just another cog in the wheel. If she quits, they'll quickly find someone to replace her. I've seen managers continue to hold that view with turnover rates of 80%. They feel that it's easier to replace people on the merry-go-round than it is to deal with the problems leading to the employee burnout.

Unfortunately, they don't want to look at any cost analysis of this kind of management philosophy. The irony is you can find these managers going around telling everyone how "people are our most important asset." I guess that could be true if the only other asset you deal with is chemical waste.

But the point of this story is that there are other costs (and benefits) related to employees that you should be thinking about. There are the human costs, the value placed on the organization's reputation and goodwill, and a multitude of extra benefits that a highly motivated workplace can provide. There are many intangible rewards for organizations that have people around who love their job.

What are some of the changes that could be made to help Mary with her situation? One option would be for her to find a way to maximize her time doing the tasks she really enjoys. If building relationships is her strength, then many of the administrative aspects of her work could be delegated to others. People who love problem solving, setting priorities, and organizing things could take over those parts of the job. Mary could be the person who provides the customer the solutions and maintains their confidence and trust.

Mary should have the opportunity to set her work goals collaboratively with her supervisor (e.g., number of customer problems solved per day) and have her effectiveness measured with constructive feedback. In the course of her day she should have the opportunity for scheduled downtime to plan and think about her priorities.

She should play a major role in creating and structuring her daily activities in order to achieve the goals set by her and her supervisor. Mary needs to be responsible for carrying out her activities and not be unnecessarily micro-managed. If she is unable to carry out her responsibilities independently, she should be coached, re-trained, and given fair timelines to get it right.

If her performance continues to fail, she should be removed from the job. Nobody wins when an employee flounders at a job. The employee usually feels bad about her poor performance, fellow employees get upset that the organization condones mediocrity (or worse), and the organization ends up losing by having poor performance. People who are unable or unwilling to offer high-quality performance in their jobs should be removed from the job (whether terminated or transferred) as quickly as possible, for the benefit of all parties. With proper counseling and assessment, low-performing employees can be directed towards types of work for which they are better suited.

In Mary's case, there could be huge benefits to having her focus more on what she enjoys, giving her more control over her job, such as by increasing her responsibility in setting and measuring goals, and by providing opportunities for advancement. In other words, Mary's happiness and job satisfaction were at a turning point. How did she fare? We'll return to Mary's story shortly.

The Case for Job Happiness

I still encounter some employers who are skeptical about the importance of work happiness. "I'm not a social worker, so why should I have to care if staff are happy? I only care about the bottom line—are they getting the job done?" This is what I was told by Frank, the CEO of a lumber company.

"Getting the job done is certainly important," I agreed, "but at what cost? How many of your people will put in more than what you want done, especially in times of crisis? How many of your people would take a bullet for you?" I asked. I didn't mean to be so morbid, but with Frank I thought that might drive it home.

"I guess I can see your point, but you'd have to convince me it would increase productivity," he conceded.

This chapter defines job happiness and how it goes beyond traditional job satisfaction and includes *feelings* about the job and workplace as well as job challenge, empowerment, and several other variables that help connect people to their work.

As evinced in Chapter 3, there has been a great deal of research in the area of job satisfaction. But job satisfaction is only a part of job happiness; job happiness implies how much someone *enjoys* their workplace in addition to job satisfaction, which incorporates the degree to which people are challenged and fulfilled by their jobs.

What is the link between job happiness and productivity?

Researchers have become increasingly interested in the relationship between "affect," or mood, and people's attachment to their work. Do an employee's stronger "emotional bonds" to their work increase what organizational psychologists refer to as "organizational citizenship" behavior? Does it make employees better ambassadors for the organization?

For his doctoral dissertation, Scott Schneider surveyed 203 managers from both private and public organizations throughout the United States.[1] He looked at job characteristics, organizational commitment, job satisfaction, and demographic variables. One question explored was, "How do good feelings about your job relate to other components of job satisfaction?" In other words, could you love your job yet be unhappy with other aspects of your work?

Well, apparently not. He found that the affective or emotional commitment to the job was related to a variety of job satisfaction components. People who felt good about their job also liked their present work, present pay, opportunity for promotion, supervision, co-workers, job-in-general, and job situation.

Another dissertation by Jane Paradowski looked at the effects of both positive and negative affect (mood) on job satisfaction.[2] She reviewed 90 research articles, looking at the relationship between affect and job satisfaction. Her meta-analysis found that 11% of job satisfaction can be accounted for by positive affectivity and 15% by negative affectivity. So, bad feelings were slightly more important than good feelings for being satisfied with your job.

Taken together, it's clear that feeling good at work will increase your satisfaction with your job as well as many other components of your workplace. However, bad feelings at work can sabotage all that goodwill, which could have a negative effect on the workplace. People's personalities and their emotional and social intelligence have a direct relationship to their moods. However, it would seem that reducing those annoyances and irritants in the workplace would go a long way to improving job satisfaction.

Do feelings about work relate to a company's financial performance?

Does any of this make a difference to a company's bottom line? Is there any real benefit to having people who love, or at least don't dislike, their jobs? In a large study looking at 35 companies over eight years, Benjamin Schneider and his associates examined the relationship between employee attitudes and an organization's financial performance.[3]

They found that three out of seven work factors were consistently related to bottom-line performance. These included overall job satisfaction, satisfaction with (job) security, and satisfaction with pay. One of the differences in their study was the reciprocal relationship they found between these factors and organizational performance. In other words, it is not simply a matter of satisfied workers leading to greater performance, but also a high-performing organization leading to more satisfied employees.

What about longer-term financial performance? In a series of studies, Daniel Denison looked at 34 publicly held firms over a five-year time frame; he found that organizations in which employees reported that an emphasis was placed on human resources tended to have superior short-term financial performance.[4] Organizations with higher-level employee participation decision-making practices showed small initial advantages which increased steadily over five years. In fact, over the five-year period during which they were followed, their financial performance increased steadily in comparison to their competitors.

So do we increase job happiness one employee at a time, or do we focus on groups of employees? Denison's study, along with a number of others, supports the idea that aggregated employee (satisfaction) attitudes are related to organizational performance.[5] While an individual employee's positive attitudes are related to organizational performance, having groups of employees feeling good about the organization shows even stronger relationships to performance.

But again, the relationship between happy workers and performance is not a simple one. Benjamin Schneider and his colleagues outline several important steps or sequences:

1. High-performance workplaces are seen as leading to financial and market performance through improvements in production efficiency;

2. Financial and market performance leads to higher levels of job security (improved benefits) and job satisfaction (through improved reputation of organization);

3. Financial and market performance leads to increased pay levels, resulting in higher satisfaction with pay, which gets improved production efficiency through greater organizational citizenship behavior.[6]

How far will companies go to make employees happy?

The importance of happiness at work can be seen in some company's efforts at promoting job happiness. Analytical Graphics, in an effort to maintain happy employees, provided washers and dryers for personal use, catered meals for breakfast, lunch and dinner, as well as candy, snacks, cereal, and coffee on every floor of its offices.

The company was reported to spend $1 million per year to provide their workers with food and other perks, over and above their salaries, health benefits, vacations, 401(k) matches, and profit-sharing benefits. Open communication and trust were also reported as part of the corporate culture.[7]

Analytical Graphics, as will be highlighted in Chapter 14, was also listed as one of the "Best Small and Medium Companies to Work for in America," based on company information collected by the Society for Human Resource Management (SHRM).

How happy are employees with their jobs?

In our surveys of workplaces we ask people how satisfied they are with their jobs. Overall, we found that 70% of people are satisfied (includes both somewhat satisfied and very satisfied) with their job. At first glance, that doesn't seem too bad—until you realize that you have 30% of employees who either don't care or dislike their jobs. Having 30% of people ambivalent or negative about their work is a huge drag on an organization.

Satisfied with my job		
No	Neutral	Yes
15%	15%	70%

How does this compare to large-scale studies in other countries? Joseph Ritter and Richard Anker carried out a study looking at job satisfaction among thousands of employees in five different countries.[8] Here's how they compared in how much they were satisfied with their work:

Satisfied with nature of my work		
Country	No	Yes
Argentina	13.2%	71.7%
Brazil	13.8%	73.4%
Chile	11.9%	70.6%
Hungary	10.8%	66.2%
Ukraine	18.8%	62.1%

One way that we get a better look at how people really *feel* about their jobs is whether or not they would recommend their workplace to others. In organizations where people really love their jobs, much of their recruiting comes from friends and relatives of employees as well as general word of mouth. These organizations usually have piles of resumes waiting to be looked at for almost any job offered.

So, if 70% of people are happy with their jobs, what percent of employees do you think would recommend their workplace to others? I would have thought somewhere close to the 70%. Well, I thought incorrectly. The actual numbers are:

I would enthusiastically recommend this organization to others		
No	Neutral	Yes
16%	26%	58%

Only 58% of people would refer others to their workplace for jobs. In other words, while 70% of people are happy with their work, only 58% are excited enough to recommend their workplace to others. Great workplaces not only close this gap, but the percentages are closer to 90%.

Are there opportunities for career advancement?

The item that universally scores the lowest in our look at work happiness has to do with opportunities for career advancement. As can be seen below, only 55% of employees surveyed feel there is an opportunity for career advancement in their organization.

Opportunity for career advancement in my organization		
No	Neutral	Yes
15%	30%	55%

Both employees and employers are responsible for ensuring career growth. This is one of the most challenging areas for small-and medium-sized organizations. Smaller organizations may have fewer career opportunities available. However, even small- and medium-size organizations have opportunities to stretch jobs. They can restructure positions, add more responsibilities, and increase compensation, as opposed to a promotion to a completely new position. Or, there may be opportunities for a lateral move to an interesting position in another part of the organization. Talented employees adapt well and learn new skills quickly.

A study on career advancement in Fortune 100 companies was recently reported in the *Harvard Business Review*. It looked at prospects of internal vs. external career advancement:

Career research also offers insights about when it's best to move on. An individual's advancement may slow for reasons beyond his or her control, such as problems with immediate supervisors and changes in company strategies that reward different backgrounds. As the average age of executives in the highest jobs decreases, delays in promotions become more damaging to a manager's odds of getting to the top. An objective look at the company's prospects can help a manager decide whether to sit tight and hope the situation improves or move to a different company or division. Take a zero-based budgeting approach, as an investor would: If you were not already an employee, would you invest your human capital in this company, given its plans and current situation?[9]

Writing in Harvard Business School's *Working Knowledge*, Linda Hill's recommendations for managers looking for advancement can be applied to many line positions as well:

People should look for jobs in which they can leverage initial fit to establish a self-reinforcing cycle of success whereby, year after year, they acquire more of the sources of power necessary to be effective and successful. They should pursue situations in which their strengths are really needed, important weaknesses are not a serious drawback, and their core values are consistent with those of the organization; in other words, the stretch should not be too big or the risk too great.[10]

According to a Mayo Clinic report on career advancement:

The times when people worked for the same company until they retired are a thing of the past. People are more mobile. Few live in the same place all their lives. Access to education is better, and people have higher expectations of what they want out of life. And since people live longer, they can pursue several different careers during their lifetimes if they wish.

If you want to transfer to a different position, move up the corporate ladder or change careers, charting your career path can help you do so with less stress. [11]

The article points out some useful suggestions for employees interested in career advancement. While employees should be responsible for plotting their own career path, there's a lot the organization can do to help the process along. If people are the organization's greatest asset, then the organization must be willing to invest in that asset. Part of that investment should be to help develop employees. Here is a digest of those suggestions:

- The first part of the plan should involve a fairly clear look at where the organization is going. Managers, when meeting with their employees as part of setting or reviewing goals, should discuss future plans. Where does the employee see themselves in six months and a year out? How does that match with where the organization is going? Managers should get a sense of whether this is a longer- or shorter-term employee, and plan their development accordingly.

- Managers should be looking for where their people might fit into longer-term plans. Some employees may be happy in their current positions for the foreseeable future, while others are already thinking about the next opportunity. If desirable, employees can meet with a human resource person in the organization to get an even wider scope of where the company is going.

- While 45% of the people we surveyed don't see an opportunity for career advancement in their organization, we really have to ask how many of them have made their intentions known. The organization's culture should be one in which people can be comfortable talking about their career goals with their supervisor. Employees should be free to talk about what skills they want to build in order to advance their career. That way, supervisors can recommend their people with the right skills to other parts of the organization. But it's important for supervisors to know what their employees' interests and skills are in order for this to happen.

- Employees should be encouraged to find a mentor. It could be their supervisor, or it could be someone from another department. The mentor can add valuable career advice on training, skill building, and career opportunities. A mentor can also review career goals and provide guidance.

- Part of the continuing growth along any career path is the opportunity to discover strengths and weaknesses. It's always a good time to honestly look at one's top two or three weaknesses. One of these areas can then be selected to work on for improvement. For example, there may be things one could change to get along better with a supervisor, co-workers, or others.

- Additionally, one could find an area of work that is currently uncomfortable or unfamiliar. It could be something like accounting or computer skills. Steps can be taken to get more experience or training in this area. Managers should be more than willing to find ways to help support employees improve in these work-related areas. In fact, this serves as a signal to the manager that the employee really cares about the job.

- Someone who is truly interested in career advancement will be more than eager to take on new challenges when the opportunity arises. It pays to listen for any talk around the organization about new projects or other opportunities. If one's skills match the needs in this area, one should talk to a supervisor about any possibility of getting involved. Proving oneself on a special project could be a big help with career advancement.

- Employees should not be reticent about talking to others at work about their accomplishments. This should not be done in a bragging manner. Rather, in the course of conversation, let people know what you've been working on. Specifically, one may want to bring up challenging situations that have been overcome.

- Employees need to stay up-to-date on what's going on in the organization. By networking with people in the company, one will be aware of new opportunities. By staying on top of the organization's needs, you can work at positioning yourself for filling those needs.

- Also, employees need to stay on top of training opportunities provided by the organization. Great workplaces regularly create and post opportunities for learning. These can be as basic as computer skills, accounting processes, customer service do's and don'ts, or other areas where there may even be in-house expertise. Using in-house talent provides current employees a chance to develop their presentation skills, enhance their own job, and make them local experts in their area. Everyone wins from giving employees opportunities to shine, especially in front of their peers and managers.

To return to the story of the customer service rep, Mary decided to take a good look at her strengths and weaknesses. On the positive side, she knew that she was good at dealing with customers. One of her weaknesses, however, was setting priorities. She knew there were ways she could improve in this area. She found someone in the organization that was willing to mentor her in this area. Another weakness was that she lacked the assertiveness to discuss her strengths, weaknesses, and goals with her supervisor. She also wanted to make suggestions on how the department could run more efficiently and with less stress. She was able to work with her mentor in improving her assertiveness skills. Her ability to confront these issues and make changes in her life made a big difference in her job happiness.

What about great companies?

In a recent *Computerworld* survey, 100 top IT companies were identified as the best places to work. From those companies, 27,108 employees were surveyed on a number of issues related to their organization.[12]

One of those questions asked employees how interesting and challenging their job was.

My job is interesting and challenging		
Disagree	Neutral	Agree
7%	13%	80%

As can be seen, 80% of these employees find their work interesting and challenging. Only 7% report their work as boring.

Company pride is another measure of great organizations. How proud are these employees to work for their company? In this case 85% of people working in these companies were proud of their organization.

I am proud to work for my company		
Disagree	Neutral	Agree
4%	11%	85%

As previously mentioned, opportunities for career growth are not too high in most companies we surveyed. What about career growth in these top 100 companies?

There are opportunities for career growth in my company		
Disagree	Neutral	Agree
12%	13%	75%

While these are mostly large organizations, 75% of employees saw opportunities for growth within their organizations.

Another area that is not generally well attended in organizations is the development of career paths for employees. How do employees rate this area in these top 100 organizations?

I have a well-defined career path		
Disagree	Neutral	Agree
22%	27%	51%

They found that 51% of employees had well-developed career paths in these companies.

It seems that great companies go to some lengths to ensure jobs are interesting and challenging. Also, it is very likely that these organizations do a good job in selecting employees who want to be challenged and do interesting work. Great companies want their employees to be proud of their organization. They also work at creating opportunities in order to retain their talent. These are areas I find that mediocre organizations neglect or only pay lip service to. By surveying the organization, you discover where the organization really stands in these areas.

How to Improve the Job Fit and Organizational Efficiency

There's a lot that employers and employees can do together to improve the job fit and, as a result, the organizational efficiency. Let's now look at some concrete steps that can be taken.

Look at carrying out job reviews. An independent consultant or HR staff member can meet with each person to review their current job and look for ways to improve their function. Core strengths and skills should be matched as much as possible with the job function. There should be a good fit between the person's strengths, skills, and the job. If the fit is not there, it's time to start looking at whether you can change the job, or find a better place for the person.

Employees should participate in reviewing their job descriptions if they have one. One way to encourage discussion is to have the individual draw a line down the middle of a piece of paper and list all the aspects of their work that they enjoy on one side of the page and all the aspects they dislike on the other side of the page. Let them brainstorm ways to increase the positive aspects of the job and delegate or change the less desirable parts.

A lack of fit between a person's knowledge, skills, and abilities and the requirements of their position results in loss of productivity and happiness at work. Matching the intellectual capacity, personality, emotional intelligence, and interest of individuals to a position is the ideal. Perhaps assessing each of these areas can help make one more aware of the type of job they are better suited for.

Consider the use of "job interest tests" to help people discover if they are generally doing what they are suited for. Let each person determine whether he or she prefers working with people, things, solving problems, or ideas.

Are there any formal mentoring/coaching programs? Often having a mentor or coach gives a person someone to discuss frustrations with and gain perspective on his or her situation.

Enhance Job Happiness in the Workplace

Managers must be alert to areas where the workplace can be enhanced. Can work schedules be improved? Can the work environment be improved? Can a new rewards system be put in place?

Are there other areas that could promote increased self-actualization? Are there formal training programs with sufficient resources to provide employees with real opportunities for learning and development? Encourage employees to pursue learning options.

Is there sufficient opportunity at work to network with others? Is networking a positive experience? Some companies offer "treat days," where one day a month each department takes a turn offering special snacks to everyone in the organization, or weekly breakfasts sponsored by the company to encourage inter-departmental networking.

Ask the individuals themselves to identify areas for change. Find out what they would like to see to make a better workplace.

Is there a formal employee suggestion program? Often, lack of a formal method of offering suggestions or feedback to management frustrates workers and results in their feeling they have no voice.

Is there a "bigger picture" that people feel they are contributing to? How has the company defined its organizational goals to benefit the community or society as a whole? Do we build houses, or "make affordable places for people to live"? Do we make water pipes, or "help provide clear, clean water for people everywhere"?

Think about how your mission can capture the hearts and minds of your people. If you can't deliver a compelling message in the nature of the work, then what cause or causes does your organization support to better the community? Do people get paid days off to help out in the community in some way? Is there something they can tell their friends and relatives about how they made the world a better place to live?

While there are people who prefer to work in places that offer perks such as cappuccino on demand, you're much more likely to win the hearts and minds of dedicated people when there is a greater cause that everyone in the organization is committed to.

Measure and Celebrate What You Do

Ensure that work is challenging enough at the individual level. Some people prefer to have a great deal of challenge in their work while others prefer more routine work. The ideal is a balance where the work is not so routine that it becomes boring, or so challenging that it is impossible to complete.

One way to determine and monitor "challenge" is to ensure that goals and standards for each position are clearly understood by the incumbent staff. All jobs have goals. In more routine positions, daily tasks and standards will make up a large component of the goals (e.g., the goal could be to exceed standards by 10%), whereas more challenging positions will have fewer daily tasks and far more goals. Ensuring that goals and standards are set and understood means that everyone knows what is expected of them and they can stay focused.

Create goals that are specific, measurable, realistic, and attainable. People work best when there are set points of accomplishment. Individuals need to be able to recognize themselves when these accomplishments have been met. Achieving success or meeting one's goals is a prime aspect of job happiness.

Establishing goals and measurements communicates to staff that what they are doing is important. Individuals who understand how their efforts contribute to the overall success of the business are generally more satisfied and productive.

If goals are not being met, the tasks may need to be broken down into smaller steps.

Ensure that individuals have a formal development plan with both a personal growth and career growth element.

Ensure that goals and measurements are reviewed on a frequent basis, and communicate to supervisors and managers the importance of setting aside time to do this thoroughly. Use these reviews as opportunities to celebrate success, and intervene early when goals are not being met.

Provide opportunities for staff to evaluate themselves against the measurement criteria. Look for areas where self-ratings are inconsistent with supervisor/manager ratings and investigate the source of the discrepancy.

When milestones or goals are met, ensure that there is an opportunity for recognition and celebration. Too often we take people's efforts for granted. People appreciate the recognition and encouragement that comes from others noticing a job well done. Celebrations need not be elaborate, but the appreciation should be genuine.

CHAPTER 8

Compensation: Show Me the Money

"Pay your people the least possible and you'll get from them the same."

Malcolm Forbes

"The buck stops with the guy who signs the checks."

Rupert Murdoch

"Do not hire a man who does your work for money, but him who does it for love of it."

Henry David Thoreau

Key #2: Compensate people fairly.

Margaret was furious. She threw her purse on her desk and turned to Richard. "I've had it. This is too much."

"What do you mean?" Richard asked, caught off guard by her anger.

"I was just talking to Nick. He told me that Mario's base pay is five thousand higher than mine. That's ridiculous. I've outperformed him every year for the past three years," she seethed.

"Yes, but he's been here a couple years longer than you," Richard replied.

"Wait a minute! When I was hired I was told that this place was about performance, not how long you've been here. Why should I get a lower base if I outsell him every year? That's not fair!"

One of the questions I often get when talking about organizational emotional intelligence is what does compensation—pay and benefits—have to do with emotional intelligence? Isn't compensation just part of any standard workplace survey?

Well, the answer is yes and no. The research on satisfaction with pay has found this area breaks into several different components. So while you may be able to say someone is happy (or, to the contrary, unhappy) about their pay, it's more important to understand which of several factors they feel this way about. One factor has to do with the amount people get paid; most surveys on pay satisfaction ask people if they're satisfied with their level of compensation.

A second factor has to do with *the way in which* people are paid: is the administration of compensation fair? People compare their pay to their colleagues' pay, as well as to those in other organizations. It's how people *feel* they are being treated that provides the emotional connection. People who feel they are poorly paid may believe they are being cheated by their employer. This can lead to upset or anger directed towards the employer about their situation. And it's not just the amount people are paid. For example, when a company is doing poorly, employees may accept lower pay if they believe it's a fair tradeoff for greater job security.

A third factor is that benefits are often separated out from pay. Benefits are regarded differently throughout the world. In some cases benefits are taken for granted and not well articulated as part of the compensation package. But more about that later.

An effective organizational survey measures people's satisfaction with their pay and the degree to which they believe remuneration keeps them committed to the organization. It includes their feelings about the opportunity for growth in the organization, fairness of assignment of pay increases, and openness of the organization in sharing financial information.

How happy are workers with their pay?

People often report unhappiness with their compensation. However, it's not so much the amount that someone gets paid that upsets them, but their *feelings* about the fairness of the allotment of pay. Having pay systems that are clear, fair, and well understood can be more important than "how much."

How many people are happy with their pay? There have been a number of studies looking at pay satisfaction.

David Sirota and his colleagues have surveyed thousands of workers and managers looking at how satisfied they are in general with their pay. While their surveys tend to focus on larger corporations, the findings provide an anchor point. In a recent summary of their large-scale surveys they found differences between managers' and non-managers' satisfaction with their pay:

> 60% of managers and executives are satisfied with their pay, compared to only 44% of non-management employees, according to Sirota's most recent survey, which covers from 2001 through 2004. This gap has widened by 45%—from an 11-point difference between managers and non-managers in Sirota's 1997-2000 survey to a 16-point difference in the 2001–2004 survey.
>
> "While pay is just one component of employee satisfaction, there is a link between greater employees' satisfaction with their pay, and overall satisfaction, as well as trust in management, and the feeling that management treats workers fairly," said Jeffrey Saltzman, Chief Executive Officer of Sirota.[1]

A Canadian study that involved interviews with 2,500 working people found that 70% of people were satisfied with their pay.

Figure 8:1
Pay Satisfaction Survey

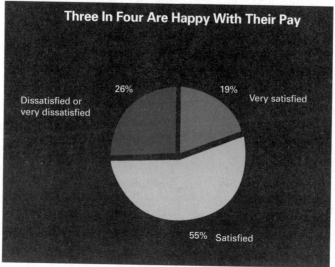

Reprinted with permission of JobQuality.ca and Canadian Policy Research Network.

As Figure 8:1 suggests, most of those surveyed indicated that they were content with the pay and benefits they received (74%), but one in four were not (26%). The significant number of employees who express dissatisfaction with their pay should be cause for concern among employers.[2]

Does it *really* matter if people are satisfied with their pay?

How important is pay satisfaction and how does it affect productivity? Studies have found that perceived employee satisfaction with their level of compensation has an important effect on the behavior of employees. Those who are unhappy with their level of pay have lower levels of job commitment, often have less faith in management, are more likely to seek work elsewhere, and will more often be late for or absent from work. Other studies have linked satisfaction with pay to greater job satisfaction, lower turnover rates, less absenteeism, fewer work stoppages, and better overall employee performance.

According to Steve Currall, a professor at Rice University's Jesse H. Jones Graduate School of Management, well-paid employees are the key to better job performances and ultimately a better-performing company:

When it comes to job choice, the most important incentive is salary. Similarly, the happier workers are with their overall pay, the more satisfied they are with their jobs and the better their company performs. According to university researchers, no single component of an employee's compensation, including health care benefits or pay raises, drives an organization's performance. Employees' overall satisfaction with their pay is key when it comes to the connection between pay and organizational performance.

Based on prior studies, Currall and his colleagues knew that pay satisfaction influences workers' job satisfaction, which, in turn, affects their job performance. As individual employees become satisfied or disgruntled over their pay, they share their attitudes and eventually influence other employees' behavior, all of which results in functional or dysfunctional performance norms and behaviors at the organizational level.[3]

Do people feel they are fairly compensated?

Is it how much you get paid, or how fair the pay system is? In our surveys over the past few years, which include approximately 1,000 employees across 17 workplaces in North America, Europe, Australia, and the Middle East, we ask people whether they believe their pay is adequate for the work they do. To our surprise, only 34% of people report that they feel they are properly paid for their work. This is 10% lower than Sirota's finding that 44% of line employees are satisfied with their pay. It would seem that a significant number of employees who report they are satisfied still don't think their pay is fair.

My pay is adequate for the work I do		
Disagree	Neutral	Agree
44%	22%	34%

Let's leave aside the issue of whether or not people really know what their work is worth. The finding that only one-third of employees *believe* their pay is fair—a day's pay for a day's work—is frightening.

Other studies have confirmed this same trend. For example, research carried out by Kathryn Bartol, a University of Maryland professor of management and organization, and her colleagues suggest that a majority of employees feel their employers compensate them unfairly. They point out how important it is that organizations understand how workers perceive the fairness of pay allocation in order to effectively motivate and retain employees. This becomes even more important with performance-based systems that have a subjective component. According to their research:

> The results ... suggest that organizations and managers need to pay increased attention to pay raise procedures and outcomes. As raises depend more on performance, which usually involves some subjective assessment by supervisors, procedural issues become more complex and are more likely to result in perceptions of inequity and unfairness. Ultimately, satisfaction with pay depends less on the dollar value of a raise than on the employee's perception of fairness, velocity and his or her own worth to the organization.[4]

As companies look more to incentive plans, the issue of fairness becomes even more important. In a study looking at group incentives for merit pay, which compared employees in the United States and Hong Kong, Sunny Fong and Margaret Shaffer from Hong Kong Baptist University found: "The fairness of treatment received will certainly have a bearing on employees' satisfaction with the actual pay raise and the way the company administers pay."[5]

As a result of their findings, they recommend: "When designing and implementing group incentive plans, companies should not only focus on the amount of the incentive, but also ensure that employees perceive the related procedures as fair and believe that the targets of the plan are achievable."[6]

Bartol suggests that the result of being seen as unfair in paying employees directly affects staff retention: " ... turnover is heavily influenced by the perceived fairness of pay allocation within an organization. 'A lot of times we hear that people leave because they'll receive more pay somewhere else, but this research indicates that people really leave an organization because of concerns about the fairness of the way they have been treated based on their pay raises.'"[7]

Do people leave their jobs because of their pay?

How likely is it that people leave their job because they are unhappy with their pay? Our own survey data shows that 30% of employees are considering leaving their organization primarily because of pay. The majority—47%—do not consider pay as a primary reason for quitting their job. If 30% of employees exercised this option, however, that would lead to a very high attrition rate.

I am considering leaving this organization primarily due to pay		
Disagree	Neutral	Agree
47%	23%	30%

In a national study of medical librarians completed by the Medical Librarians Association and consultants from Hay Group, one of the factors looked at were reasons for turnover. While the study examined the attraction of better pay with a different organization as a reason to leave a job, it did not include perception of fairness of pay at their existing job. But one of the areas looked at, quality of management, would certainly support this possibility.

> While the reasons for leaving a position are many and varied, the single biggest reason for turnover for medical librarians continues to be for better pay elsewhere. Beyond pay, the next five reasons for leaving a position included areas within management's ability to change (poor leadership, lack of career development and organizational climate).[8]

But it's not only about pay. Bartol's group points out that employers need to be more creative and find complementary means of rewarding employees.

> "There are other types of rewards than pay, and managers need to get away from the notion that everyone needs the same exact set of rewards," says Bartol. "One employee may value a certain training opportunity, while another wants flex time and a third wants a particular office location. As long as they are comparable and done in an upfront manner, such reward combinations can help managers creatively meet workers' needs to feel their contributions are valued and the organization is concerned about their well-being."[9]

In fact, according to the research by the Canadian Policy Research Network, it's more about respect and other more intrinsic rewards. According to their survey, as seen in the chart in Figure 8:2, 70% or more of employed Canadians consider respect, interesting work, meaningful work, and good communications with co-workers as key ingredients of a good job.

The survey also found, surprisingly, that economic (extrinsic reward) aspects are considered relatively less important. For instance, only 62% of those surveyed indicate that job security or pay is very important, and slightly more than one in two indicate that fringe benefits are very important (54%). This does not imply that the financial package doesn't matter. Rather, it suggests that many employees tend to place greater importance on intrinsic aspects of work.[10]

Figure 8:2
What Employees Want

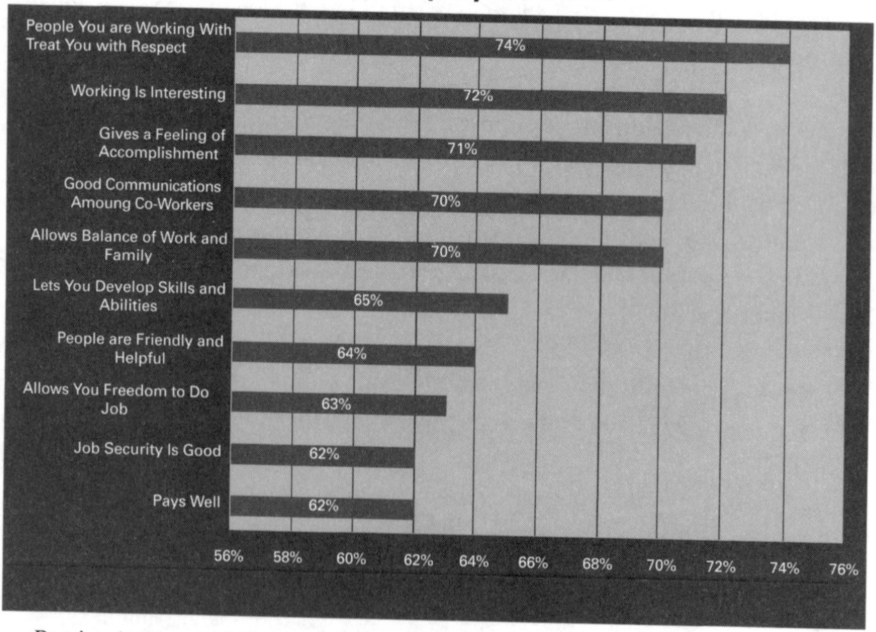

Category	Percentage
People You are Working With Treat You with Respect	74%
Working Is Interesting	72%
Gives a Feeling of Accomplishment	71%
Good Communications Amoung Co-Workers	70%
Allows Balance of Work and Family	70%
Lets You Develop Skills and Abilities	65%
People are Friendly and Helpful	64%
Allows You Freedom to Do Job	63%
Job Security Is Good	62%
Pays Well	62%

Reprinted with permission of JobQuality.ca and Canadian Policy Research Network.

How do we know if pay is fair?

How do we know if our pay system is fair? What if employees were heavily involved in designing the job evaluation process during the implementation of a compensation system? After all, if employees are substantially involved in setting up their job evaluation system, it should be seen as fair. Frederick Morgeson, Michael Campion, and Carl Maertz examined this in a study of 168 employees in a manufacturing firm. Making comparisons over time and between groups, they found that participation had no effect on pay satisfaction.[11]

We often determine how fair our pay is by comparing it to others. How important is the amount you get paid compared to what others you know are getting paid? Gordon Brown, a professor at the University of Warwick in England, and his colleagues carried out a study looking at this issue. They sampled more than 16,000 employees at all kinds of workplaces throughout England. They found that the amount you are paid and your comparisons to others are both important.

> In summary, wage satisfaction in this sample of over 16,000 employees from almost 900 separate organisations was predicted by (a) the absolute level of pay, (b) the ranked position of pay within the organisation, and (c) the position of pay with respect to the lowest and highest pay levels that were sampled.
>
> The survey-based study produced results consistent with the hypothesis that an individual gains utility from the ranked position of his or her wage within a comparison set. The absolute level of pay and the distance of his or her wage from a "reference" wage also both matter.[12]

Does paying people more money increase their satisfaction?

According to Rob Heneman, a management professor at Ohio State University's Fisher College of Business, increasing pay accelerates satisfaction more than the actual dollars warrant. In fact, you receive more satisfaction than expected for each additional amount of increase. He studied the effects of pay increases on 456 nurses at a hospital in the American Midwest. However, the amount of satisfaction in this case may have been higher than usual due to the lack of an adequate performance appraisal system: "'When employees aren't given a lot of feedback about how they are doing, they have to use pay as their only measure of worth,' he said. 'This magnifies the importance of salary as a way to feel appreciated and for employees to gauge their importance.'"[13]

In fact, it may not be easy to gauge the effect a pay increase will have on satisfaction. According to Heneman, "the results show that employers can't assume they know how the pay raises they give workers will affect satisfaction. Satisfaction may rise at an increasing rate along with pay—as it did in this study—or at a steady rate, or even a decreasing rate. Employers need to consider characteristics of the job, the employees, and of the pay system administration to fully understand the link between pay and satisfaction."[14]

Rob Heneman strongly recommends that an organization tailor the pay system to the specific needs of the organization. Organizational surveys are a critical method for helping determine the nature of these specific needs.

> Companies should do an analysis of their employees and pay system to find what works best for that organization ... The results may show the need for flexibility in spending priorities. For example, some companies may find they need to spend more on salaries for the lowest-paid workers—because they would get the most satisfaction—while the higher-paid workers would not need as much of an increase.
>
> "By knowing how pay is related to satisfaction in their companies, managers can learn how much they need to spend to keep their workers happy," Heneman said.
>
> "The problem is that very few employers evaluate the effectiveness of their pay systems. Given the huge investment companies make in salaries, it's amazing to me that more of them don't evaluate their pay systems."[15]

What if you build rewards into your pay system?

Do employees believe their pay package provides incentives for working hard? It would seem from our surveys that not very many do. This is another of those areas that really differentiates the great companies from the rest. We found that only 20% of employees feel their pay package encourages them to work harder.

My pay package provides incentive for those who work hard		
Disagree	Neutral	Agree
60%	20%	20%

How important is it to provide employees with pay incentives? The research seems to suggest that it's pretty important. Mary Jo Ducharme and Parbudyal Singh carried out a study of 15,000 working people and found that "pay satisfaction is the highest when performance pay is tied to the employee's performance and the lowest when there are no performance appraisals in organizations, even if there is performance pay."[16]

Looking at the prevalence of pay for performance in the medical librarian field, the Hay Group found:

> As compared to 2001, the number of 2005 respondents who agree or strongly agree that better performers receive higher pay than average performers increased slightly from 34% to 39%. However, this still means that over 60% of respondents continue to experience sub-optimized pay-for-performance systems.
>
> Recent ... research indicates that many of America's most admired companies [per Hay Group's collaboration with *Fortune* magazine] and those companies that view their pay-for-performance programs as being effective differentiate pay increases for top performers by as much as one-and-a-half to two times that of average performers. These results indicated that this issue continues to be an important opportunity to improve the link between pay and performance for 60% of organizations surveyed.[17]

Studies have been carried out looking at the relationship between performance and satisfaction that take into account the importance of pay for performance. University of Houston psychologist John Ivancevich carried out a series of studies looking at the importance of intrinsic versus extrinsic rewards among different types of workers. For example, he looked at differences between employees involved in stimulating jobs and workers who carry out monotonous work.

Overall, Ivancevich found that jobs in which rewards are based on performance are more satisfying than jobs where pay is only weakly related to performance. However, in complex jobs, intrinsic rewards may be more important while in simpler jobs pay may be more significant. So, depending on the nature of the job, the intrinsic rewards become an important part of the compensation picture.[18]

Nico Van Yperen at the University of Groningen in the Netherlands looked at the importance of the success of the organization itself. An important part of the pay-for-performance equation has to do with how successful employees feel their company is. He surveyed 198 employees from 22 different firms in his study. He found that employees at successful firms had much better buy-in of their pay-for-performance system than employees at unsuccessful firms.[19]

In another study, Alexander Stajkovic and Fred Luthans from the University of Wisconsin looked at the effects of different incentives on work performance. They set up a behavior-modification program where employees were rewarded with money based on performance, and another which used a combination of money, social recognition, and performance feedback. These were compared to a routine pay-for-performance system. The system using the organizational behavior modification program outperformed the routine pay-for-performance system by 37% to 11%. It also surpassed the social recognition and performance feedback conditions.[20]

Many of the studies looking at the relationships among pay, job satisfaction, and performance have involved white-collar workers. One study, by Christopher Lowery, N. A. Beadles, and Thomas Krilowicz, involved tradespeople. They examined the relationship between job satisfaction and a concept known as organizational citizenship behavior among a sample of 91 machine operators.

Organizational citizenship behavior refers to positive contributions to colleagues or to the workplace that go above and beyond expectations of the job. It involves going out of one's way to do good or altruistic things that benefit the organization or co-workers. Lowery and his colleagues found that citizenship behavior in this group was most affected by satisfaction with co-workers, satisfaction with supervisor, and satisfaction with pay. Surprisingly, satisfaction with opportunities for advancement, satisfaction with the work itself, and organizational commitment were not related to citizenship behavior in this group.[21]

In our surveys we looked at how employees view their bonus plans. We found that only 22% of employees regard their bonus plan as satisfactory. Just over half (51%) of employees believe their bonus plan is unsatisfactory. This is definitely an area in need of attention in most organizations.

My organization's bonus plan is satisfactory		
Disagree	Neutral	Agree
51%	27%	22%

Are salespeople any different?

It's often suggested that salespeople operate from a different set of rules when it comes to compensation plans. Their pay is the most often tied to their performance, whether through commissions or bonuses.

How do salespeople make judgments of commission fairness? Sridhar Ramaswami and Jagdip Singh recently studied this issue in a group of industrial salespeople in a Fortune 500 firm. They found that being treated fairly by supervisors and management was more important than having fair procedures and rules in place for distributing merit pay in influencing job outcomes or performance. They also found that job satisfaction was an important aspect in enhancing loyalty to the organization. The perception of fairness of current rewards and potential for rewards were a direct influence on sales performance.[22]

In another study looking at pay fairness perceptions among salespeople, Jerald Greenberg of Ohio State University found that a formal pay-for-performance system was perceived as fairer than a salary-only pay system. However, the importance of implementing the system transparently was stressed as not undermining the perceived fairness of the implementation.[23]

Another study looked at whether salespeople change in their preference for variable pay as they get older. Interestingly, this preference remains consistent throughout a salesperson's career. Salespeople, young and old, are primarily driven by monetary rewards.

Research by Neil Ford, Orville Walker, and Gilbert Churchill from the University of Wisconsin looked at rewards desired by more than 100 industrial salespeople. They looked at a variety of options that included both internal and external rewards, such as job security, recognition, promotion, feelings of accomplishment, and personal growth. They found support for the long-held conventional wisdom in sales management: salespeople are motivated by money. What was surprising was that money does not appear to lose its attractiveness as salespeople reach the later stages of their careers.[24] The expectation that job security would increase in importance as a salesperson gets older did not hold up. It seems that among salespeople—young and old—money is the most important motivator.

Lawrence Chonko and his associates carried out a number of studies looking at what motivates salespeople. They concluded that pay was the most important motivator of salespeople. The basic pay package, however, seems to be the main motivator. The incentive package gives salespeople that extra effort to go over the top:

> The pay package "is the basic motivator, whereas other financial incentives, such as bonuses and contests, operate only to induce effort over and above that produced by the basic plan in certain circumstances." While pay is not the only motivator, it still remains an important (if not most important) component of sales force management.[25]

They go on to point out that salespeople, just like other employees, who are unhappy with their remuneration are likely to quit their jobs.

> The results ... established the ... relationship between a salesperson's satisfaction with pay and intent to turnover. It was found that the less satisfied a salesperson is with his/her pay, the more likely they are to seek new employment. Satisfaction with pay explained 26% of the variation in the sample's intent to turnover.[26]

How do salespeople judge what is fair pay? Well, pretty much the same as everyone else. They look within their own organizations and outside to other organizations. According to Chonko's research:

> It appears that internal and external perceptions of pay equity are the most important contributors in explaining variations in salespeoples' satisfaction with pay.
>
> The primary contribution of the present research was the finding that internal and external perceptions of pay equity were the most important variables in explaining salespersons' satisfaction with pay—even more important than level of pay. As perceived levels of pay inequity increased, satisfaction with pay decreased. Consistent

with previous research and theory, satisfaction with pay was found to be a significant predictor of intent to turnover.[27]

Just how important is fairness in salespeople's pay?

Jerald Greenberg of Ohio State University carried out a study where salespeople were moved from a salary-only system to a salary-plus-commission system. While he found that salespeople viewed the movement to the pay-with-commission as more fair, they then saw their managers as less fair.[28] Essentially, the "system" is now perceived as "fair" since it operates from a set of rules that are defined. However, the supervisor, who is seen as interpreting these rules, is now in the position of being "subjective" and perhaps unfair. This explanation stems from a psychological theory known as correspondent inference theory.[29]

How can fairness be determined in salespeople's pay?

To arrive at equitable pay decisions, sales managers need to conduct thorough job evaluations, use objective industry data on pay (e.g., *Dartnell's Survey of Sales Force Compensation*), interview salespeople individually or in small groups about standards of comparison, and/or hire a pay consultant. Sales managers must provide objective data which shows the salesperson is being paid equitably both inside and outside the organization and discuss any other personal pay standards the salesperson might use.

This suggests that, in addition to perceived internal and external equity, sales managers need to gauge the pay level an employee feels he or she deserves and get some feel for a minimum acceptable salary as well. A minimum acceptable amount has promise as a standard for evaluating pay satisfaction because it implies instrumental uses of money (to purchase desired goods and services, for status and prestige, for self-validation).

When rewards are contingent on performance, the inverse relationship between performance and turnover is stronger. This pattern suggests that sales managers who choose to reward good performance can encourage better performers to stay and poorer performers to leave (Williams and Livingstone, 1994). The most frequently offered explanation is that reward contingency influences turnover through employee satisfaction (Dreher, 1982; Wells and Muchinsky, 1985). Poor performers will be less satisfied than better performers when rewards are tied to performance (Podasakoff and Williams, 1986), hence poor performers should have stronger intentions to quit and should quit more often.[30]

What can management do about the issue of fair pay?

Managers must investigate whether pay levels within the organization are fair and are *perceived* as fair. Sometimes the issue is as simple as a lack of understanding on how pay levels are determined.

Check pay levels of various occupational groups against industry norms. Surveys are available by industry and location. Ensure you are comparing to organizations of similar size in terms of revenue and staff.

Is the organization's "Compensation Policy" clearly formulated and communicated? A clearly articulated philosophy on compensation, whether or not lauded by staff, goes a long way to managing realistic expectations and eliminating time-consuming frustrations.

Organizations choose how they wish to be perceived in the marketplace. Some examples are:

- High pay but low job security
- Low pay but high job security
- Medium pay but opportunities to increase earnings through participation in organizational performance

Does your organization fit into any of these categories? If so, is it clearly communicated to employees?

Make sure that pay adjustments are driven by factors that support the achievement of corporate goals. Loyalty in the form of long service may be a factor in company success, but not at the exclusion of productivity. Your pay policy needs to acknowledge this dynamic.

Find ways for employees to share in the success of the organization. Consider bonus plans, profit sharing, employee share options, or other plans.

General salary surveys may not be enough, particularly if you are in a unique industry or marketplace. Sometimes an outside consultant is required to complete a review of the job pay scales and develop a strategy and a communication plan for pay.

Clear communication is essential. Employees may have an unrealistic idea of what reasonable pay is for certain jobs. Anecdotal information can lead to inappropriate comparisons, therefore, investigate whether your employees' pay ideals are based on realistic facts.

If in fact pay scales are low, you may want to explore options for increases, or implement profit sharing or other participatory plans.

When employees think about pay, they often don't factor in benefits and other non-financial aspects of compensation. For example, sometimes pay is balanced by other factors that can include a lower-stress environment, good work-life balance, great teamwork, learning opportunities, and so on. Look at your scores in these areas to determine if they provide a balance to the results on pay.

What about benefits?

When surveying an organization, it's important to evaluate employees' perception of the organization's benefit package, its competitiveness, flexibility, and its importance in retention.

The average organization provides fringe benefits worth approximately 40% of an employee's salary.[31] It definitely makes sense to look closely at what type of benefits are being offered, why the organization values the goods and services supported through benefits, and how benefits can improve job satisfaction and performance.

Typically referring to any non-pay incentives for employees, tangible benefits vary greatly among organizations. Generally, they fall into one of three categories: health protection, financial security, and conditions of work.

More and more organizations are moving towards "total rewards," which includes everything that an employee can value about the employment relationship. This ranges from direct compensation to more subjective incentives, such as recognition and development opportunities.

While fringe benefits aren't what connect employees to their organization, they are believed to be an integral part of many employees' total rewards strategy. An appealing total rewards package should play a large part in attracting and retaining the best talent.

There are some research studies that link benefits and performance. For example, working with a German service company, Simone Kauffeld, Eva Jonas, and Dieter Frey found that flexible work times resulted in lower absenteeism, higher work quality, and increased adherence to company goals.[32]

According to some researchers, an employee's satisfaction with benefits is determined by the difference between how the employee perceives the amount of benefits currently received and the amount the person thinks they should receive. It's this difference that has an impact on the employee's emotional commitment to the organization.[33]

How flexible are benefits?

The biggest problem we found with benefits in our surveys is their flexibility. More than half the people we surveyed (53%) believe their benefit package is not flexible enough to meet their needs.

Benefit package should provide more flexibility to meet my needs		
Disagree	Neutral	Agree
18%	29%	53%

The traditional "one-size-fits-all" benefits program may not meet all of the employees' benefits needs. By offering benefits that are valued by employees, organizations hope to entice the best people to their company. They also want to retain these people once they've been hired.

In larger organizations, flexible benefits programs are one option to help improve employee's satisfaction with benefits. These flexible programs allow employees to choose from a range of benefit options. This enables each employee to select a package of benefits individually tailored to his or her needs. For example, shifting the coverage of certain benefits to a health-care spending account is not only an effective way to change how benefits are provided, but it also sends a clear message regarding employees' responsibilities regarding benefit consumption and the choices made.

Psychologists have referred to expectancy theory when describing the flexible use of benefits. This theory states that "the strength of a tendency to act in a certain way depends on the strength of an expectation that the act will be followed by a given outcome and on the attractiveness of that outcome to the individual."[34]

This means that organizational rewards should be linked to each individual's goals because different people have different motivators. In a study by Edward Lawler, 80% of the employees at a company changed their benefit package when a flexible plan was put in place. He goes on to suggest that flexible benefits can be a powerful motivator.[35]

Providing benefits that are consistent with an organization's culture, strategic plan, and overall rewards philosophy contributes to the organization's total rewards—as well as its organizational emotional intelligence. For example, an organization that offers new parents a subsidized child care center (or vouchers for a nearby daycare center), flexible work-from-home options, and time off to care for family might see improved work-life stress management compared to an organization without similar benefits.

Similarly, a company that never covers the costs of professional conferences, professional dues, or training workshops is likely to be rated by employees as inferior in training and innovation than an organization that supports professional development.

A study by Barton Weatherington and Lois Tetrick looked at how employee perceptions of their benefits influenced employee attitudes. They found that employee benefit satisfaction and the perceived motive of the organization in providing a benefit has a direct relationship with employee attitudes. Selecting benefits that are appropriate and worthwhile to staff, and in keeping with the organization's objectives, is key to a successful benefits program.[36]

Once the right benefit program is in place, the organization needs to communicate the value of the reward offerings to employees. Unfortunately, many employees undervalue their benefits either because they are unaware of them, or they were not involved in the benefits decision-making process.

A recent article in *Canadian HR Reporter* magazine states, "similar to misunderstandings that occur in personal relationships, the disconnect between employers and employees regarding their attitudes towards benefits can often be traced to a breakdown in communication."[37] As part of being an emotionally intelligent organization, it's important to put out a cohesive message involving front-line managers that educates staff on the value of the organization's benefit program.

What about vacations?

One thing we know from our surveys is that people are generally happy with the amount of vacation time they get. This is the most positively rated aspects of employee benefits.

Amount of vacation time is acceptable		
Disagree	Neutral	Agree
22%	14%	64%

As seen in the chart, 64% of employees are satisfied with the amount of vacation time they get. However, close to a quarter of employees (22%) are not happy with their vacation time.

As can be expected there are significant differences in vacation times internationally as seen in Figure 8:3. Interestingly, the United States and Canada, countries whose employers offer the least number of vacation days, are also the countries with the most unused vacation time. According to the same survey, American and Canadian workers average three days a year in unused vacation time while Germans and French only give back one day. In the Netherlands, workers give back two days and in Great Britain only half of one day.

Figure 8:3
Comparison of Vacation Days

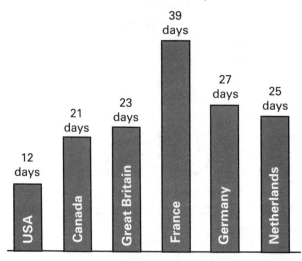

Based on data from Harris Interactive and Ipsos-Reid for Expedia.com [38]

A finding from another survey found that 39% of Americans would prefer extra time off rather than a $5,000 raise. One of their recommendations is that "successful companies will recognize that their employees value forms of compensation beyond money and the most successful employers will be the ones that perfect ways to handle this."[39]

It's very important for organizations to respect vacation time. All too often, work is piled on and employees are unable to resist either taking work with them or forgoing some of their vacation time. Opportunities should be made available to ensure there is enough flexibility for employees to use their vacation time.

What can the organization do about benefits?

Benefits are an important part of any compensation package. The appreciation of the true value of benefits by staff will vary by a number of factors, not the least of which is your employees' understanding of the cost borne by the company and the services provided. Appreciation of benefits will also vary significantly by the overall and individual demographics of your company.

It may be time for your organization to do a benefits review. Are benefits perceived as too rigid? Are there major aspects of a benefit package that you are missing? If cost is a factor and a particular benefit is of great importance to your staff, is there a way to share the costs of the premium or have a co-share clause on the actual expense?

Perhaps people are not fully aware of their benefit package. It's a good idea to have the person in charge of benefits meet with groups of employees to go over the plan. This provides useful feedback on people's accessibility to the plan, benefits they like and those that are not useful. Suggestions can be taken for any additional benefits.

Continuous updates (through memos, newsletters, email) on the changes to the benefits package will provide people with up-to-date information.

Are the benefits a good match for the age group or life stage of your staff? Flexible benefit plans can be overwhelming in cost and administration and may not be an option for all companies. However, there are other ways to add flexibility. Would a health spending account address the needs for flexibility? Can the money be found for it by eliminating low-usage benefits or increasing the cost share?

Once employees appreciate both the value and the cost of benefits, changes can be made that shift spending, without increasing it, to better meet the needs of your company.

CHAPTER 9

Work/Life Stress Management: *I've Been Workin' Overtime*

"The best and safest thing is to keep a balance in your life, acknowledge the great powers around us and in us. If you can do that, and live that way, you are really a wise man."

Euripides

"I've learned that you can't have everything and do everything at the same time."

Oprah Winfrey

"In order that people may be happy in their work, these three things are needed: They must be fit for it. They must not do too much of it. And they must have a sense of success in it."

John Ruskin

"It's not enough to be busy, so are the ants. The question is what are we busy about?"

Henry David Thoreau

Key #3: Don't overwork (or underwork) people.

The strike was a bitter one. It was in a sector that could really do without labor strife. The union represented child welfare workers—the people who provide protection to some of the most vulnerable in our society. They deal with abused children. They make decisions about whether or not families can safely manage their children. The alternative is taking the children into protective custody.

"Our strike was simply about overwork," recalls one of the striking intake workers.

"There was never enough time to do good client assessments," she adds. "One visit and you're out. Also, my own health care went completely out the window. We had no lives. We worked days, nights, weekends, virtually without any kind of breaks." That further compounded the stress leading up to the strike.

"Quite regularly the social worker just shows up because there is no time for a transfer meeting," said one of the family service workers. "You say hello to a five-year-old. 'Hey! Guess what? I'm your new worker. A complete and utter stranger will be working with you now.'"[1]

Work Stability

Concerns about workloads have become a major trigger point between unions and management, especially in the public sector. But the problem is not restricted to unionized environments.

We all know someone close to us, relative or friend, who has concerns about being overworked. Having a reasonable workload is an important aspect of a good job. While having too little work is boring and can cause financial difficulties, having too much work is a recipe for stress, which is bad for a person's health and wellbeing over the longer term. Determining what is a reasonable workload is the subject of ongoing discussions and negotiations among workers, employers, unions, and professional associations. Generally speaking, it means having enough time to do your job well, being able to balance work with your personal life, and not being constantly stressed.

How prevalent is high workload?

What is overwork? One definition of overwork has been provided by Christina Maslach and Michael Leiter, pioneers of the concept of "burnout," as the following: "having too much to do, not enough time to perform required tasks, and not enough resources to do the work well."[2]

In our own surveys of workplaces, we look at the amount of change in both responsibilities and workload that people have been experiencing. Sixty-seven percent of our sample reported that people's responsibilities had increased over the six-month period in which the survey was conducted. The implication of this is that jobs do not remain static. There is greater pressure to change and adapt as jobs fluctuate. As responsibilities change, learning is also required.

I've had an increase in work responsibilities		
Disagree	Neutral	Agree
18%	15%	67%

Interestingly, the percentage of people increasing their work hours over this same time period is 37%. So while 30% of employees have increased their responsibilities without increasing their workload, another 37% found their workload did increase.

I've had an increase in work hours		
Disagree	Neutral	Agree
49%	14%	37%

Having 37% of workers increase their workload over a six-month period has a big impact on the workplace. How does this compare to other surveys on workloads?

A Canadian survey entitled the Changing Employment Relationship Survey included telephone interviews with a sample of 2,500 employed respondents. The sample was representative of Canada's employed population 18 years of age and over.[3]

The survey found that the work lives of many employees fall short of what they consider a healthy balance. Almost one-fifth (18%) of employed Canadians say that they "often" or "very often" have difficulty keeping up with their workload. There is little difference in this respect between men and women, or between paid employees and self-employed workers. Younger workers are less likely to feel overworked than those over age 25.

Figure 9:1 illustrates the difference among occupational groups. Overall, managers and others in the health occupations report being the most over-worked. More than one-quarter of all managers and health care workers report often or very often having difficulty keeping up.

The same is true for just under one-quarter of those in various profes-sional occupations (e.g., natural, applied, and social sciences). These are the people we generally refer to as "knowledge workers," reflecting their relative-ly high skill levels and education. The importance of this is that it shows that workload problems are a result of excessive demands, rather than a worker's lack of skills.

For managers and healthcare workers, the key issue in workload is the de-manding nature of their work itself—a point seen in indicators on work hours. By comparison, a much lower percentage of individuals in arts and culture, sales and service, and processing and manufacturing jobs, has difficulty keep-ing up with their workload.

Figure 9:1: Occupational Differences in Workload

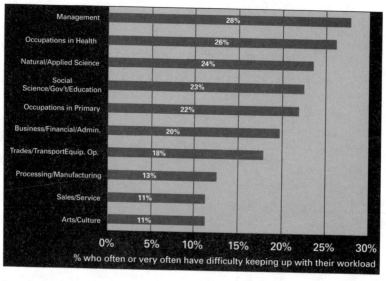

Printed with permission, Canadian Policy Research Networks, JobQuality.ca, 2006.

What effect does the size of the organization have on workload? One school of thought is that people in smaller organizations, often being more generalist and having to wear several hats, would have greater workloads. The Changing Employment study, however, as seen in Figure 9:2, found just the opposite.

There is quite a variance across different-sized workplaces. The biggest difficulties in keeping up with workloads is in the largest workplaces (500 or more employees), where 24% of employees say they often or very often have difficulty keeping up. Compare this to 14% of individuals in small workplaces.

One explanation for the variance due to size of workplace may be the result of staff reductions and restructuring in large corporations and public-sector organizations throughout the 1990s that created a "doing more with less" work culture. As organizations pruned the ranks of management, while expanding the scope of the remaining managers' responsibilities, it is not surprising that workloads and hours increased. As a result other workers also face these issues—overworked managers raise the bar for all their staff.

Figure 9:2: Workload Related to Size of the Organization

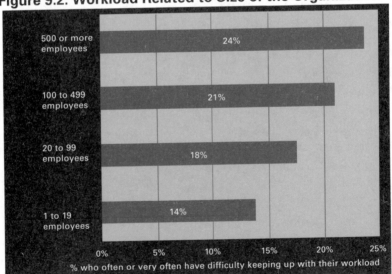

Reprinted with permission of JobQuality.ca and Canadian Policy Research Networks, 2006.

Finally, according to a 2005 report from the Families and Work Institute in the United States:

- 44% of US employees are overworked often or very often according to at least one of the definitions described below:

    - 26% of employees were overworked often or very often in the last month
    - 27% were overwhelmed by how much work they had to do often or very often in the last month
    - 29% often or very often didn't have time to step back and process or reflect on the work they were doing during the last month

- 36% of employees do not plan to use their full vacations
- 43% return from vacations feeling overwhelmed by what they have to do
- 44% of those who are in contact with work outside of normal work hours are highly overworked versus 26% who have little or no contact.[4]

What happens when employees are overworked?

Does it really matter that one in three employees reports being chronically overworked? Does it create problems for employers, employees, and society at large? The Families and Work Institute looked at some of overwork's effects on employees. The institute divided employees into three groups—those who experience high, mid, and low levels of being overworked—and then compared them on a series of work-related outcomes. According to its findings, overworked employees were:

- More likely to make mistakes at work. Twenty percent of employees reporting high overwork levels say they make a lot of mistakes at work versus none (0%) of those who experience low overwork levels.
- More likely to feel angry at their employers for expecting them to do so much. Thirty-nine percent of employees experiencing high overwork levels say they feel very angry toward their employers versus only 1% who experience low overwork levels.

- More likely to resent co-workers who don't work as hard as they do. Thirty-four percent of employees who experience high overwork levels versus only 12% of those experiencing low overwork levels say they often or very often resent their co-workers.[5]

It's clear that overwork has become a serious issue in North America as well as in many places I have visited internationally. While there are those who love their work and have difficulty tearing themselves away from what they do, there are many who resent the additional time they feel forced to contribute. And while there are those who claim to work optimally under pressure (remember those people in college who coasted along until a day or two before the exam and then pulled the all-nighters?), many others find it overly stressful.

One of the surprises I have found is that few executives accurately predict the amount of overwork in their organization. Only after surveying the organization does the true nature of the problem become exposed. Is it worth surveying your workplace to get a better handle on overwork? Well, let's look at the consequences of ignoring this issue.

What are the costs of work overload? (Or, How much pain can you tolerate?)

Many studies report relationships between workplace stress, employee burnout, increased healthcare costs, lower productivity, dissatisfaction with work, and more work-family conflict, especially for mothers.[6] These effects have a negative impact on the work environment.

- Twenty percent of employees who experience high levels of overwork say they make a lot of mistakes, and over one-third feel angry toward their employer and resentful of their co-workers.[7]
- High stress costs U.S. employers about $300 billion per year in absenteeism, employee turnover, productivity, and direct medical costs.[8]
- Burnout is responsible for job dissatisfaction, low organizational commitment, absenteeism, desire to leave, and turnover.[9]
- Employees are less likely to want to advance. In a study of global leaders, 67% of executives have reduced their career aspirations due to the anticipated sacrifices that would be required in their personal lives.[10]

- The worst news for employers is that they may be burning out their best performers. Since top performers are often given the toughest assignments with the biggest challenges, they are the most likely to struggle with overwork, but the least likely to ask for help or set limits.[11]

How do you cope with being overworked?

There are different ways of coping with increases in workload. One option is for employees to take work home with them. The percentage of workers who take work home, based on the Canadian Policy Research Networks study, is given in Figure 9:3. As the figure shows, 39% of people often or very often take work home. In many countries, working at home is becoming easier due to the greater penetration of the internet and the ability to stay "wired" to work. But one of the personal costs of taking one's work home is that it cuts into the amount of time one has for family and friends and for oneself.

There is considerable debate over the effects of having increased access to the internet through BlackBerries and other such devices. At a recent CEO conference I attended, Jim Balsillie, the chairman and co-CEO of Research In Motion (RIM), the company that created the BlackBerry, challenged us on this issue. He asked the group when the last time was any of us had gone to the office on a Saturday for a meeting. He made the argument that while more time at home was spent checking and responding to BlackBerry messages, those who used a BlackBerry were still able to spend more time at home and less in meetings at the office and elsewhere. Balsillie claimed that being wired actually reduces the number of meetings that people have to attend in person.

Others, such as those at the Families and Work project, see increased accessibility differently. They are more concerned about the effect of technology (cell phones, beepers, computers, email, etc.) and flexible work schedules, which they see as blurring the lines between work and so-called non-work times. In their survey they found that one in three employees (33%) is in contact with work once a week or more outside normal work hours. Those who are in contact with work once a week or more outside of normal work hours are more often highly overworked (44%) than those who have little or no contact (26%).

Many employees, especially unionized workers, are concerned about increasing workloads. According to one union survey of 700 of its members, "the effects of the workload increase are staggering," the survey showed. About 94% reported feeling run down, while 87% feel exhausted and 89% have headaches. Amazingly, about half said their symptoms were caused by work.[12]

Figure 9:3:
Who takes work home?

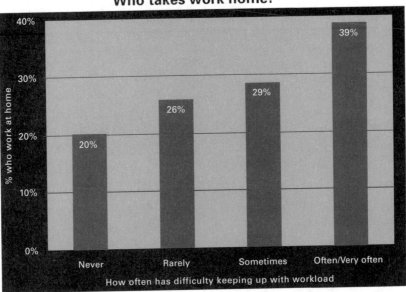

Reprinted with permission of JobQuality.ca and Canadian Policy Research Networks, 2006.

According to a Canadian study carried out at the Centre for Families, Work and Well-Being at the University of Guelph, child care workers regularly contribute an extra day's (unpaid) work a week, with teachers doing an average of 5.3 hours of unpaid work each week.[13]

A number of studies have looked at the effect of "workload" on employees. Australian psychologist Wendy MacDonald carried out a study where she found that workload was a key factor determining stress and fatigue levels among employees performing repetitive, manufacturing work tasks.[14]

Other effects attributed to unrealistic workloads include stress, musculoskeletal injuries, fatigue and related accidents, exhaustion, anxiety, depression, gastrointestinal disorders, and increased exposure to health and safety hazards such as noise, temperature extremes, and hazardous substances.

In addition, people who are overworked are likely to contribute less to their communities. When people are stressed at work, they stop contributing to community activities. They lack the energy to coach a Little League baseball team or lead a Girl Guide troop. They may just be too exhausted to do these things.

There are many benefits to the organization in having employees active in their communities. First, it introduces more people to the organization. People always talk about what they do and where they work and this is a very inexpensive form of public relations. Second, it demonstrates to others that people who work in your organization care about their community and voluntarily contribute to make it a better place. Third, people often make contacts that can be useful from a business perspective. You can meet potential clients or customers, suppliers, and even talent for your workforce.

Clearly, work overload isn't a new problem, nor is it an exclusively North American problem. For example, in Japan, it is now possible for families to get compensation for "death by overwork" when a family member dies from conditions related to overwork. It's not a pleasant option, but it underlines the seriousness of the problem. There is a recognized set of symptoms for workload-related deaths.

The word *karoshi*, which means "death from overwork," is now an internationally recognized term. *Karoshi* is used to describe deaths or work-related disabilities due to cardiovascular attacks (including strokes and heart attacks), which are aggravated by heavy workloads.

In 1987, Japan's ministry of labor began to publish statistics on *karoshi*. So far the Japanese ministry has awarded compensation for about 20 to 60 deaths each year resulting from overwork. Japanese unions say the compensated deaths are actually much lower than the number of *karoshi*-related deaths. They estimate that 10,000 *karoshi* deaths occur each year.

In fact, a recent American study on *karoshi* was reported in the medical journal *Hypertension*.[15] The study, led by Haiou Young at the University of California's Irvine Center for Occupational and Environmental Health, surveyed 24,000 Californians. They found that working 10 hours more than a 40-hour week may increase a person's chance of having high blood pressure by 17 percent, compared with those who work 40-hours or less. The risk increased to 29 percent for people who worked 51 hours or more a week compared to employees who worked between 11 and 39 hours.

They compared rates of high blood pressure across different levels of workers. For example, service workers had the lowest percentage of high blood pressure cases (13.2%) while managers and unskilled workers reported the highest amount of hypertension (17%). Professional employees and semiskilled workers such as machine operators were in between with 14 percent.

Overall, they support the claim that people who put in long hours on the job are more likely to suffer from hypertension than those who work less. Comparing international work rates in 2003, they report that U.S. employees worked roughly 2,000 hours a year, Europeans worked 1,650 hours, and Japanese worked 1,950. Only workers in Thailand, Hong Kong, and South Korea worked longer hours.

The Costs of Overwork

In the United Kingdom, social worker John Walker made legal history in the 1980s when a high court decided his employer had caused his nervous breakdown by overworking him. His union, UNISON, successfully argued that the breakdown was caused by employer negligence. He was compensated to the tune of almost $400,000.[16]

In 1960, a Michigan court upheld a compensation claim by an automotive assembly line worker who had difficulty keeping up with the pressures of the production line. To avoid falling behind, he tried to work on several assemblies at the same time and often got parts mixed up. As a result, he was subjected to repeated criticism from the foreman. Eventually he suffered a psychological breakdown.

By 1995, nearly half of all U.S. states allowed worker compensation claims for emotional disorders and disability due to stress on the job (note, however, that courts are reluctant to uphold claims for what can be considered ordinary working conditions or just hard work).[17]

A current union campaign in the United States calls for an end to "skyrocketing burnout" and the "most hazardous work-related illness: vacation deficit disorder." Campaigners argue that what is needed is "more free time" by amending the law so that every American gets three weeks of vacation after a year, rising to four weeks after three years.

An Australian union has taken up the workload cause with a campaign to tell workers not to "swallow dangerous hours." The campaign literature insists that "reasonable hours are safer hours."[18]

Excessive workloads or work overload isn't just having too much work to do or working longer hours. It may include workplace changes that lead to employees working harder and faster. Some jobs have become more intense because of, for instance, demands for superior customer service. Employees can be under greater pressure to serve customer needs, yet at the same time be required to follow company rules and procedures.

Work overload may also include long and difficult hours, unreasonable work demands, pressure to work overtime (paid and unpaid), fewer rest breaks, days off and holidays, faster, more pressured work pace, unrealistic expectations, additional tasks imposed on top of "core" duties (doing more than one job), and no replacements during sick leaves or vacations.

What can be done about unrealistic workloads?

Workplace support is important. According to the Families and Work Institute survey:

> Employees who have less supportive workplaces—inadequate materials and equipment to do a good job, inadequate support from people at work to do a good job, inadequate flexibility to manage work and family responsibilities, inadequate support from supervisors, and lack of respect—feel more overworked.
>
> For example, 51% of employees who *somewhat* or *strongly disagree* that they "have the flexibility in their work time to manage their personal and family responsibilities" report high levels of feeling overworked versus 29% of those who *somewhat* or *strongly agree* with the statement.
>
> In addition, 51% of employees who *somewhat* or *strongly disagree* that their "supervisor really cares about the effect that work demands have on their personal and family life" report high levels of feeling overworked versus 28% of those who *somewhat* or *strongly agree* with the statement.[19]

With some jobs the workflow can be uneven. There may be certain periods of time when people feel they are being overloaded. Many people, when overloaded, do not perform at their best. Others, however, prefer to work under pressure, even though this may not be the healthiest way to function. One option is to create a team leader position to manage the workflow. This would be a person within the work area to whom an employee could go if it seemed there was too much work. That person could objectively evaluate the situation and help negotiate a reasonable solution.

Thoughtful planning of workflow can also reduce stress and increase effectiveness. Better planning has many advantages, including reducing staff burnout. When managers and line staff work together to negotiate reasonable time frames for reaching various milestones and goals, more realistic workloads can be determined.

Managers must evaluate the resources assigned in each area to determine if resources are sufficient to meet workflow. Temporary employees can provide a cost-effective solution to handle cyclical spikes in workload.

If the problem is one that has escalated beyond control of team leaders and supervisors, then the assistance of an outside consultant might be worthwhile to help analyze the workflow. Perhaps together with the consultant you can identify inefficiencies and opportunities for improvement.

What about low-value work?

One of the problems companies have identified is the amount of time employees spend doing low-value work. Basically, this is work that does not add value or help accomplish the organization's business goals.

What contributes to low-value work? Why would any organization want their employees to be wasting time? Organizations may contribute to this without even realizing it. When a company operates with a culture of "face time," where presence is rewarded as opposed to performance, outcomes such as productivity and work quality suffer.

Some managers are "transaction focused" instead of strategic and big-picture oriented. They expect employees to constantly report what they are doing, so that employees spend as much time telling others what they are doing as they spend doing the work.

How prevalent is this problem? There have been a couple of surveys that have looked at this issue. They have found:

- 20% of employee time is spent on low-value work.[20]
- 29% of employees report that they do a lot of work that is not necessary.[21]

Some companies have identified and started implementing solutions for dealing with this problem. For example, Marriott International found that a facilitated, well-defined work redesign process was important to gain employee commitment and sustainability in their organization. By streamlining low-value work and focusing on results, managers reported less stress, greater work commitment and a more supportive work environment.

Also, IBM's People Oriented Work Redesign Tool—or "POWR"—has enabled teams to pinpoint and resolve unnecessary, low-value work at the department level and improve productivity among team members. The groups that have used POWR report increased clarity, teamwork, and improved processes, which result in the reduction of time and effort spent on activities that do not provide creative and innovative client solutions.[22]

What about stress management?

There are a number of reasons for stress at work. One reason is that people don't have the basic materials or resources they need to do their job. In technical positions this can be specific tools or equipment. In more knowledge-related jobs, it can involve physical or informational needs that aren't being met. In our surveys we find that almost one-third (29%) of employees lack the resources they need to do their jobs properly.

Lack of resources makes it difficult to do my job		
Disagree	Neutral	Agree
57%	14%	29%

Additionally, we have surveyed people to try and determine how many believe their stress is caused by the job itself. In this case, 33% of employees report that their job creates so much stress that it interferes with their being productive at work.

My job creates stress that makes it difficult to get my work done		
Disagree	Neutral	Agree
49%	18%	33%

How much stress is caused by unrealistic deadlines at work? Again, we have one-third (33%) of our worker sample reporting that unrealistic deadlines prevent them from completing their work. This can be a costly drag on efficiency.

Unrealistic deadlines make it difficult to get my work done		
Disagree	Neutral	Agree
49%	18%	33%

How big is the problem of stress in the workplace?

There have been a number of national and regional surveys looking at how widespread the problem of stress in the workplace is. Some examples are presented in Figure 9:4.

Figure 9:4:
What Workers Say About Stress on the Job

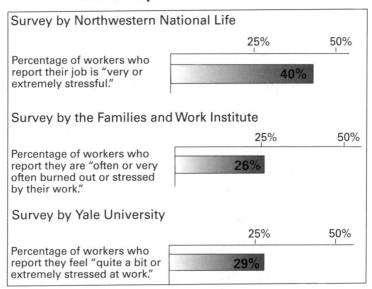

Reprinted from National Institute for Occupational Safety and Health (NIOSH)/Stress at work. [23]

Here are some additional findings from studies of stress in the workplace:

> "One-fourth of employees view their jobs as the number one stressor in their lives."
>
> Northwestern National Life[24]

> "Three-fourths of employees believe the worker has more on-the-job stress than a generation ago."
>
> Princeton Survey Research Associates[25]

> "Problems at work are more strongly associated with health complaints than are any other life stressor—more so than even financial problems or family problems."
>
> St. Paul Fire and Marine Insurance Company[26]

Lawrence Murphy and Steven Sauter wrote a major review on the impact of work stress. They report that throughout the United States, workers continue to report relatively high levels of stress. They cite national estimates showing that in excess of one-third of U.S. workers report their jobs are "often" or "always" stressful.[27]

What are the effects of the stressful workplace?

What's the relationship between work stress and burnout? It is fairly well acknowledged that there are negative effects of emotional exhaustion from work. In a review of the research in this area looking at seven studies, Raymond Lee and Blake Ashforth found that there was a strong relationship between organizational commitment and burnout, accounting for about 16% of the variance. Also, emotional exhaustion was highly related to a person's intention to leave his or her job, accounting for about 16% of the variance.[28]

Russell Cropanzano and his colleagues carried out two field studies looking at the effects of work exhaustion or burnout. In the first study, they looked at the effect of emotional exhaustion on work commitment by examining survey feedback from 204 hospital workers. In a second study, they looked at 232 private- and public-sector workers. They found that high emotional exhaustion was associated with lower organizational commitment, higher turnover intentions, poorer job performance, and reduced organizational citizenship behavior.[29]

East Meets West

Are there cultural boundaries to stress? What about in Hong Kong? In a study examining the cultural aspects of job stress, Oi-ling Siu examined two samples of workers in Hong Kong. The first sample included 386 people and the second had 145. She found that job pressures had a negative relationship on self-rated job performance. She also found that it is essential to nourish work values among employees and cultivate employees' commitment to their organizations.[30]

In another study Siu and her colleagues took another look at work and job stress in Hong Kong and also included Beijing. Once again, she found that employees with higher levels of stress reported worse wellbeing—which includes job satisfaction as well as physical and mental health. The good news was that employees who had traditional Chinese work values were better able to mediate their stress. These Confucian work values include collectivism, hard work, endurance, and *guanxi* (relationships or interpersonal connections). Employees with Chinese work values are also inclined to have more harmonious social relationships.[31]

Is there good stress as opposed to bad stress?

There has been some discussion around differentiating good stress from bad stress in the workplace. That is, there may be some aspects of a stressful environment such as impending deadlines, a sense of urgency, and importance attached to projects that motivate people in positive ways. This is in contrast to negative stress, which involves overloading people with more work than is possible to complete, unrealistic deadlines, and so forth.

A study by Wendy Boswell and her associates looked at challenge- and hindrance-related stress in the workplace. They evaluated 461 university staff employees, looking at the effects of these kinds of stress on their work performance. They found that the two types of stress related differently, as expected, to work outcomes, yet both were related to psychological strain.[32]

What's the emotional intelligence connection?

How does emotional intelligence relate to work stress? In a study looking directly at the relationship between employee emotional intelligence and work stress, Victor Dulewicz and his colleagues, using the EQ-i as one of their measures, found significant relationships between various measures of morale, stress at work, and emotional intelligence.[33]

In another study, Mark Slaski and Susan Cartwright looked at the relationship between emotional intelligence and subjective stress, distress, general health, morale, quality of working life, and management performance in a study of 224 managers in England using the EQ-i. They found that managers who scored higher in EQ suffered less subjective stress, experienced better health and well-being, and demonstrated better management performance.[34]

One of the interesting findings in this study was the link between emotional intelligence and exercise. Exercise was a likely mediator in these managers' ability to moderate their stress. They found that 29% of their sample exercised often while 43% did little or no exercise. The emotional intelligence components that were significantly related to exercise included self-actualization, optimism, and happiness.

How do you get employees (whether managers or front-line) to exercise more? One of the suggestions from research like this would be to focus your intervention on more than the exercise itself. Pay attention to increasing self-actualization—people's desire to improve themselves, optimism—the ability to focus on positive effects, and happiness—the ability to be satisfied with yourself. By including emotional intelligence variables in your employee program you can increase the chances of its success. As seen in this study, the success pays off significantly in terms of health and wellness benefits.

Does stress affect quality of work?

At one time fear was used as a way of keeping people in their place and at their job. Does being fearful and tense at work keep people in their jobs today? One study looking at job stress went beyond the usual study of work performance and looked at the effects of being tense at work.

Suzanne Zivnuska and her colleagues collected data from 270 hotel workers looking at the relationship between job tension and their intention to leave, how much they valued their job, and how satisfied they were with their job. Not surprisingly, being on edge and tense are factors that will motivate you to change jobs. In fact, the tenser an employee is, the more likely he or she intends to leave their job. Also, being anxious is related to valuing their job less and having lower job satisfaction.[35]

In a study of psychological strain (feelings of conflict and tension) and work performance, Linn Van Dyne and associates looked at the effects of work strain and home strain over six months in 195 hair salon stylists. They found that workplace tension was helpful in driving sales and attracting new customers. However, stress carried into their home in turn created stress that interfered with their creativity and performance at work.[36]

What about interventions for work stress?

In the previously mentioned report by Murphy and Sauter, they discussed the importance of examining job stress associated with emerging human resource practices, such as flexible employment contracts and new work systems, such as lean production. Many of the interventions described are aimed at individual workers, including muscle relaxation and meditation. They prefer interventions that involve job/organizational change as they more directly address the stress at work. Other areas mentioned as important include efforts at achieving better work-life balance.[37]

What can be done to reduce stress in the workplace?

There are two aspects of dealing with stress. First, there are responsibilities of the organization, which include practices, procedures, and opportunities that can be implemented. Second, there are responsibilities of individual employees who can take a more proactive role in managing their own stress.

Organizational Activities

What can organizations do about recognizing stress in the workplace and its impact on performance and productivity? One of the first things an organization can do is recognize the role management plays in the stress-work equation. Setting a policy stating the position of the organization on this issue sends a strong message to employees that the employer is concerned. This process can include the following steps:

- Senior managers and employees should meet to acknowledge the importance of the issue and agree to a corporate policy on work stress.
- The policy should be jointly "owned" by the organization and those it protects.
- The policy should begin with a statement of goals that are linked to local health and safety legislation.
- Management outlines areas that the organization can take responsibility for implementing.
- Employees outline areas that they can take responsibility for implementing.
- Management determines the need for carrying out risk assessments.
- Specific steps should be delineated to eliminate work-related stress injuries.
- The organization must ensure there is support for confidential health monitoring.
- All stakeholders agree on a process for publicizing the policy.[38]

Stress-reduction Strategies

- **Job Conditions**: With some jobs, the nature of the work can lead to stress. Management should ensure that workloads are not too heavy, build in rests or breaks, and avoid overly long work hours. With routine tasks or overly hectic jobs, the organization should emphasize how meaningful the work is by putting it in the context of organizational goals and performance. People should have access to the big picture of what they are trying to accomplish. Also, allow them as much of a sense of control over their work as possible. Controlling the timing of breaks, the setup of the workspace and various other issues can give the employee a greater sense of ownership and pride in the work.

- **Management Style**: A great deal of stress at work can be a result of a manager's style in dealing with employees. Managers should have appropriate training or skills in dealing with others. Employees should be part of a decision-making team with their manager. Managers should be more like coaches or mentors, and should be good communicators and sensitive to family issues of employees.

- **Interpersonal Relationships**: Employees who are isolated from others should have opportunities to connect with co-workers. The social environment at work is important. While little work will get done if the workplace is excessively social, there should be some ability for people at work to bond with others.

- **Work Roles**: People's job responsibilities should be clear. Conflicting or uncertain expectations should be avoided. Often people have too many hats to wear or too many competing tasks to complete. An effort should be made to rationalize the job and work expectations.

- **Career Concerns:** It's important for people to have some sort of career plan. Whenever there is job uncertainty or lack of opportunity for growth, some employees will experience stress. Also, changes to the workplace can be worrying to many people. Whenever there is restructuring or reorganizing, ensure the plan includes timely and individual feedback to everyone affected.

- **Environmental Conditions**: The workplace should be as pleasant as possible. Avoid crowding, too much noise, noxious odors, or ergonomic problems.

Taking Action

What can you do when problems with stress in the workplace are identified? Simply acknowledging the existence of a high level of stress can be a relief to staff and a good first step in emotional awareness.

Meet with groups of staff and explore the causes of the stress. Listen to staff suggestions on how the workplace can be made less stressful. Those closest to the stress will often have useful ideas on dealing with some of the difficult issues.

One source of stress is a lack of proper tools or equipment. It's important to ensure that people have the proper resources to do their jobs. This includes workspace, tools or equipment, software, and information. Another stressor relates to people resources. For example, it's important to establish appropriate reporting relationships and communicate team members' responsibilities so workers know who to go to for information. Many people are frustrated by the lack of knowledge transfer and not fully understanding how their teammates' skills should be utilized. They might find they spend a lot of time reinventing the wheel unnecessarily because they didn't have access to the right person.

Set realistic deadlines. These should be reviewed with employees to ensure they can be met.

Sometimes stress can't be removed (during restructuring, for example), so it is important to provide access to information on stress management techniques. See if it would be useful to build in rest times for people. Often, just having a place to relax for brief periods can help people refocus.

How to Combat Work-Related Stress

Workplace stress affects employees' abilities to meet deadlines, make decisions, and manage professional relationships. What are some steps that can help combat stress at work? A report from the American Psychiatric Association (APA) says that one in four people report that they have missed work as a result of work-related stress.

To combat the problem, the APA recommends the following strategies: cultivate a positive work environment; prioritize and set manageable goals; and be efficient with your time at work. The association also recommends taking five-minute breaks between projects, communicating effectively with colleagues; and dividing large projects into smaller tasks. Most of all, it says, be flexible and take criticism constructively.

If workers show stress-related symptoms such as irritability, anxiety, headaches, or poor work performance, business owners should consider recommending professional care, the group says.[39]

Similarly, a report in the *American Psychologist* had a set of recommendations for a less stressful workplace. The article by Steven Sauter, Lawrence Murphy, and Joseph Hurrell, suggests the following:

- Clearly define workers' roles and responsibilities.
- Give workers opportunities to participate in decisions and actions affecting their jobs.
- Improve communications or reduce uncertainty about career development and future employment prospects.
- Provide opportunities for social interaction among workers.
- Establish work schedules that are compatible with demands and responsibilities outside the job.[40]

Work-Life Balance

For all of us, our overall quality of life depends largely on finding a healthy balance between our jobs and other aspects of life. There is a great deal of concern that working people everywhere are finding it increasingly difficult to balance personal responsibilities with job demands.

The "struggle to juggle" is taking a toll on companies, families, and workers. This toll is showing up as increased job stress, declining physical and mental health, increased absenteeism, declining job satisfaction, weakening employee commitment, lower workplace morale, and reduced satisfaction with family life.

What have our surveys told us about work-life balance? For more than a third of our respondents (34%), workloads are making it harder to get their jobs done. So by giving people more work than they can handle, we find that they seem to get less work accomplished.

My personal workload makes it difficult to get my job done		
Disagree	Neutral	Agree
50%	16%	34%

One issue is predictability of work hours. We found that for 20% of people the unpredictable nature of their work interferes with their home life. The ability to plan for work activities, as much as possible, would go a long way to help manage this issue.

Unpredictable work hours cause significant problems for my personal or family life		
Disagree	Neutral	Agree
66%	15%	20%

More than one-quarter (27%) of our survey group report having problems balancing their work and personal lives. This is a considerable percentage of the workforce.

Due to job demands, I find it difficult balancing work and life issues		
Disagree	Neutral	Agree
57%	16%	27%

While we found that 64% of employees we've surveyed feel they have enough time for family and friends, there are 18% who believe their personal time is inadequate.

Due to job demands, I rarely have enough time for friends or family		
Disagree	Neutral	Agree
64%	18%	18%

An interesting set of data on work-life balance was collected in a recent study for the Canadian Policy Research Network (CPRN) by professors Linda Duxbury of Ottawa's Carleton University, and Chris Higgins from the University of Western Ontario in London. They compared results from two large surveys they conducted, one in 1990-1992 (21,228 employees) and the other in 2000–2001 (6,502 employees), in different organizations and across various sectors of the economy.[41]

What they found was that during the 1990s work-life conflict showed up in two areas: role overload and work-to-family conflict. Role overload occurs when people have too much to do, and too little time to do it; work-to-family conflict occurs when the demands of work make it difficult for employees to meet their family responsibilities.

The fact that both intensified during the 1990s may not be surprising, given the trends in the world of work in that decade. During the 1990s, many employers downsized, leaving those who remained to "do more with less." Earnings declined in most of the decade, so many families needed more paid work hours to pay the bills. The "digital revolution" introduced technologies that blurred the lines between work time and personal time—laptops and cell phones made work possible anywhere, anytime.

As Figure 9:5 shows, while work-to-family conflict increased somewhat between 1991 and 2001, role overload rose sharply during that period. While high levels of role overload affected 47% of employees in 1991, 10 years later the rate had increased to 59%.

Moreover, only one in 10 respondents in 2001 characterized their level of role overload as "low," a slight drop from 13% in 1991 (data not shown). At the same time, the proportion of employees surveyed who reported high levels of job stress jumped from 13% to 27%. The 1990s also saw a drop in the number of employees who say they are highly satisfied with their jobs, from 62% to 45%.

Figure 9:5:
Canadians Are Increasingly Stressed from Work

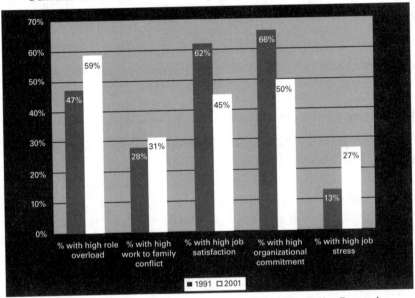

Reprinted with permission of JobQuality.ca and Canadian Policy Research Networks.

The Role of Emotional Intelligence in Work-Life Balance

In a study looking specifically at managers' emotional intelligence and their ability to balance work and family, Abraham Carmeli had some interesting findings. While there is an expectation that organizations adopt better policies and do more to balance employees' lives better, this study also looks at the importance of the role of the employee. He found that emotionally intelligent employees may better handle these conflicts. The integration of work-family programs and an emotionally intelligent workforce can better achieve the desired balance. Both high and low emotionally intelligent managers were sensitive enough to know how their work is affected by family matters. However, high emotionally intelligent managers were better able to balance their career commitment to a healthier midpoint. Low emotionally intelligent managers, while sensitive enough to be aware of how their work is affected by family matters, felt no need to reduce their career commitment.

One implication of this study is that implementing work-family balance programs in organizations without taking into account the emotional intelligence of managers can, in fact, be counterproductive. Other important findings were that emotionally intelligent managers were better "role models" for employees and performed better on the job than the less emotionally intelligent managers.[42]

What can you do to better manage work-life balance?

There have been a number of strategies proposed for managing work-life balance. One study by Shelley Haddock, Toni Schindler Zimmerman, and associates developed 10 strategies for families. Based on their study of 47 middle-class dual-earning couples, they reported that these successful couples structured their lives around 10 major strategies: valuing family, striving for partnership, deriving meaning from work, maintaining work boundaries, focusing and producing at work, taking pride in dual earning, prioritizing family fun, living simply, making decisions proactively, and valuing time.[43]

Management Strategies for Managing Work-Life Balance

- Review workloads to ensure that people are not taking on more than is reasonable. If people are being given more work than is realistic for the time allotted, then nobody wins. The organization will not meet its deadlines and performance will suffer.
- Set predictable workloads. Try to prepare for unexpected shifts in workload, schedules, and responsibilities for at least the next three months.
- Explore the possibility of flextime with staff that may be eligible.
- Ask what steps the organization has taken to show it recognizes family and personal obligations of employees. Explore or communicate these programs or actions.

- Many organizations have work-life balance programs that assist employees in taking care of personal issues that often detract from their efficiency and productivity at work. Generally, these programs improve employee satisfaction and loyalty. Explore the possibility of offering programs that focus on improving employees' physical and mental wellness. Programs may include weight training or cardiovascular activities, stretching and relaxation sessions (e.g., yoga, visualization), and artistic focused courses (e.g., photography classes, dance classes). These programs can be implemented in-house or with outside resources such as exercise clubs or art studios.

What are some solutions to work-life imbalance?

What steps can be taken to reduce, or eliminate, role overload and work-to-family conflict? Several workplace factors uncovered by JobQuality.ca surveys are directly associated with high role overload and high work-to-family conflict: work hours, the ability to refuse overtime, the extent of work flexibility, and the financial situation of families.[44]

Hours of Work

Longer working hours are related to increased role overload and work-to-family conflict. For example, while 45% of those working under 35 hours per week report a low level of work-to-family conflict, only 18% of those who work in excess of 45 hours characterize the level of work-to-family conflict as low. Similarly, while 25% of those working under 35 hours per week characterize their work-to-family conflict as high, a full 60% of those working in excess of 45 hour weeks agree that this is the case.

In practical terms, ensuring that employees do not work excessively long hours will likely have the effect of reducing the number of employees who feel highly overloaded or who experience a high level of work-to-family conflict.[45]

The Ability to Refuse Overtime

Being able to refuse overtime hours is associated with an employee's level of role overload and work-to-family conflict. For instance, while 46% of those reporting low role overloads cannot refuse overtime, 87% of those reporting high role overloads say they are unable to refuse overtime hours. Likewise, 54% of those reporting low work-to-family conflicts cannot refuse overtime, but 82% of those reporting high conflict cannot.[46]

These survey findings suggest that providing employees the right to refuse overtime hours can help reduce the incidence of role overload and work-to-family conflict. However, recent changes to employment standards in some areas have actually extended the normal workweek and made it easier for employers to require overtime hours of their employees.

Job Flexibility

Providing employees with greater flexibility regarding when and where they work also may reduce role overload and work-to-family conflict. Employees with a high level of flexibility in their work are more likely to report low role overload and low work-to-family conflict than those with limited flexibility. According to the JobQuality.ca survey, while 20% of those with low role overload say that their job is highly flexible, only 3% of those who have little discretion over when and where work is performed enjoy a low level of role overload. Similarly, while 60% of those who report that their job is highly flexible also say they experience little difficulty in balancing work and family, only 16% of those in jobs they deem inflexible experience a low level of work-to-family conflict.[47]

In terms of solutions, these findings suggest that providing employees with increased autonomy regarding when and where they work can contribute to a healthy balance between work and family life, and can have the effect of reducing role overload and its negative effects.

The Family's Financial Situation

Finally, a family's financial situation appears to mediate, or buffer, role overload and work-family conflict. While 68% of families reporting high role overload say that "money is an issue," this is reported by only 52% of employees where money is "not an issue."

Similarly, while over one-third (36%) of employees reporting high work-to-family conflict also said that money was an issue, high work-to-family conflict was less common (25%) among employees who said that family finances were not an issue. The fact that more well-off families are less likely to indicate high levels of role overload or high levels of work-to-family conflict may reflect, in part, the ability of wealthier families to afford child care or eldercare services.

Families with fewer resources may be less able to leave non-supportive work environments or to buy goods and services that make it easier to balance competing demands. These families may need to work longer hours simply to "make ends meet." One solution for reducing high role overload and high work-to-family conflict, then, would be ensuring workers are better paid, or at least have access to vouchers for daycare or eldercare services.[48]

Examples of Good Practice Workplace Programs

According to the Boston College Center for Work and Family, the home electronics chain Best Buy provides a good example of practice in this area. At their corporate campus, overwork syndrome is gradually being eradicated by giving workers some control. Their new Results-Oriented Work Environment lets employees adopt a fluid way of working, free from the focus on time. Flexibility is a key factor of this strategy where getting results are valued more than simply dictating how people spend their time. Employees at all levels are systematically challenging their own deeply held assumptions about how work works.[49]

According to a study by Steve Harvey, Kevin Kelloway, and Leslie Duncan-Leiper, workload and the tension around it are mediated by the degree to which employees have faith in management. In their study of accountants, work overload was related to burnout, psychological strain, and work's interference with family. "Trust in management" was found to moderate these effects.

Employees who have a high degree of trust in management may experience reduced strain because they do not fear punitive repercussions for failure to complete their assigned work.[50]

Another example of an exemplary program described in the Boston College Center for Work and Family can be found at Alcan Inc. Alcan's Work Life Effectiveness Strategy is part of EHS FIRST, the company's global Environment, Health and Safety Management system. Workload issues and the culture of long hours are the main issues being addressed by its strategy.

This includes increased focus on working hard but smarter; identifying and eliminating unnecessary or low value work; and utilizing 6 Sigma Continuous Improvement techniques to drive process improvement. Effective workload management, process improvement and culture change do not happen overnight, so senior executives are receiving executive coaching to improve their leadership skills while employees receive resilience coaching.[51]

Finally, the findings from the AstraZeneca Pharmaceuticals Work Environment Flexibility and Effectiveness study show that having flexibility is strongly related to resilience and the ability to handle workload. Employees who have the flexibility they need are more likely to "strongly agree" or "agree" on defined resilience indicators concerning managing pressure and pace. Also, they are more likely to agree that they have control over their work and have a manageable workload.[52]

What can be done to reduce overwork while meeting business goals?

Employees

- Regularly analyze the tasks that you perform and distinguish between the vital and the disposable.
- Make adjustments that will ease work pressure without significant sacrifice of quality.
- Take vacations; take sick time if needed.
- Assess the best fit between your work and personal life.
- Set firm boundaries between work and non-work time.
- Take care of your health—exercise regularly, eat for health, sleep adequately.
- Minimize interruptions and distractions.
- Expect recognition and rewards from co-workers and managers.
- Insist on being treated with respect and fairness.

Managers

- Rethink workflow and division of labor. Is there a better way to achieve results without overtaxing your resources?
- Consider cross-training as both a developmental and coverage strategy.
- Provide learning and retraining opportunities.
- Give employees some choice over their work and control over their schedule.
- Assess the fit between job requirements and employee needs.
- Ask employees for input about management decisions.
- Support and encourage vacations.

- Focus on performance outcomes, not "face time" (simply showing up).
- Thank people and recognize them publicly.
- Ask employees about their workload and work with them to reduce their workload if necessary.

Teams

- Determine expectations about how accessible members need to be (evenings, weekends, holidays).
- Reduce low-value work.
- Set realistic work plans.
- Develop boundaries around interruptions.
- Create solutions that meet employee, team, and business needs.
- Establish flexible ways to get work done with a focus on outcomes.

Organizations

- Reward leaders that effectively manage human resources and their own time towards the achievement of goals.
- "Disincent" unproductive management behavior that encourages overwork.
- Embrace a performance-based culture.
- Create a culture of flexibility.
- Articulate clear organizational values.
- Establish effective ways to resolve conflict.[53]

Getting your organization to work towards a better work-life balance means more productive workers; giving a day or two here can mean the difference between months of work affected by bitterness and stress, and months of quality work by someone who feels they've been treated fairly. It's much more important to have a loyal workforce than it is to police their time at work. If you have employees who are irresponsible about work time, they should be let go. But treat the rest as professionals and their attitude will add to the organization's bottom line—both financially and in human resource terms.

CHAPTER 10

Organizational Cohesiveness: *We're All in This Together*

"The important thing to recognize is that it takes a team, and the team ought to get credit for the wins and the losses. Successes have many fathers, failures have none."

Philip Caldwell, CEO of Ford Motor Company
from 1979 to 1985

"Teamwork is the ability to work together toward a common vision. The ability to direct individual accomplishments toward organizational objectives. It is the fuel that allows common people to attain uncommon results."

Andrew Carnegie

"Individual commitment to a group effort—that is, what makes a team work, a company work, a society work, a civilization work."

Vince Lombardi

Key #4: Build strong teams with shared purpose and viable goals.

Bernard was furious. He had put in late nights for the past two weeks in order to get his sales presentation ready. He had depended on Hilary, a colleague in the marketing department, to provide him with the numbers he needed to round out his slides. But she didn't come through. He couldn't present the client with his best shot. He lost the sale.

"How could you do this to me?" Bernard roared.

"What do you mean? I've been sick," Hilary said indignantly.

"You weren't sick last week. You could have assigned someone else to get the numbers to me," he said.

"I started getting it together last week, and then I got sick, nobody else knows where to look or how they could have been pulled together. I'm sorry, what could I do?"

People at work often depend on each other. They support each other in both formal and informal ways. Bernard and Hilary had actually been good friends at work. They had lunch together at least a couple of times a month. The goodwill between them had led to many successful transactions at work. Now Bernard's trust in Hilary had been damaged.

How important are co-worker relationships at work?

How much attention do organizations pay to these informal networks at work? Do companies see any advantages in nurturing a culture at work where people get along? The good news is that many relationships at work form naturally and seem to work well.

Organizations have become much more team focused. Work has become much too complicated for the "lone wolf" to be successful. When identifying "star performers" as part of a star profile analysis, I now try to include those people who can galvanize and direct teams smoothly towards their goals and higher. This chapter explores what you need to know about fostering strong interpersonal relationships at work and the role emotional intelligence plays.

When evaluating co-worker relationships, I look at the degree to which people in the organization get along, trust each other, and can depend on one another for support.

When we surveyed workplaces and asked employees if they believed they could rely on their co-workers, 78% agreed that they could. Only 10% reported being in a situation where they could not depend on others at work.

I can rely on my co-workers		
Disagree	Neutral	Agree
10%	12%	78%

How deep are these relationships? How well do employees know each other at work? How well can employees "read" their co-workers? And, of course, how important is any of this? Part of any social relationship is the importance of knowing each other. The better you know someone, the better you can anticipate their reaction to situations, requests, and events.

For example, knowing that a certain request will upset your co-worker should make you think twice before initiating it. You may want to think of alternative people you could ask, or other ways that you could phrase the request. Your goal is to find the most efficient way of getting what you need and leaving relationships either intact or stronger.

Suppose you have to make an unpleasant request of a co-worker, such as asking him to give you a report of his work activities over the past month. You need the information because of a budget request you are working on. The simplest option is to approach Nigel and say:

"Nigel, could you please give me all your hours and activities for the last month?"

Now, Nigel does not report to you, so the request may be puzzling to him, and he has no obligation to provide you with the information.

"Why do you need it?" he asks.

"I'm doing a report and need to know people's activities," you respond.

"Okay, but I've got some pretty important projects I'm working on right now, so it may have to wait," Nigel answers.

How would you rate Nigel's level of cooperation? Would you predict that the information will be forthcoming soon? How will that impact you and your responsibility to get the budget in on time?

Even small interactions can affect work productivity. Sometimes the smallest exchange could lead to huge consequences. Not getting the information on time from Nigel could delay the submission of a critical proposal for a government grant worth tens of thousands of dollars. How would you explain to senior management that you missed the grant's deadline because you and Nigel were unable to agree on getting the information you needed in a timely way?

Suppose instead that you approached Nigel this way: "Nigel, I'm sorry to bother you but I'm working on this proposal for the state of Texas. It's worth about $250,000 and there's a lot of paperwork involved. In fact I've been working day and night all week in order to get it in by Friday. One of the requests, which is a real pain, is to include time sheets for all our technical people who would be working on the project. I know you're really busy right now, but is there some way you could get me your time sheets for the last month by Friday?"

While this may seem to be a more long-winded approach, it has the advantage of keeping Nigel in the loop, making him feel a part of the process. It also gives him some background on how hard you've been working on this proposal and how important it is to the company. By giving him more information than he needs, you increase motivation to cooperate.

How well do your co-workers know themselves?

We all have our ups and downs at work. Knowing when someone else is upset helps us better prepare to deal with them—or not deal with them until they're ready. We asked employees if they believed their co-workers were aware of those times when they lost control of their emotions. A slight majority (54%) reported they were. However, 21% reported that they did not believe their co-workers were aware of those moments when they lost control.

My co-workers are aware of when they lose control of themselves		
Disagree	Neutral	Agree
21%	25%	54%

In any organization, as we've shown, the informal social relationships are important. They are part of the glue that keeps the organization functional. In an attempt to look at how strong this glue is, we asked employees if they have times when they feel unable to talk to their co-workers. Almost one-third (28%) of employees experience times during which they are unable to speak to their co-workers. On the other hand, 59% feel free to talk to their colleagues at any time.

At times I feel I can't talk to my co-workers		
Disagree	Neutral	Agree
59%	13%	28%

How can we improve co-worker relationships?

Does your organization experience high turnover (either company wide or in a specific area)? Have you conducted and reviewed exit interviews for trends or indications of causes related to co-worker relationships?

Do the work processes, physical work environment, or management styles reinforce isolation among co-workers? How is information transferred from one person or area to another? Are there opportunities for people in different parts of the organization to get to know each other and their role within the organization? There need to be mechanisms within the organization that allow for the smooth transfer of information. Fostering relationships among employees is one step in smoothing out that process.

Is the work group newly formed? If so, what steps have been taken to build trust and a common culture? Explore the possibility of engaging in team-building activities.

If the workgroup has been newly formed, what steps have been taken to define the structure of the group? Have workers been given specific job descriptions and job responsibilities?

Group cohesiveness, or a sense of unity and loyalty among co-workers or teams, is a powerful antidote to occupational stress. Are there scheduled activities or events that support the development of these types of relationships among workers? Encourage unity by fostering these events.

What makes teamwork tick?

How productive are work teams? What do they contribute to organizational success? How well do they get along? How can they work better?

We measure the degree to which people who work as a team work well together. It's important to look at trust, morale, complementary skills, group pride, ability to communicate, and productivity.

The bottom line on teams is, of course, are they productive? Are teams a good use of people's time and resources? People represent a huge line item on most organization's balance sheets. What level of accountability do we have on the success of teams?

The first level of assessment is to survey the teams themselves to see how productive team members feel they are. We find that 82% of employees believe their teams are highly productive. Only 8% of workers feel their team is unproductive. This is pretty good news for most of the teams that we have invested in.

My workgroup is highly productive		
Disagree	Neutral	Agree
8%	10%	82%

What happens when a team doesn't work well?

Mario knew there was a problem with the inventory. On a number of occasions he noticed sales and marketing people removing stock from the warehouse to show customers. He had also seen customer service people looking for products in order to answer customer questions.

Ellen was perplexed. She spent hours trying to reconcile the inventory count. There were a number of different product categories that just didn't add up. She called her team together.

"Something's wrong—the inventory count is off. I've gone over a number of products several times and it just doesn't add up. Does anyone know why we're short on the count?"

Mario looked down at his feet. He was the junior member of the team and still didn't feel he could speak up. He looked over at Gino, a more senior shipper. Gino was quiet as well. Mario was sure that Gino had seen the sales and customer service people take products from the warehouse shelves. If Gino said nothing, how could Mario mention it?

Mario and Gino's silence, for whatever reason, was about to cost thousands of dollars in time and effort, not to mention the frustration. Ellen wanted a total recount of all the products that were short.

All Mario or Gino had to do was mention that they saw products leaving the warehouse without being signed out. But would that be considered snitching on fellow employees? Would the salespeople get upset? On the other hand, getting to the bottom of the problem could save considerable time and money as the numbers could quickly be reconciled.

We looked at some of the problems that teams may be experiencing, or issues that prevent them from being even more productive. The biggest problem we identified in teams was the feeling that there were team members who had difficulty speaking up when there were problems. We found that 37% of employees reported team members who had difficulty speaking up.

Members of my workgroup have difficulty speaking up when something is wrong		
Disagree	Neutral	Agree
49%	14%	37%

Not speaking up can be problematic. When there are issues that need to be dealt with, it's important for team members to inform each other. What could be done to empower people such as Mario and Gino to speak up?

There has to be an atmosphere of openness in the team. People have to feel they are free to contribute. Team leaders have to be able to invite team members to contribute without putting them on the spot. Each member has to feel their contribution is valued. All members, junior and senior, have to be encouraged to participate and be part of the team.

This takes us to team morale. How important is the morale of the team? High-morale teams are much more productive than teams with low morale. How high is morale generally in teams? Our surveys have found that 65% of employees feel the morale of their team is good.

My workgroup has good morale		
Disagree	Neutral	Agree
20%	15%	65%

We also found that 20% of teams have poor morale. There can be a number of reasons for poor morale. Often it's because team members feel they are not full participants in the team or they are not heard. Team leaders, in order to be successful, need to make each member feel they are an important and contributing member of the team.

Organizational Cohesiveness

Peter Jordan, Neal Ashkanasy, and their colleagues in Australia set out to relate workgroup performance to emotional intelligence. They specifically looked at the relationship between emotional intelligence and team process effectiveness and team goal focus. They found that emotional intelligence of team members was related to the initial performance. Over time, however, teams with low average emotional intelligence raised their performance to match teams with high emotional intelligence.[1]

A study by Lawrence Fredendall and Charles Emery looked at the relationship between self-directed work teams and profit and customer satisfaction. They also looked at leadership style and compensation systems. Examining 54 service departments (22 with teams and 27 without teams) of automobile dealers they found that service garages using teams had higher profits than service garages not using teams. There were also differences in customer satisfaction favoring those using teams.[2]

Craig Pearce and Michael Ensley looked at innovation in work teams. Studying 71 product and process-innovation teams, they looked at team dynamics. They concluded that a shared vision was a key part of longitudinal success.[3]

There have been many studies showing a link between group cohesion and performance. One interesting study was carried out at a Harley-Davidson plant. After converting from a "command and control" structure in the late 1980s, the company moved to a very successful culture of work teams. In a study involving 233 employees, Phillip Chansler and Paul Swamidass found that employee control over team staffing and perceived fairness accounted for 42% of the variance in group cohesion.[4]

Employees' attitudes towards working in teams can significantly affect team success. Sandra Kiffin-Petersen and John Cordery looked at data from 218 employees in 40 self-managing work teams to examine this relationship. They found that two forms of trust — trust in co-workers and trust in management — were strong predictors of an employee's preference for teamwork. Their opportunity for skill utilization was also found to be important.[5]

In a study looking at adapting to self-managed work teams, Peg Thoms and her associates found characteristics such as conscientiousness and attitude toward self-managed work teams predictive of long-term adaptation to the team. They also found that team members focus on internal feelings to assess their long-term adaptation to the team.[6]

In a study looking at innovation among senior executives in high-tech companies, David Caldwell and Charles O'Reilly reported that teamwork, along with support for risk taking, tolerance of mistakes, and speed of action were key factors.[7]

Flavia Cavazotte examined diversity in workgroups. She also looked at group mean and variability in empathy and ability to express emotions. One of her findings was that group cooperation was higher when group members were more emotionally competent: groups where members had greater ability to express emotions and to empathize with others were more cooperative than groups faring lower on these indicators of emotional competence.[8]

How can we improve teamwork?

There are clear barriers to the productivity of work teams. As a manager, you need to determine: 1) if there are conflicts within or among the teams or unhealthy competition within the organization, and 2) whether teams are set up to be cooperative or competitive within the organization.

What are the team's goals? Create goals that are SMART: specific, measurable, attainable, realistic, and tangible. Individual goals should support the team's goals, and should be revised if major changes to the team take place. Team goals should, in turn, support the mission, vision, and goals of the entire organization. In an organization with poorly communicated objectives, a person might have SMART goals, but those goals won't necessarily translate to the bottom line for the organization.

Is there a mixed message? Are people rewarded as a team or individually? Is there a shared goal and vision within the teams? Have the team leader or manager meet with the team to determine staff perceptions.

What strengths does each worker bring to the work team? How can co-workers complement each other in order to work more effectively together? Sometimes developing areas of specialization can foster harmony and take advantage of individual strengths.

What type of needs must be met to motivate individuals? Explore and then identify motivating factors that affect job satisfaction within the organization.

Do leaders talk about teamwork but fail to model it? If a leader fails to model the practices of proper teamwork, staff will become less motivated to obtain team goals. It is important that leaders be aware of how individuals within the organization feel about the status of team unity. Look into having 360-degree assessments (such as the EQ 360®) of the organization's leaders. This is a valuable way to learn more about the leaders' strengths and weaknesses.

Teams should be formed with consideration to work or personality styles. Failure to acknowledge and appreciate style differences can lead to conflict and lack of success. You may want to examine the personality makeup in current teams that may require facilitation.

When teams are formed, it is beneficial to establish ground rules on basics such as communication, keeping each other informed, and conflict resolution.

Examine the problem-solving styles that are being used within current teams. Some people prefer to follow gut feelings through to action in solving problems. Others prefer a more systematic approach of generating alternative solutions, evaluating the positives and negatives of each, implementing one that is agreed upon by the majority of the team, evaluating the results, adjusting the implementation as needed, keeping everyone in the loop, and rewarding successes. It's important to get agreement among team members on the rules of the game and how decisions will be made.

People may be having problems getting along with each other. It would be useful to have candid talks with people individually to find out where clashes in personality or other disagreements are occurring. Interpersonal difficulties among staff can be costly in terms of getting work completed.

Times of change can be stressful within organizations. However, this is when teams and co-workers need to be together. It's important to work through change together, supporting each other along the way.

When change occurs, leaders need to be there to explain why the change is occurring, what direction the organization is headed, and why that particular direction. Leaders need to involve teams in the evolving process of change. They need to have a role in helping to define the future.

When feelings of low cohesiveness occur, managers need to meet both individually and together with team members. It is important to go over their concerns, fears, or objections. The goal is to bring team members on board together to collectively work towards solutions.

How Managers Can Nurture Emotional Intelligence

If there is a specific emotional intelligence characteristic that managers need to nurture in their teams it is empathy. In order to avoid conflict, which can derail any potential progress, team members must be willing to hear each other out. It is the manager's responsibility to model and cultivate a culture that is empathic. Team members need to understand that being empathic does not mean agreeing with what others say. It means being able to understand where their beliefs or feelings are coming from. By understanding other members of the team and their points of view, one is better prepared to present his or her own view.

For some individuals, emotional self-awareness precedes empathy. When hearing contradictory opinions or points of view, some people automatically move into a reactive mode. They react emotionally with anger or anxiety and cease functioning rationally. By being more self-aware, and developing the ability to better regulate their emotions, they will be better able to appreciate other people's opinions and beliefs and react in a more thoughtful and positive way.

While it would be nice to think that co-workers will just get along and teams will work things out, great companies take the time to ensure these things happen. They understand the importance of strong relationships within the organization and the power of these relationships to drive the organization forward. As well, it is these relationships that make the organization resilient in times of crisis. Everybody wins when people work together in the same direction with shared goals.

CHAPTER 11 | # Supervisory Leadership: You're Not the Boss of Me

"Management is nothing more than motivating other people."

Lee Iacocca

"Leaders need to be optimists. Their vision is beyond the present."

Rudolph Giuliani

"Good management consists in showing average people how to do the work of superior people."

John D. Rockefeller

"Outstanding leaders go out of their way to boost the self-esteem of their personnel. If people believe in themselves, it's amazing what they can accomplish."

Sam Walton

Key #5: Make sure managers can manage.

Juan saw himself as the commander of his troops. He ran the accounting department of a medium-size manufacturing company. He was an extremely hard worker. It was not uncommon for him to put in 12-hour days. The dozen staff reporting to him all had ranks and their importance was measured by, among other things, their length of service. Juan loved gathering together the troops and rattling off orders based on new initiatives that he was to enforce. He even enjoyed taking questions from his troops and trying to convince them that all new policies were really for their own good.

When any of the troops made suggestions, or tried to recommend improvements, Juan politely thanked them for their efforts and promised to take their comments into account. But it did not take long for everyone to realize that their contributions were not really taken seriously and that it was not worth the effort in trying to add their thoughts or improve upon ideas. When any of the troops left the fold for greener pastures in other organizations, Juan saw them as traitors, and could never understand why any of his troops would be unhappy at work.

Juan would probably have been described as an effective leader 20 years ago. He did well at following orders from his superiors. He was compelled to keep his people in line and have everything below him run smoothly. He was smart and technically proficient. Why, then, does he have so much trouble keeping his people loyal today?

We've spent years promoting people into management positions for all the wrong reasons. What does it really take to be a good supervisor? As I've mentioned before, more people leave their jobs because of a poor manager than any other reason. Supervisory leadership is the key to retaining great staff and reducing restructuring costs.

Dealing with Poor Performance

One of the most difficult aspects of supervising others is dealing with poor performance. A significant part of any management-training program deals with how to motivate employees. Motivation involves setting and reviewing goals with each employee. Goal setting should be a cooperative exercise where both the manager and employee buy into the desired outcomes.

What happens when goals are unmet? First, it should be determined if the goals set were reasonable. If not, then they may have to be adjusted.

However, if the goals are reasonable, and performance is lower than expected, then you will have to problem-solve around what is preventing acceptable performance.

How well do supervisors deal with poor performance? In our surveys of workplaces we found that almost half of employees feel that their supervisors handle poor performance appropriately. Alternatively, 27% say their supervisors do not handle it well. Handling poor performance involves giving good, honest feedback. It's important to let someone know what behavior you want more of.

Ultimately, you will need to let go of poor performers. Great companies not only try and select great people, they know that when people fail to contribute, there's a point at which they need to be let go. One of the most difficult aspects of managing is ensuring you have a high-performing team. When one or two poor performers continue to get rewarded, or no action is taken to mitigate poor performance, a negative message is sent throughout the organization. As seen here, nearly one-third of employees report that their supervisors do not deal adequately with employees performing poorly.

My supervisor deals appropriately with employees who are not performing		
Disagree	Neutral	Agree
27%	24%	49%

Mediating Disagreements

Another important skill set for managers is the ability to mediate conflicts or disagreements among staff. We found that 21% of employees feel their supervisor is ineffective in this area. On the other hand, more than half (56%) of employees feel their managers deal effectively with disagreements. Negotiating skills is another important aspect of managing others. Once again, these results are taken from our own surveys of thousands of working people across a number of different countries over the past several years.

My supervisor effectively mediates conflicts/disagreements		
Disagree	Neutral	Agree
21%	23%	56%

Managers have to often deal with competing interests. The ability to navigate these interests successfully goes a long way towards winning the trust of employees. This is an opportunity to demonstrate fairness and gain employee respect. Badly handling conflict by not being even-handed, or by taking sides, can demoralize all those around.

Knowing the Effect You Have on Others

Part of being emotionally intelligent involves understanding the way you come across to others. Some people just seem angry all the time, even when they believe they are nicely making a request. Self-awareness is important for everyone, but especially important for leaders. We found that 24% of employees report that their supervisor is unaware of how their words and actions affect others.

My supervisor is aware of how his/her words and actions affect others		
Disagree	Neutral	Agree
24%	16%	60%

Anthony needed his shift of workers to stay late one night to help finish off a large order that had to be shipped the next day. He gathered his crew together right after lunch.

"Look, guys, I don't think you've been pulling your weight this week. We don't have the Ridgefield order even close to ready and it's due out tomorrow," he told them.

"But it just came in this morning," Maurice answered.

"I wasn't asking for excuses—I just want to make sure everyone is available to stay late tonight to finish it up," Anthony replied.

Ricardo quickly jumped in: "I got plans tonight with my wife."

How do you think Anthony saw himself in this situation? If you asked him he would probably say he was just trying to let his guys know he needed them to work late. He had no intention of arguing or putting his crew under pressure. But at this point he likely saw them as getting quite defensive towards him.

How could he have handled this situation differently, or at least come across better to his staff? He might have tried something more like this:

"I'm sorry to ask this of you so late, but we just got a large order today that we have to ship out tomorrow. As you know, Ridgefield is an important customer and we need their order in order to make our numbers this month. Could I ask any of you stay late tonight to help get it ready to ship tomorrow?"

This is a much more positive tone and he is less likely to get people's backs up. Rather than throwing out statements that are likely to challenge and sidetrack his crew, he deals with them in a more straightforward way. This will likely increase their willingness to be cooperative.

What happens if nobody voluntarily comes forward at first? Well, Anthony needs to know how to be persuasive and may have to add some sort of incentive as well. He'll have to know his staff well and who he can depend on at times like this.

Can you bully your way to compliance?

Probably one of the most common ways of getting compliance at work has been through bullying others. A recent series of articles in the American Psychological Association *Monitor* focused on the issue of bullies in the workplace.

It has been difficult to come up with a universally accepted definition of the bully at work since the concept is relatively new. But psychologist Gary Namie, who directs the Workplace Bullying and Trauma Institute in Bellingham, Washington, describes workplace bullying in this way: "Repeated, health-harming mistreatment of an employee by one or more persons, manifested in one or more ways: verbal abuse, threatening and intimidating conduct (verbal or nonverbal, nonphysical) that interferes with work and undermines legitimate business interests."[1]

This definition was expanded by Charlotte Rayner, a professor of human resources at the University of Portsmouth in England. She adds: "Bullying is as much about what people don't do, such as excluding targets from meetings, withholding information or leaving them off an important e-mail, as what they do, such as yelling, name-calling, making threatening statements, micromanaging or undermining somebody's reputation."[2]

How then do organizations prevent bullying from becoming part of their supervisory culture? While bullying behavior should not be tolerated in organizations, there are better ways to deal with it than by setting up rules of dos and don'ts. First, once again, it's important for the organization to recognize that bullying behavior is occurring and to take the temperature of the organization. Is there a high level of anger or anxiety going on within the organization? If so, this will need to be addressed and defused.

In a pilot program at the U.S. Department of Veterans Affairs involving 11 workplaces in the VA system, improving the work climate decreased aggression and bullying.[3] In this program, groups collected data on a problem and then cycled through stages of action and reflection. The outcome not only reduced aggression but also increased employee satisfaction.

When supervisors are identified as bullying their staff, it is the responsibility of the organization to take action. These individuals should be asked about their behavior by their supervisor. If a problem is discovered, then individual coaching with an outside management coach should be recommended. Supervisors should be properly trained and coached in order to manage others effectively.

Know Your Strengths and Weaknesses

Another aspect of emotional intelligence is the ability to know your strengths and weaknesses. I have found this skill to be highly associated with successful leadership. Managers who have personal blind spots are more likely to make bad decisions. By ignoring weaknesses, they are likely to press ahead in areas where they have no knowledge or ability.

How do employees rate their supervisor's awareness of strengths and weaknesses?

My supervisor is aware of his/her strengths and weaknesses		
Disagree	Neutral	Agree
16%	19%	65%

A majority of employees (65%) agree that their managers are self-aware. However, 16% believe their supervisor is unaware of their strengths and weaknesses. It's likely that these employees see their managers as intruding in areas beyond their expertise.

Open-door Policy

There's been a lot of talk about "management by walking around" and "open door" policies of managers. How available are managers to their employees? We found that 77% of employees feel their manager is available to them. Only 13% disagree. This is a good sign in that supervisors, for the most part, aren't hiding behind closed doors.

My supervisor is available when I need to talk		
Disagree	Neutral	Agree
13%	10%	77%

Managers need to be aware of what is happening around them. By shutting down direct reports, or by being unavailable, they miss the opportunity to find out valuable information about both people and the operation. Also, employees who feel they are not being heard by their managers often end up retaliating in various ways. It could be through nonperformance, wasting time, or in extreme cases by behaving negligently or sabotaging the workplace.

Be a Good Coach

Are supervisors behaving like coaches, or are they more like old-style military commanders? We found that 65% of employees report that their supervisor is a good coach or mentor. Seventeen percent disagreed with the statement that their manager is like a good coach.

My supervisor is a good coach/mentor		
Disagree	Neutral	Agree
17%	18%	65%

Coaching is a good way to motivate employees. Good coaches want to see their protégés succeed. They help them increase their performance. They usually do that by telling them what to do more of, or what behaviors to increase. They also give good feedback on performance. They help by providing suggestions for correction or improvement. The relationship is seen on both sides as a win-win relationship.

Are you satisfied with your supervisor?

Overall, how satisfied are employees with their supervisor? We found that 78% are satisfied with their supervisor. What does this mean to the organization?

Good supervisors are able to retain good employees. Let's assume that most employees who were unhappy with their supervisor have already left for greener pastures. That would help explain the high numbers who are currently satisfied.

I am generally satisfied with the person who supervises me		
Disagree	Neutral	Agree
12%	10%	78%

However, we still found that 12% of employees are not satisfied with their supervisor. Perhaps these are the people who are contemplating change. If your organization triggers a high score on this item, it is a good time to implement management training. It's likely that the managers are deficient in one or more of the areas discussed previously.

Leadership and Emotional Intelligence

There are a number of ways in which today's leaders are different from yesteryear. A comprehensive study looking at the role of emotional intelligence in leadership was carried out by Dr. Marian Ruderman and her colleagues at the Center for Creative Leadership in Greensboro, North Carolina, an internationally renowned research and training center for leadership.

Studying 302 leaders and senior managers, both successful and struggling, she measured their emotional intelligence with the Bar-On EQ-i® and their on the job performance with Benchmarks®, a 360-degree tool designed to get a clear picture of leadership performance from superiors, peers, and subordinates.[4]

Based on their study, Bar-On has suggested the presence of four pillars or competencies that were of significance in determining leadership performance. The pillars are: 1) being centered and grounded, 2) action-taking, 3) participative, and 4) tough-minded.[5]

Each of these pillars was significantly related to aspects of emotional intelligence as measured by the Bar-On EQ-i®. In percentage terms, research results indicated that emotional intelligence accounted for somewhere between 25% and 28% of leadership performance. So, if you're measuring leadership performance using traditional objective benchmarks, you could be missing out on almost one-third of what makes your managers great.

Centered and Grounded Leaders

The first pillar of successful leadership I'll refer to is being centered and grounded. These individuals are in control of themselves. They are seen as stable in mood and do not fly off the handle when things get difficult. People describe these leaders as predictable in their disposition. In other words, you don't go into their office to say good morning and then get berated for something you forgot to do the day before.

Successful leaders are more aware of their strengths and weaknesses. Dangerous are the leaders who propose to know it all. While it's important to know your strengths and use them wisely, it's equally important to know your weaknesses and not inflict them on everyone around you. While I find that not all leaders are willing to invest the time to improve their weaknesses, the next best alternative involves ensuring that there are people close at hand who excel in the skills lacking.

Another aspect of this pillar is being balanced between work life and personal life. In the past there has been an overemphasis on the workaholic lifestyle of leaders. In the Ruderman study, balance was associated with better-performing leaders. If a leader can manage her or his own life well— managing stress, home life, fitness, diet—then chances are higher that the workplace is well managed also.

Grounded leaders are also straightforward and self-aware. People know where they stand on issues. They tend to not be vague or wishy-washy. They are also aware of their own feelings and motivators. These leaders are consistent in their approach to issues as they know how and what they feel and believe about issues.

Finally, these leaders are composed under pressure. They do not flare up or lose control, even under difficult circumstances. The most important emotional intelligence skills in this pillar are social responsibility, stress tolerance, impulse control, and optimism.

Action-taking Leaders

The second pillar of leadership success is action-taking and includes the ability to be decisive. Successful leaders make decisions and have a track record of making good decisions. These leaders take into account the views of others but, in the end, make the best decision they can with all available information.

Additionally, leaders high in this competency persevere in the face of obstacles. They do not give up easily once they have decided on a course of action. They realize follow through is a critical part of the decision-making process. As well, they evaluate the effectiveness of their decisions and make adjustments as needed.

This competency relates directly to three factors of a person's emotional intelligence: assertiveness, independence, and optimism.

Participative Leaders

Command-and-control is no longer in style in today's military, let alone in business environments. People resent being told what to do and certainly do not appreciate being ignored. Successful leaders today focus on winning the hearts and minds of the people around them. Without getting "buy in" for their ideas, plans, and tactics, there's little incentive for those around them to perform optimally. People want to be involved in the plans and their implementation. As well, they have to feel they can contribute. After all, if people feel they have some ownership of the initiative, they are more likely to want to see it succeed.

The ability to succeed in this aspect of leadership involves having good listening and communication skills. While many leaders know how to present their ideas and directions to others, fewer know how to actively listen to their people to ensure they are onboard. Good leaders are sensitive to what may even seem minimal objections to ideas and requests. They can pull out the objections and attempt to deal with them, even adjusting plans when flaws are pointed out. The leader must aim for what is best for the whole organization, not just her or his own ego.

Great leaders can put people at ease. Bad leaders scare people. When people are at ease, they are more likely to speak their minds and offer suggestions and ideas. Great leaders give people credit for their contributions and make them feel like an important part of the team. Even greater leaders take responsibility for bad decisions and mistakes.

The important work of building consensus follows hearing everyone out. Successful leaders, after ensuring they are aware of people's position, both pro and con, use their skills to get everyone on board with whatever decision is made. If team members feel that they have participated in the process, presented their case and gotten a fair hearing, they are more likely to go with the prevailing consensus.

What was surprising about this pillar of leadership was the nature of its relationship to specific factors of emotional and social intelligence. While related to several aspects of emotional intelligence, the strongest relationship was with empathy and social responsibility. Leaders who are socially responsible — that is, those who care about their community and people who are less fortunate — and respect society's rules, are more participatory in their leadership style. These leaders also have better interpersonal relationships, better impulse control, and higher empathy.

Tough-minded Leaders

The fourth pillar of successful leadership is tough-mindedness. Tough-minded leaders are confident and know their strengths and weaknesses. They manage stressful situations well. These leaders are resilient. They are good at overcoming obstacles. They are also composed under pressure. Their impulse control is high.

A good example of tough-mindedness in a leader was shown by Mayor Rudy Giuliani during the September 11 terrorist attacks. In the face of unbelievable pressures and while being constantly scrutinized by the world media, he kept his composure, worked unbelievable hours, and continued to be effective in accomplishing his goals.

In describing the characteristics of great leaders during his address to the 2004 Republican National Convention, Giuliani had this to say, "There are many qualities that make a great leader. But having strong beliefs, being able to stick with them through popular and unpopular times, is the most important characteristic of a great leader."

How does one have strong beliefs yet still be flexible as described in the earlier chapter on CEOs? The beliefs referred to here relate more to core characteristics of the individual — believing in democracy, human rights, fairness, and other matters of principle. The ability to make decisions (i.e., business decisions) will be dependant on the information at hand. Your decision at any given time depends on what you know about a situation, and that decision will be guided by your principles (beliefs). New information may come along that causes you to change your decision, yet you are still guided by the same principles in making that choice.

The good news about these findings is that both the pillars of leadership competencies and the emotional intelligence building blocks can be developed. The starting point is clear: the first step for improving as a leader is to increase self-awareness. By learning more about your strengths and areas for development you will be on your way to developing yourself as a better leader.

More Research on Supervisory Leadership and Emotional and Social Intelligence

What is the relationship between emotional intelligence and effective management practices? Abraham Carmeli carried out a study of 98 senior managers employed as chief financial officers in local government authorities in Israel. They all completed emotional intelligence questionnaires along with other work-related surveys. He found that higher emotional intelligence increases positive work attitudes, altruistic behavior, and work outcomes, and moderates the effect of work-to-family conflict on career commitment but not the effect on job satisfaction.[6]

Thomas Sy, Susanna Tram and Linda O'Hara carried out a study looking at the relationships among employees' emotional intelligence, their manager's emotional intelligence, employees' job satisfaction, and performance among 187 food service employees from nine different locations of a restaurant franchise. They also tested the personality characteristics of managers and employees.

They found that the higher an employee's emotional intelligence, the better their job performance. They also found that the manager's emotional intelligence had a stronger relationship to the job satisfaction of employees with lower emotional intelligence than those with higher emotional intelligence. In other words, if you have employees who have lower emotional intelligence, it is even more important to have managers with high emotional intelligence. The findings for emotional intelligence were much stronger than the relationships they found for personality characteristics.[7]

There is a lot of support for participative management. Kim Soonhee, for example, studied 1,576 employees from a number of government agencies. He found that managers' use of a participative management style and employees' perceptions of participative strategic planning processes were positively associated with high levels of job satisfaction. He concluded that participative management that incorporates effective supervisory communications can enhance employees' job satisfaction.[8]

In a study looking at the relationship between organizational culture and empowerment among 331 nurses, Esther Mok and Betty Au-Yeung found that, of the six factors they examined, leadership and teamwork proved to be the most predictive of employee empowerment.[9]

Are there cultural boundaries to participative leadership styles? In a Chinese study looking at employee involvement, Zhang Zhen, Ma Li, and Ma Wenjing examined 148 organizations throughout Mainland China. They found that non-bureaucratic, supportive and communicative climates were the strongest predictors of employee involvement.[10]

In my work with the BOEI (Benchmark of Emotional Intelligence), we measure the effectiveness of supervisors as seen by the people they supervise. It includes the ability to share information, involvement in decision making, coaching, providing feedback, mediating conflicts, trustworthiness and confidence, self-awareness, and general satisfaction with immediate supervisors.

How does leadership impact organizational culture?

Interesting research carried out by Carl Bryant of the Center for Creative Leadership (CCL) helps shed more light on the relationship between leadership and culture. It has recently been popular to downplay a leader's weaknesses and focus only on her or his strengths. In this study Bryant assessed leaders' strengths and weaknesses using Benchmarks®, a 360-degree feedback survey. In addition, their organizations were surveyed with a cultural survey.

The CCL study supported the notion that lower ratings of an organization's culture were associated with a greater likelihood that the leader would become derailed. They looked at 500 leaders from a wide range of organizations that included education, manufacturing, transportation, health and human services, government, and finance.

The study also surveyed 2,872 workers in these organizations.

They not only found a strong relationship between the managers' leadership capabilities and corporate culture, but they found that the strength of the relationship increased with the level of the executive. In other words, the higher level the executive, the more impact the leader has on culture.

The study goes on to stress the importance of a leader's personal development. It points out that leaders with deficits can have a negative impact on the entire organization.[11]

How can you improve supervisory leadership?

There are several things we can do to improve the quality of supervisory leaders.

- Using a facilitator to meet and have candid discussions with employees (without leaders present) can help bring out the major issues around their immediate supervisor. Prevent blaming in these discussions, but try to determine specific impediments to effective leadership. One approach to keeping the discussion productive and focused is the use of the STOP, START and CONTINUE model. This model allows individuals to focus their comments on three things: features they find unhelpful and would like to see stopped; features that are not present but which they like to see started; and features that are working well for them, and which they would like to see continued.

The facilitator should meet with the supervisor and discuss leadership issues. The supervisor's perspective on why ratings are low should be elicited. Do supervisors in the organization make decisions autonomously or do they involve others? Is there a pattern in the organization of supervisors making decisions impulsively or under stress?

- Specific aspects of leadership should be explored with the supervisor, including sharing of information, decision-making processes, coaching opportunities, providing effective feedback on performance, and conflict mediation. Issues such as integrity, confidence, and self-awareness should also be discussed.

- Does your organization value strong supervisory/managerial leadership? If yes, do you invest in these people through training and coaching? How is successful leadership measured and rewarded?

- Consider the use of a 360-degree assessment for all leaders, which will allow for employee, peer, and supervisor evaluation of leaders.

It's clear to me, after meeting with so many leaders and managers, that the best leaders are excited about learning. Not only do they continually learn about the world around them, but they learn more about themselves as well. They are interested in how others see them and what they do that works well in their relationships. Managing is hard work and requires persistence. There will always be good times and times of challenge, but the best supervisors will ride these waves as smoothly as possible.

Diversity and Anger Management: It's a Wide, Wide World— Take This Job and Shove It

CHAPTER 12

"Diversity is the one true thing we all have in common. Celebrate it every day."

Anonymous

"Anyone can become angry—that is easy. But to be angry with the right person, to the right degree, at the right time, for the right purpose, and in the right way; this is not easy."

Aristotle

"If you are patient in one moment of anger, you will escape a hundred days of sorrow."

Chinese proverb

Key #6: Treat people with respect and leverage their unique talents.

Angelo, a partner in a boutique architecture firm, had a unique opportunity for a major project that he and his team were very excited about. As a small but specialized architectural firm in San Francisco, they were invited to bid on a major development project in Hong Kong. This was their first project opportunity in the Far East.

Their initial drawings made it to the finalist stage. They were now competing against one other firm, which was based in Houston. Angelo and his top designers were going back and forth with the client trying to finalize details before flying out to make their presentation.

Myrna, one of the architects on the team, was having difficulties around some of the specifications. The team had two weeks before the presentation. They were too professional to try and wing it. Everything had to be perfect. Myrna suggested to Angelo that they bring Sue-Lee, a junior draftsperson on the team. She was born in Hong Kong and spoke fluent Cantonese.

"I don't know," said Angelo, "she's still pretty junior and we really need her on the Adamson project. It's at a pretty critical stage right now."

"That's true," replied Myrna, "but this is a huge potential project for the firm. We could replace Sue-Lee with George on the Adamson and she could help us liaise with Hong Kong. She's bilingual, she knows how we work, and I think this would really impress the client."

"But how would it look if she was picked over the other drafters? We have people who have been with us for five years who would jump at a chance like this. It would cause dissent. You want to give her this opportunity just because she's Chinese?"

"Being Chinese is a big part of it. But she's also talented and works hard. I wouldn't want her on my team unless I knew she could produce quality work," replied Myrna.

After going back and forth over the possible repercussions, it was agreed that Sue-Lee would join the team. It meant she would work not just on the drafting side but would also be a senior liaison person and the main point of contact with the client.

It turned out that Myrna's instincts were right. The client appreciated dealing with Sue-Lee. She flew to Hong Kong with the team and played a major part in the presentation. In fact, it was one of the few presentations where Angelo had less to say than the other members of the team, especially Sue-Lee. Fortunately, Angelo's ego wasn't too big and he saw the big picture in winning this deal.

Sue-Lee was also able to make the team more relaxed when they arrived. She knew her way around Hong Kong and helped the others with various issues in adapting to the culture. She advised them on the best ways to approach the client, what to say and what not to say.

Of course, they won the contract. This proved to be a major break for the firm. None of the other people at the firm resented Sue-Lee's role in the project. Everyone saw that it was best for the company, especially when new projects were getting more competitive.

In this chapter I will look at the importance of employee diversity and its effectiveness in managing employee anger and frustration. The three areas I'll discuss are diversity climate, gender/racial acceptance, and anger management. While it may seem strange that these areas came together in our statistical analysis, it does make intuitive sense. Underlying each of these areas is the importance of treating people fairly and respecting their differences.

How much attention do organizations pay to their diversity climate?

Diversity climate refers to the degree to which people feel they are treated fairly by the organization regardless of age, race, gender, physical limitation, or disability.

How sensitive are organizations today to cultural issues in the workplace? In our surveys, we have found that 63% of employees believe their organization is sensitive. On the other hand, 16% of employees feel their organization is insensitive.

This organization is sensitive to cultural issues in the workplace		
Disagree	Neutral	Agree
16%	21%	63%

Being sensitive to cultural differences is only the first step in being able to leverage these differences to benefit the organization. People bring different talents to the organization. Many of these talents are shaped by cultural differences.

Another set of differences are due to age. In Chapter 1, I discussed the different generations of workers we find in organizations today. How sensitive are organizations to employees of various age groups? We find that 71% of employees feel their organization treats all age groups fairly. Another 13% say their organizations discriminate on the basis of age.

People are treated fairly regardless of age		
Disagree	Neutral	Agree
13%	16%	71%

How well are people with physical disabilities being integrated into the workplace? From our surveys, it looks like 74% or nearly three-quarters of employees feel their workplace is fair to people with physical disabilities. Only 8% were reported as having problems in this area.

Employees with physical disabilities are treated fairly by this organization		
Disagree	Neutral	Agree
8%	18%	74%

We need to spend more time focused on the diversity of the workplace. Smart companies are using diversity to leverage their products and services to new markets. Diversity-friendly workplaces can also be more productive.

Research on Diversity in the Workplace

What does research tell us about diverse workplaces? For a number of years now it has been argued that work climates should be created in which diversity is not just present, but highly valued.

In one study, Susannah Paletz and her associates looked at two types of ethnically heterogeneous groups on their enjoyment of and performance on an interactive creative task. They found that teams made up of mostly ethnic minorities rated working with the group to be more enjoyable and experienced more positive and fewer negative emotions compared to homogeneous Caucasian groups, although in this case ethnic composition did not predict task creativity.[1]

Warren Watson and his associates looked at the effect that ethnic diversity had on learning team leadership, group process, and team performance. They examined 75 ethnically diverse and 90 ethnically non-diverse teams over four months. They found that in diverse teams, emergent interpersonal leadership activities were more important for team performance, while for non-diverse teams, task leadership was the critical leadership factor. Over time, self-orientation was reported more by non-diverse teams including a more individual focus. By the end of the team's life cycle, the ethnically diverse teams performed more effectively on team project tasks.[2]

In a study looking at the effects of gender and ethnic diversity on team-based work structures, Fredrick Panzer examined 264 people in 66 four-person teams. He found both ethnic and gender homogeneity in teams resulted in increased interpersonal cohesion. Higher levels of interpersonal cohesion also enhanced coordination between team members, which ultimately improved performance. This study, which used undergraduate students as subjects, involved a flight simulation game with two aircraft that needed to coordinate their course. Here, unlike the Paletz study, homogeneity of gender and ethnic type increased performance.[3]

Kristine Rand looked at the importance of valuing diversity in work groups in 211 employees in 27 work teams. She identified two factors in valuing work groups; these included solidarity and individuality. A predictor of a work group's favorable climate for individuality was a highly involved team leader. Work teams with more favorable solidarity climates were more satisfied with their co-workers and had higher levels of team performance, as assessed by both team leaders and the team members themselves.[4]

In a study trying to link team diversity to team effectiveness, Virgil Metts found that diversity was directly related to team members' ratings of overall quantity of work.[5]

In an interesting study focusing on how diverse groups get along, Jeffrey Polzer looked at interpersonal congruence — the degree to which group members see others in the group as others see themselves. Looking at 83 work groups, he found that diversity tended to improve creative task performance in groups with high interpersonal congruence. However, diversity undermined the performance of groups with low interpersonal congruence. By expressing members' unique characteristics, interpersonal congruence was improved.[6]

This means that empathy is an important aspect of working successfully in a diverse team. One way of determining how well members of diverse teams may work together would be by using an instrument such as the EQ-i to gauge the empathy scores of team members. Individuals high in empathy will likely work well in a diverse team. People who are low in empathy should be given training in how to understand others better before being placed in a diverse team.

A study on cross-functional groups by Robert Keller examined 93 research and new product development groups from four companies. He found that functional diversity improved technical quality, schedule and budget performance, but reduced group cohesiveness. However, he felt that group cohesiveness could be improved.[7] Once again, by increasing the empathy level of individual members of the team, group cohesiveness should improve. Taking the extra time to prepare people for this experience can result in significant productivity gains.

How can you improve the diversity climate in an organization?

As a manager, you must be aware of the cultural mix within the organization. Acknowledge special days and events of different cultures. Informal social events such as potluck lunches are one way of experiencing and appreciating other cultures. Look for the strengths that people of different cultures bring to the organization. These strengths can include languages and awareness of culture-specific behaviors and values.

Better understand the benefits of a diverse workplace. For example, there may be advantages for customers to be more aware of the cultural diversity within the organization.

If people in the organization perceive that they are not being treated fairly, you may want to review the priorities the organization places on dealing with diversity. Check with senior management as to whether the organizational goals, mission, or internal policies deal with diversity.

If an organizational survey determines that this is a real problem, consider introducing a diversity-training program. Often diversity problems are caused by ignorance of cultural norms.

How accepting is your organization of people's gender and race?

The room was crowded and the wine and hors d'oeuvres flowed. It was an alumni event celebrating a major donation to a new university program by a very successful alumnus. Sam, who rarely attends these events, struck up a conversation with a female accountant named Jill who worked as an executive for a major bank.

Jill started telling him how her bank, while not the largest in the country, had been the most profitable bank for five years running. In fact, it was recently ranked as one of the most profitable banks in the world. She gave the impression that she was quite proud to be an executive working for this institution. That was the good news. After a few more glasses of wine, Jill then confided how, after several years there, she desperately wanted to leave the bank for another job.

"But you just told me how great your bank performs," Sam said, quite surprised.

"Yes, but we just completed an organizational survey. It's not just me; everyone scored them at the bottom of the list on benefits and pay. They really don't treat us very well at all. Nobody below the level of Executive Vice President has shared in the bank's success. In fact, every one of our EVPs are multi-millionaires."

Jill continued to unload: "The bank is so cheap managers aren't even allowed to reward their staff with donuts after putting in long hours of overtime. A senior director wasn't allowed to take a key employee out for lunch after she worked flat-out for weeks on a complicated merger deal."

"And the way they treat women—not a single female VP in the place. The only place I know that compares to this was when I used to work in the oil and gas industry," she continued.

"People must be leaving there in droves," Sam responded.

"No, most of them are staying. They're afraid to rock the boat. In fact, the person I confide in the most agreed to speak out on behalf of a number of us about the low survey results on pay and benefits. The opportunity came during the survey feedback session with the consultants who administered the survey. But when she spoke up to the senior consultant, she actually said the low score was probably because a few unhappy people brought the average down. Then she told the consultants that she believed that pay and benefit scores are the lowest in surveys for all companies. I was shocked! These people are too scared to complain—they just want to keep their jobs."

"Then why do you stay?" he asked.

"Well, actually, I'm kind of looking around for something else," she confided. "Could you introduce me to your friend?"

With that, Sam introduced her to the donor, a friend of his, whose billion-dollar company was known for rewarding all the high performers in his organization—regardless of gender, race, or culture.

When looking at gender and racial acceptance in an organization it's important to look at the degree to which people are harassed or discriminated against due to race or gender. One of the more surprising findings of our surveys in this area is the high rate of sexual harassment or intimidation reported in workplaces. We found that 22% of employees reported sexual harassment in their organization.

Someone has experienced sexual harassment or intimidation at this organization		
Disagree	Neutral	Agree
48%	30%	22%

How does this compare to other surveys on the topic? One of the problems is that the questions asked in this area are not quite the same and the variations can cause some big differences.

For example, in a 1994 study of U.S. federal employees, 44% of women and 19% of men reported that they had experienced some form of unwanted sexual attention during the previous two years.[8] Adam Malamut and Lynn Offerman carried out a survey of approximately 15,400 members of the U.S. military—89.5% of whom were women and 10.5% men. They reported that 54% experienced gender harassment.[9]

Another study, of private-sector workers in the Los Angeles area, reported that 53% of women respondents had experienced at least one incident that they considered to be sexual harassment during their work lives.[10]

Sandy Lim and Lilia Cortina surveyed two groups of female employees within a large public-sector organization. In one group, 22% reported experiencing gender harassment and general incivility (defined as disrespect, rudeness, or condescension); in the other group 16% experienced both gender harassment and incivility.[11]

What are the consequences of sexual harassment? According to *Working Woman* magazine, a typical Fortune 500 corporation can expect to lose $6.7 million annually. Losses can result from absenteeism, lower productivity, increased health-care costs, poor morale, and employee turnover. These losses do not include litigation costs or court-awarded damages. Also not included is damage to a company's image. Bad press, which often accompanies such cases, can cost a business not only its reputation but also its customers and revenues.[12]

How prevalent is racial discrimination?

How do employees perceive racial discrimination in their workplace? Our results find that 7% of employees report incidents of racial discrimination in their workplace. Alternatively, 79% of employees report being unaware of any racial discrimination.

People here have been discriminated against due to race		
Disagree	Neutral	Agree
79%	14%	7%

How does this compare to other surveys on racial discrimination? Hispanics are becoming more assimilated into mainstream American culture, but a large percentage polled recently say that discrimination is a problem and prevents Hispanics from succeeding.

The National Survey of Latinos, conducted by the Washington, D.C.–based Pew Hispanic Center, with the assistance of the Kaiser Family Foundation, found 31% of the approximately 3,000 Hispanics polled reported that they or someone close to them had suffered job discrimination in the past five years because of their racial or ethnic background. Fourteen percent reported experiencing employment-related bias personally, including not being hired for a job or not being promoted because of their race or ethnicity.

Eighty-two percent of Hispanics responding to the survey, as reported in *HR Magazine*, said that discrimination is a problem that keeps them from succeeding in general, while 78% see bias as a problem in the workplace and 75% see it as a roadblock in the schools. The language they speak was the most frequently cited reason for this discrimination, followed by physical appearance.[13]

The Costs of Discrimination: Companies Are Paying the Price

In recent years, companies have been hit with huge verdicts—or have agreed to pay massive out-of-court settlements—to employees who have been discriminated against or harassed on the basis of race or national origin. For example:

- In 2004, the Equal Employment Opportunity Commission (EEOC) announced a $50-million settlement of a race and sex discrimination lawsuit against the clothing retail company Abercrombie & Fitch. Among the allegations was a claim that the clothier refused to hire female and non-white applicants because they did not fit the image or "look" the company was trying to project in the marketplace.

- Consolidated Freightways Corporation of Delaware agreed to pay $2.75 million to settle a racial harassment lawsuit filed by the EEOC. Twelve African-American employees alleged that they were subjected to racial intimidation, threats, assault, racist graffiti, and property damage, among other things.

- Coca-Cola settled a class-action race-discrimination lawsuit for $192.5 million. African-American employees said that Coke imposed a racial "glass ceiling" by discriminating against them in pay and promotions. Of the total settlement, $36 million was earmarked for monitoring the company's employment practices to make sure that the discrimination stopped.

- In 2000, Commonwealth Edison Company agreed to pay $2.5 million to settle a lawsuit brought by a group of Latino employees alleging discrimination based on national origin. The employees charged that the company failed to promote them to middle management positions.[14]

According to the U.S. Department of Labor, by 2005, 85% of new employees entering the workforce would be women or minorities. By 2006, Hispanics would be the largest minority group in the workforce in the United States. Unfortunately, discrimination still exists in the workplace, whether on the basis of gender, race, weight, religion, or sexual orientation. Its effects are usually more obvious at upper-level positions where higher salaries, benefits, and perks come into play, although there are still reports of discrimination in entry-level positions.[15]

How prevalent is gender discrimination?

In our survey of workplaces we found a higher percentage of discrimination due to gender than to race reported. We found 12% of employees reporting gender discrimination in their organization. However, 73% of employees report being unaware of any gender discrimination in their workplace.

People have been discriminated against due to their gender		
Disagree	Neutral	Agree
73%	15%	12%

What about sexual orientation? In 2001, the latest year for which statistics are available, the U.S. Human Rights Commission identified about 2,000 companies, colleges, and government bodies with written nondiscrimination policies covering sexual orientation, up 17% from the previous year. Nearly 300 of these were Fortune 500 companies. "The closer a company is to the top of the Fortune 500 list, the more likely it is to have such a policy," according to a 2001 HRC report, *The State of the Workplace*.[16]

The Business Case for Diversity

Great companies are benefiting from diversity in their workplace. There are a number of good business reasons for supporting diversity. Some of these have been documented by Marcus Robinson, Charles Pfeffer, and Joan Buccigrossi.[17]

First, it is only natural to have a more diverse workforce. Developed countries around the world are becoming much more diverse. Countries such as the United States, Canada, Australia, and the United Kingdom have been transforming and are becoming much more multicultural. This transformation is happening much faster than was anticipated. Companies that want to be competitive in the future will need to understand and actively attract merging-market customers, which include people of color, gays and lesbians, and people with disabilities.

Second, by getting involved in these emerging market groups, companies send a strong message of support for these potential customers and employees within their communities and beyond. Involvement can be at a number of levels, including business supplier and philanthropic activities.

Third, organizations need to recruit, train, and promote diverse employees. This should not be done at the expense of getting the best talent available. This should be a planned effort.

Fourth, any corporate diversity efforts should have buy-in from the top of the organization, particularly the CEO. Without high-level support any initiatives like this are not likely to succeed.

Finally, organizations need to pay more attention to the details of the quality of life in the communities in which they operate. In this way they can nurture young talent developing nearby. They can help build apprenticeships, suppliers, and distribution relationships.

According to a *Fast Company* article, a year-long study was conducted by a team from McKinsey & Company that included 77 companies and 6,000 managers and executives. They concluded that the most important corporate resource over the next 20 years will be talent: smart, sophisticated business people who are technologically literate, globally astute, and operationally agile.[18]

Studies by the Gallup organization have identified factors, across companies, which are clear "satisfiers" and "dissatisfiers" for diverse workers. These factors, not unlike those that are important for any worker in any place, include:

Satisfiers
- Getting to do what I do best
- Caring managers and supervisors
- Positive co-worker relationships
- Adequate resources to do my job
- Trust and fair treatment by upper management
- Opportunities to learn and grow
- Clear expectations about the work requirements
- Competitive compensation, reward, recognition

Dissatisfiers
- Prejudice and discrimination for arbitrary reasons
- Poor career development opportunity

- Poor work environment or climate
- Low organizational savvy on the people issues
- Pressure to conform or assimilate.[19]

According to Robinson and his associates: "Organizations that are successful in leveraging the diversity of their people are better able to adapt to changes in the external environment. They are more innovative in anticipating and responding to these changes."[20]

Building a Culture of Gender and Racial Acceptance

What are some of the steps that can be taken to eliminate gender and racial discrimination in your workplace?

- Be aware of gender and racial differences with the organization. Examine the strengths people of different genders and racial backgrounds bring to the group.

- Find out to what degree the organization has policies and procedures that deal with race and gender discrimination.

- When scores on organizational surveys are low in this area, consider bringing in a specialist with expertise in race or gender discrimination to increase knowledge and awareness.

- Make absolutely certain your managers, and any other employees with the power to hire others, are aware that that unwelcome sexual activity tied to employment decisions or benefits is sexual harassment. They should also be aware that sexual jokes, vulgar language, sexual innuendoes, pornographic pictures displayed in the workplace, sexual gestures, physical grabbing or pinching, and other unwelcome or offensive physical touching or contact constitute harassment.

- Realize that men as well as woman may be sexually harassed.

- Understand that employees may delay lodging sexual harassment charges.

- Implement a sexual harassment policy. You and your company can be held liable if your employees engage in sexual harassment.

It is important for the organization's gender/racial mix to closely mirror that of the larger society. The organization should evaluate the current composition, and proactively seek to balance with societal gender/racial composition.

Implementing a Sexual Harassment Policy

Does your organization lack a clear set of guidelines as to what constitutes sexual discrimination? Or are the policies there for show, but rarely enforced? Taking the following steps can help create a culture of gender acceptance in your workplace:

- Issue a strong policy from the CEO against sexual harassment that provides a clear definition of sexual harassment using examples of inappropriate behavior.

- Review the policy with your employees on a regular basis, and discuss the policy with all new employees.

- Appoint a senior corporate official to train your supervisors and managers to recognize and prevent sexual harassment and outline procedures to use in reporting sexual harassment. A personnel officer or other appropriate manager, rather than a direct supervisor, should receive sexual harassment complaints.

- Enforce the policy by keeping all sexual harassment charges confidential, investigating all sexual harassment charges quickly and thoroughly, and by taking immediate action when sexual harassment is discovered or suspected.

- Remember that employees who bring charges should never face retaliation. It's your organization's responsibility to safeguard the rights of the accused.

Sexual discrimination results from a lack of respect for others. Similarly, I see anger and violence in the workplace as yet more symptoms of lacking respect for others. Both of these issues pertain to a very important aspect of emotional intelligence that we call impulse control.

Getting a Handle on Anger in the Workplace

Linda was shocked when she read the email. She couldn't believe someone would write something like that—especially about her.

> Paul, you won't believe what that bitch Linda did today. I heard her blabbing on the phone cutting up half the office. I don't know who she was speaking to but she called Joe a "fat ass," Mary the "Queen Mary," and she called you "the loser."
>
> I don't know what's with her but she seems to think she's better than everyone else around here. I just hope she doesn't ask me to help her with her work. – Sue

It seems that Sue unintentionally circulated the email to an internal list. What could have got her so upset about Linda? What effect could her hostility towards her have in the workplace? How much anger is there in the workplace? And who is it directed at?

But first, what is anger?

Anger usually occurs as a reaction to a real or perceived threat. Physiologically, our heart rate speeds up. Our cheeks may become flushed and we might clench our jaws. When we get angry we might start slamming doors, or confront the person whom we perceive to have caused our anger. In this age of speedy computer technology we might fire off an angry email without thinking of the consequences. Those who easily fly off the handle are usually aware of this tendency and should take steps to react differently to adverse situations.

One well-known researcher in the area of anger, Ray Novaco, defines anger as a "negatively toned emotion subjectively experienced as an aroused state of antagonism toward someone or something perceived to be a source of an aversive event."[21]

According to Robert Baron and Joel Neuman, workplace aggression is more often relatively verbal, passive, indirect, and subtle as opposed to physical, active, direct, and overt.[22]

Another model of anger has been proposed more recently by psychologists Raymond DiGiuseppe and Raymond Chip Tafrate. They have done extensive research into anger among normal and also psychiatrically disturbed populations. Anger, in their definition, goes beyond just "feelings."

They have identified five dimensions of anger. The first is *provocations*. These are the events or stimuli that give rise to the anger. Anger is always preceded by some real or imagined provocation. The second is the *cognition domain*. These are the statements we tell ourselves about the stimuli or events. Third is the *arousal domain*. These involve the actual experience of the anger emotion itself. It includes the physiological response—heart beating, sweating—as well as the intensity and duration of the response. The fourth domain is the *motivational aspect*. These involve the use of emotions to cope with threats and stressful events—the motivating component. It can include revenge, acting to reduce tension, or coercing someone in some way.

Finally, there is a *behavioral component* to anger. This includes the outputs that we see. It can be brooding, verbal aggression, physical aggression, relational aggression, passive aggression, or indirect aggression (such as Sue sending emails to colleagues).[23]

Why control your anger?

At the least, anger can cause hurt feelings. Anger makes us less productive at work. It increases stress, which in turn can lead to illness and absenteeism. At its worst, anger can spark physical violence. There have been more and more instances of employees "losing it" at work. There has been a significant increase in workplace violence in recent years.

In a study that looked specifically at the role of emotions at work, Alicia Grandey and her colleagues found that negative emotional reactions were associated with intentions to leave the job. Interpersonal mistreatment from customers was the most frequent cause of anger. Recognition from supervisors for work performance was the main cause of pride.[24]

How does anger affect productivity in the workplace? In looking at the relationship between productivity and anger among New York City Department of Transportation traffic enforcement agents, Caren Baruch reported that a suppressed anger-management style was negatively associated with productivity. There were also significant relationships between productivity and frequency of conflicts with the public and anger-management style.[25]

You need to defuse your anger before it goes too far. This is especially true in the workplace, where losing your temper can get you fired. And, if your anger turns violent, you can face legal action.

Of course, anger can get us out of control. When we are angry we are blinded to everything else but the focus of that anger. That's when you hear the expression "I was so mad, I couldn't see straight." We can learn to use the energy created by our anger positively. Rather than letting it get the best of us, we can transform our anger to make our needs known. That means turning our anger into assertion, not aggression.

How prevalent is anger?

DiGiuseppe and Tafrate collected large samples of responses to their anger scale throughout the United States and Canada. Their data helps us estimate the prevalence of anger problems in the population. For example, the American Psychiatric Association typically defines a clinical syndrome as a problem if it has a *duration* of six months or longer. That is, people must have experienced the diagnostic symptoms of the problem one or more times over a period of at least six months. So it could be one long bout of six months, or many occurrences over the six-month duration.

DiGiuseppe and Tafrate found that 12% of the population at large reported problems with anger that had been happening for longer than six months' duration. If these findings are further replicated, that means that 12% of the population can be expected to have problematic anger experiences of a sufficient length of time to represent a potential clinical disorder.

In making a diagnosis, the length of time of each occurrence is also a consideration. This is the difference between experiencing something for a few minutes at a time or over the course of several days or more. So in this case, the length of time an anger episode lasts is also an important consideration. Their research found that 11% of people experienced anger episodes that lasted for several days or longer. This finding suggests that 11% of the population experienced anger episodes of sufficient length to consider it a clinical problem.

Another important aspect of anger is the intensity of the emotional experience. Most people reported a high intensity of anger at least some of the time. More telling, however, are the number of stimuli or triggers that elicit these angry responses. They found that 12% of people reported that their anger was triggered by several, many, or almost any event. The breadth of events may be an important factor in identifying people with serious anger problems.

Finally, the frequency in which anger occurs is important in understanding the prevalence. A serious anger episode once a week or more represents a frequency high enough to deem it a clinical problem. Their study identified that 5% of the sample reported anger experiences serious enough to interfere with their thinking, work or daily activities once a week or more. In terms of the expression of this anger, 2% displayed it through physical aggression, 2.5% through verbal means, and 3% through passive-aggressive means — once a week or more.[26]

As the result of several high-profile cases of workplace violence in the U.S. Postal Service, the term "going postal" has become widely known, since about 1994, as a description of workplace violence. For the period between 1993 and 1999 in the United States, an average of 1.7 million violent victimizations per year were committed against people who were at work or on duty according to the National Crime Victimization Survey.[27]

According to the Bureau of Labor Statistics Survey of Occupational Injuries and Illnesses, there were 16,664 nonfatal assaults in the workplace and violent acts with lost workdays in 1999. Workplace aggression is generally defined as employee behavior that is intended to harm current or previous co-workers or the organization to which they are presently or have previously been employed.[28]

In my work in this area I survey the degree to which conflicts in an organization have been successfully managed over the previous six months. Conflicts measured include verbal and physical aggression as well as subtle attempts at "getting even" with others or the organization.

We looked at the amount of serious anger in the workplace reported by employees in our surveys. One-third (33%) of employees reported seeing people so upset at work that they lost control of themselves.

Some people have been so upset that they lost control of themselves at work		
Disagree	Neutral	Agree
53%	14%	33%

How often do these tantrums lead to damaging the organization? We found that 20% of employees reported that the organization was hurt as a result of anger.

Some people have been so upset that they did things to hurt the organization		
Disagree	Neutral	Agree
65%	15%	20%

How often do co-workers suffer as a result of someone's anger? Once again, 20% of employees report having people so upset at work that they feel the need to get back at co-workers.

Some people have been so upset at work that they did things to get back at co-workers		
Disagree	Neutral	Agree
65%	15%	20%

This is the nature of Sue's attack on Linda. Poor co-worker relationships can lead to this kind of aggression at work. It's important for everyone at work to be aware of any anger among employees and the harm it can produce. Staff, however, typically do not report these kinds of disagreements or personality conflicts to supervisors. However, employees are more willing to raise these concerns in anonymous surveys. Once they are identified, either a manager or human resource professional can intervene. If disagreements cannot be mediated, employees may need to be separated into different parts of the organization.

Sometimes people get so upset at work they try to get back at their supervisors. This was reported to occur by 13% of employees.

Some people have been so upset at work that they did things to get back at their supervisor		
Disagree	Neutral	Agree
70%	17%	13%

The most dangerous result of anger, of course, is physical violence. We find that violence is reported by 4% of employees.

There have been physical confrontations between people here at work		
Disagree	Neutral	Agree
87%	9%	4%

Incidents of workplace violence have attracted the attention of not only the media and the general public, but also of organizations and researchers interested in studying workplace aggression.[29]

Research in this area is still at an early stage with few empirical studies available. There have been a number of studies looking at the general relationship between aggressive behavior at work and general measures of workplace.[30] In these studies employees are asked about the frequency with which they experienced aggressive behaviors. These are then related to relevant organizational and individual variables.

What's at the root of workplace aggression?

In a study that looked at aggressive encounters at work, Theresa Glomb documented specific antecedents of aggression. She found a variety of organizational, job-related, and personal antecedents, such as job stress and conflicts, and job-related outcomes, such as dissatisfaction. She also found a pattern in which aggression tends to escalate from less severe behaviors to more severe aggressive acts.[31]

In another study of causes of workplace anger, Kirk Calabrese identified major influences from corporate culture, work environment, psychological defense mechanisms, leadership decisions, stress, task orientation, and personality differences.[32] In a study looking at anger-provoking situations at work, Irene Gianakos identified the following examples: work performance of co-workers, work performance of supervisors, relationships with co-workers, relationships with supervisors, dealing with the public, and work performance of subordinates.[33]

But is the organization or the individual responsible for workplace aggression? Research has found that both organizational and individual characteristics play a role in workplace aggression. Scott Douglas and Mark Martinko reported that specific dispositional factors predict workplace aggression. For example, trait anger, attribution style, negative affectivity, attitudes towards revenge, self-control, and previous exposure to aggressive cultures accounted for 62% of the variance in self-reported incidents of workplace aggression.[34]

How much responsibility for workplace aggression is due to the individual? In a study by Willie Hepworth and Annette Towler, looking at 213 employees from a variety of organizations, individual difference variables accounted for 27% of the variance explained in workplace aggression.[35] Specifically, trait anger and self-control were related to workplace aggression. They supported the assumption that employees are less likely to retaliate against their employers when they perceive procedures to be fair.[36]

Do people who interact more with others show more anger at work, or is it the loner? Melissa Sloan in a study looking at a number of factors related to anger at work found that individuals who spend much of their time interacting with others at work report experiencing workplace anger more frequently than other workers. However, if the "loner" is also characterized by, perhaps, some suppressed anger, how likely is it that he or she will report feeling angry? This type of survey may not account for those who aren't even aware that they feel angry. People at higher positions at work are more likely to confront the person they are angry with than people of lower status are.[37]

What's the relationship between anger and emotional intelligence? John Mayer and Peter Salovey have reported that people with higher emotional intelligence are likely to be more aware of their own feelings as well as the feelings of others, better able to identify their feelings, and better able to communicate them when appropriate.[38]

How does emotional intelligence relate to levels of aggression in the workplace? Paul Thomlinson tested the relationship between emotional intelligence and workplace aggression. By assessing 347 employees at a behavioral health organization on a variety of measures that he related to workplace aggression, he found that emotional intelligence accounted for approximately 5% of the variance. That is, higher levels of emotional intelligence were associated with lower levels of workplace aggression. He also found that males with shorter job tenure were more inclined to engage in general workplace aggression, verbal aggression, and hostility. Less formal education was also predictive of higher levels of physical aggression.[39]

Managing anger in the workplace has become much more important in light of the increase of violence around us. There are specific steps you can take to gauge and defuse the anger, whether it's simmering or overt, in your workplace.

How can we improve anger management in organizations?

When faced with a situation that we get angry about, it is much better to be proactive in dealing with it. Rather than let the anger get the best of us, we must get the best of it. We can take steps to get our anger under control. Otherwise, we need to be able to walk away until we cool down. Following are proven techniques for improving anger management and workplace aggression.

- Determine whether managers are aware of the nature of any conflicts occurring in the workplace.

- If management is aware of the conflicts, explore the range of solutions or interventions that have been tried in the past.

- If management is unaware of the nature of any conflicts, explore this area in small groups or individually. Sometimes people do not want to raise these issues in front of others, so candid one-on-one sessions can be useful.

- If there have been physical altercations, the safety of the workplace is in jeopardy. An employer is exposed to serious legal repercussions if no action is taken. Develop a policy to handle such altercations and enforce it consistently across all levels of the organization.

- Evaluate the level of organizational stress, workload, task saturation, etc. Anger is often a symptom that has a specific root cause. If scores in any of these areas on an organizational survey are very low, consider introducing a training program or consult a specialist outside the organization to help with stress management, conflict resolution, and problem solving.

Great organizations are respectful of their people. People are appreciated for their unique talents and contributions. Emotionally intelligent organizations effectively manage situations that may lead to anger. Assertiveness is highly valued so that people are free to express their thoughts, feelings, and beliefs without fear of repercussions. Being overly passive or aggressive is not acceptable in these organizations. Bad feelings or grudges should not be allowed to fester. It's important for managers or facilitators to step in and implement conflict-resolution strategies. Dealing with gender, racial, and anger problems effectively helps build co-worker relationships, teamwork, and organizational trust.

CHAPTER 13 Organizational Responsiveness: Big Brother Is Looking Out for You

"For myself I am an optimist—it does not seem to be much use being anything else."

Sir Winston Churchill

"Leadership and learning are indispensable to each other."

John F. Kennedy, *speech prepared for delivery in Dallas the day of his assassination, November 22, 1963*

"The best leader is the one who has the sense to surround himself with outstanding people and the self-restraint not to meddle with how they do their jobs."

Author unknown

Key #7: Be proactively responsive by doing the right things to win the hearts and minds of your people.

Organizational responsiveness gets right to the bottom of my definition of organizational emotional intelligence. Responsiveness links directly to the organization's ability to be "responsible to its people, customers, suppliers, networks, and society."

Organizational responsiveness goes a long way towards motivating people's performance. A responsive organization builds trust among its people. Being responsive means showing you care by providing things that matter at a higher level. These include opportunities for training and advancement, providing an optimistic environment, embracing innovation, demonstrating integrity and honesty from the top down, showing the courage to make changes in the organization when needed, and being supportive of people.

Your organization's brand is important in its ability to attract the right people. Having a responsive organization helps build your brand, both internally and externally, now more than ever. The topics in this section focus on key areas that affect the way employees think and feel about your organization.

Training and Innovation

"This is third time I've been here to complain about these service charges. I was told this would be dealt with and obviously it hasn't been. How do you get something fixed at this bank?" fumed Clayton.

"Yes, Mr. Fryer, how are you doing today?" Cheryl asked with a smile.

"I just told you: I'm upset about not getting this problem looked after."

"Yes, of course, Mr. Fryer. Are you making any transactions today?"

"No, I want these service charges taken off, and I don't want to see any more service charges on this account," Clayton replied.

Still smiling, Cheryl looked down at her computer briefly, and then replied, "Oh, I'm sorry, Mr. Fryer; our system is down right now. Is there something else I could do for you?"

"No," Clayton yelled in disbelief, "and I don't want to have to come back here again over this."

"Yes, I understand, Mr. Fryer, but I can't enter anything right now," she replied, still smiling and looking right at Clayton.

"You know, I think I've had it with this bank!" Clayton yelled as he stormed out of the bank. Everyone turned to see what was going on.

"Have a nice day," Cheryl replied, without missing a beat.

Two senior members from the bank's training department, who had witnessed the whole interaction, came over to Cheryl in disbelief.

"Cheryl, how do you think that interaction went?" asked one of them.

"I thought it went great. I did everything we learned from the training consultant. I greeted him when he came in; I smiled, had good eye contact, and wished him a nice day at the end of the interaction."

"So you think the interaction went well? But he stormed out of the bank and he didn't get his needs met," said the other executive.

"Yes, but we were taught to make the interaction a pleasant experience."

The executive, in shock, said, "But I don't think he found it too pleasant."

In this case, the bank had spent over $200,000 on the outside training consultants for this customer service program designed for bank tellers. The question arises: how much of the training done in organizations today is well executed?

What do we know about training and innovation?

In our surveys I have found that 54% of employees feel that the training they receive at work is relevant to their job. Almost one-third (27%) feel the training is not based on what they need.

Training is based on what I really need to get the job done		
Disagree	Neutral	Agree
27%	19%	54%

A survey conducted by the Canadian Policy Research Networks shows that while three-quarters of those surveyed agree or strongly agree that the workplace training offered to them is adequate, another one in four say they do not receive necessary training.[1]

Do organizations pay attention to the career needs of individuals? The most challenging item in this area I found on our survey has to do with developing career paths. Only 32% of employees feel their organization has a well-developed career path program that provides training to help them progress. Almost half (47%) do not have such a plan.

The organization has a well-developed career path program that provides training to help employees progress		
Disagree	Neutral	Agree
47%	21%	32%

How well do organizations use the talents of their employees? This gets to the heart of innovation. Being innovative requires organizations to leverage the talent they have. I found that over half (55%) of employees feel that their talent is well used. Almost one-third (28%) feel that the organization does not fully utilize the talent available.

The organization uses the training, skills, and knowledge of its employees		
Disagree	Neutral	Agree
28%	17%	55%

Annual surveys on the state-of-the-industry of training in organizations are undertaken by the American Society for Training and Development (ASTD). In a recent survey they reported:

- The annual training expenditure per employee increased to $955 per employee, up from an average of $820 per employee in 2003 and 2002. (This increase reflects, in part, better accounting of training expenditures.)

- Employees are receiving more hours of formal learning—32 hours of learning per employee in 2004, up from 26 hours in 2003.

- Training delivery via learning technologies increased to 28% in 2004, up from 24% in 2003.

- In all categories of organizations that provided data for this report, profession- or industry-specific content was allocated the most learning content in 2004. Managerial/supervisory training and business processes were the second- and third-largest content areas.[2]

The importance of training in organizations has increased significantly. "The perception of the value of learning in driving organizational performance is increasing, as is the level of investing in learning," said Brenda Sugrue, senior director of research for ASTD and author of the ASTD 2005 *State of the Industry Report*. "More so than ever before, an organization's learning function is being run like any other business function with increased attention on operational efficiency, accountability, and connection to organizational strategy."[3]

In a national survey of businesses across New Zealand in 2003, about 90% of firms were currently providing training to employees, while 95% reported that they would likely provide training within the next 12 months. This represented a more modest 59% of all associated employees. Note, however, that this includes job orientation training.

Training is a key part of the overall business strategy for 49% of respondents. For large firms (100 or more employees), 66% claim that training is a key part of strategy. Cost was reported by 52% of respondents to be the number-one factor preventing firms from providing any or even less-than-desirable training. However, nearly three-quarters of responding firms conclude that training improves firm performance.[4]

The Learning Organization

One of the leading advocates of continual learning in organizations has been Peter Senge. He has promoted the concept of "learning organizations," which, according to Senge, are "organizations where people continually expand their capacity to create the results they truly desire, where new and expansive patterns of thinking are nurtured, where collective aspiration is set free, and where people are continually learning to see the whole together."[5]

The basic rationale for such organizations is that in situations of rapid change only those that are flexible, adaptive, and productive will excel. For this to happen, it is argued, organizations need to "discover how to tap people's commitment and capacity to learn at *all* levels."[6]

Senge describes five disciplines of learning, one of which he calls mental models. According to his theory, mental models are "deeply ingrained assumptions, generalizations, or even pictures and images that influence how we understand the world and how we take action."[7]

We are often not that aware of the impact of these assumptions on our behavior, so according to this model, a major part of the task is to develop the ability to "reflect in action." Basically, Senge means that we need to unearth and scrutinize certain mental models. He goes on to say: "The discipline of mental models starts with turning the mirror inward; learning to unearth our internal pictures of the world, to bring them to the surface and hold them rigorously to scrutiny. It also includes the ability to carry on 'learningful' conversations that balance inquiry and advocacy, where people expose their own thinking effectively and make that thinking open to the influence of others."[8]

Basically, this means that people have to be more reality oriented and flexible in their thinking. They need to be able to question their ingrained thinking. Reality testing and flexibility are two of the components of emotional intelligence as well that allow us to be better problem solvers.

There has been a fair degree of support for Senge's model of organizational learning and its importance for an organization's success. In a study looking at this model in practice, Nancy Da Silva and her colleagues surveyed 172 employees and 71 supervisors from six not-for-profit organizations. These included a variety of jobs, from receptionist to counselor. They found that the most significant learning factor related to supervisors' ratings of employee overall job performance was individual management of mental models.[9] In other words, the ability to take responsibility for challenging old assumptions and create new ways of thinking was most effective.

Once again, this relates to specific aspects of emotional intelligence that include emotional self-awareness, flexibility, and independence.

If organizations are to develop a capacity to work with mental models then it will be necessary for people to learn new skills and develop new orientations, and for there to be institutional changes that foster such growth. To quote Peter Senge again: "Entrenched mental models ... thwart changes that could come from systems thinking."[10]

Moving the organization in the right direction entails working to transcend the sorts of internal politics and game playing that dominate traditional organizations. In other words, it means fostering openness.[11] It also involves seeking to distribute business responsibility far more widely while retaining coordination and control. Learning organizations are localized organizations.[12]

What's the connection between the learning organization and innovation? Learning and keeping up to date on developments in the field are key to innovative organizations. In an academic study of innovation in organizations, Wesley Cohen and Daniel Levinthal point out: "The ability to exploit external knowledge is thus a critical component of innovative capabilities."[13]

According to a study co-authored by Canadian Policy Research Networks (CPRN) director Graham Lowe and senior researcher Grant Schellenberg, good relationships in the workplace are more important to job satisfaction than pay or benefits. Their study is entitled *What's a Good Job? The Importance of Employment Relationships.*

They stress that it's more than money that's required to win over employees. Trust and commitment cannot be bought. It's the work environment that has to be improved. One of the significant aspects of developing a positive work environment, according to their research, is training. According to Lowe:

> What we discovered was that training emerged as one of the important resources that people need in order to be effective in their work. It's one of the key ingredients of a high-quality work environment that will contribute to people having a strong sense of trust and commitment, feeling that they have an influence and that there is good communication.[14]

In fact, Lowe and Schellenberg outline four elements—trust, commitment, influence, and communication—that constitute the pillars of what the authors define as positive workplace relationships. They report that in order to create a healthy work environment it is important for employers to attain high levels of all four elements. According to Lowe: "One of the messages of this research is that a single program aimed at one of the work environment factors isn't sufficient. HR departments must instead have comprehensive plans in place as opposed to piecemeal, reactionary approaches."[15]

Improve Your Organization's Training and Innovation

There are a number of things you can do to improve the training and innovation in your organization, such as encouraging formal and informal continuing education. On the informal side, this can include lunch-and-learns with internal or external speakers and subject experts. More formally, employees could be compensated either partially or completely for completing relevant courses at local community colleges or universities. A simple 50/50 split of cost on successful completion of pre-authorized courses demonstrates the employer's commitment to learning and shares the responsibility with the employee.

Take advantage of seminars and workshops in specialty areas that can include new technologies, specific work-related skills, or soft skills (e.g., getting organized, being more productive, management skills).

Reward people for upgrading their skills and knowledge through simple company-wide acknowledgement and recognition, one-time completion bonuses (for designations, for example), or tailoring a salary plan based on skills and knowledge.

Foster a learning organization by allowing people to experiment, and try new approaches or ideas. You must be willing to allow people to learn from mistakes.

Consider coaching programs for middle and senior managers, which can improve their on-the-job performance. This approach allows for the targeting of specific skill sets that are required by the individual with direct benefits and payback to the organization.

Make sure that each employee has a formal training plan, clearly detailing areas of growth, method to get there, support structure to enable development, and the potential use of a mentor/coach to guide development.

Ensure managers and supervisors have sufficient financial resources to support training plans.

Often in times of financial cutbacks, training is the first budget item to be reduced. Ensure that you are not jeopardizing the company's financial future by failing to provide important investments in training and development.

Looking at Organizational Optimism and Integrity

Julian had sent his new idea for a marketing campaign for an important client to the rest of his department. He was responsible for coming up with a plan to grow his division's revenues by 20%. He already had several successes under his belt and felt pretty confident about this one. But he thought that maybe some of his colleagues could add some extra punch to it. Anxious to get some feedback, he stopped Julie as she walked by his office.

"Julie," he called, "have you had a chance to review my proposal?"

She stopped and looked his way, "Oh yeah, I just took a quick look. Haven't had a chance to review it carefully yet. But from what I've seen, I think it still needs some work. The campaign is a bit fluffy, and the numbers don't quite fit, but I'll get back to you."

"Thanks," Julian replied, a bit dejected.

Suddenly Roger came by, "Hey Julian, just saw your proposal, I don't really think it's what they had in mind upstairs. Looks to me like you should rework it quite a bit."

"Well, do you have anything specific?" he asked.

"Not really, I just think the idea is off, there might be one or two things in there that are pretty good, but I'd do a major rewrite. Sorry I can't help you any more, gotta go."

"Well, thanks, I'll see what I can do," he said, feeling even more despondent.

Is it necessary to praise everything everybody does at work? Aren't Julie and Roger just being honest? Shouldn't Julian know what his colleagues really think? Why let work that we believe is substandard get by?

In this case, Julian's work is quality work. As with any document, there is always room for improvement. But the comments from his colleagues demonstrate an especially negative work environment. Worst of all, this is in a creative industry, where negative, non-specific criticism can do the most harm.

Are there other, more constructive ways Julie and Roger could have provided feedback? Sure there are. For one thing, they could have started out with one thing that they liked about the proposal. For example, "Yes, Julian, I haven't gone over it in depth yet, but I really like the way you introduce the new campaign and the redesigned logo. I still need more time to review the numbers and the customer proposition." Or, "I haven't had time to really go over it yet, but it looks like you've put a lot of effort into it."

How positive are our work environments?

People do their best work in a positive, supportive environment. In our survey of workplaces, we found that only 41% of employees felt their workplace was positive and energized them. Another 30% stated that the atmosphere in their workplace was not positive and stimulating.

My organization's positive atmosphere energizes me		
Disagree	Neutral	Agree
30%	29%	41%

How do employees view their organizations? Do they believe their organization has a winning attitude? We found that 58% of employees believe their workplace has a winning attitude. Almost one-quarter (22%) do not feel they work in a winning organization.

My organization has a winning attitude		
Disagree	Neutral	Agree
22%	20%	58%

Do employees view their organizations as optimistic? Do they think they are headed for a bight future? The majority (68%) of employees see their organization as optimistic. A smaller, but sizeable number (12%), see their organization as being pessimistic about the future.

This organization has an optimistic outlook towards the future		
Disagree	Neutral	Agree
12%	20%	68%

Honesty and Integrity

More than ever, organizations must strive for fairness in its dealings with all stakeholders, including employees, customers, suppliers and the community. The optimism and integrity measure in the Benchmark of Emotional Intelligence (BOEI) reflect an employee audit of this perceived fairness. When this score is low, further in-depth interviews could shed more light on any inequities.

The executive leadership of a multinational manufacturing company decided that it would be a good idea to set up a blog so that employees from around the world could communicate with the top leadership. This would be an opportunity for any employee to post questions that would get answered directly by senior management.

There was a great deal of fanfare as notices were sent out to thousands of employees inviting them to take part. This would be their opportunity to get their questions answered directly from the top.

The first questions started to trickle in. They were fairly innocent queries about certain pricing policies, product issues, and health benefits. Then one employee wanted to know why certain executive vice presidents received such generous salary increases when company performance was flat. Another employee asked why she had to cut back on salaries for her group when there were others in another department getting increases.

The first few questions were responded to quickly in the excitement of demonstrating the utility of the new technology. Then there were delays as the questions got more pointed. Delays then turned into silence. The blog was pulled off the intranet two weeks later. The executive management announced that the blog would be replaced with a new "filtered" system that would make it easier to manage the questions.

It didn't take too long before the employees started to draw their own conclusions. The integrity of the senior team dropped several notches throughout the organization. Unfortunately, once integrity goes down, it's extremely hard to win it back.

Suggestion boxes have been around in organizations for decades. But they never had the immediacy of today's inter- and intranet modalities. When I was doing work for the Pentagon I was stationed for a couple of weeks on the aircraft carrier USS *George Washington*. Once a week the commander of the ship and his senior team were beamed throughout the television monitors all over the ship. I remember the commander retrieving questions randomly from a suggestion box.

Every single question was given an answer by the commander or one of his team. If there were specific details they didn't have available, they promised to complete the answer by a certain day and time. I remember one question was a complaint about the sailors sometimes having to wait a long time for their food while officers seemed to be readily served.

The commander apologized for that impression. He then pointed out that the mess could be busy 24 hours a day feeding the different shifts of sailors, marines, pilots, and flight crews, but the health and safety regulations required the mess be closed for a certain number of hours each day for cleaning. He immediately came up with a plan to have at least one place set up with food available even if he had to use part of the officers' mess to make it happen. It was no surprise to me that there was so much respect on board for the commander and the senior team. They were seen as making decisions and following through on them.

Perhaps if companies such as Enron, WorldCom or Tyco had used an employee survey such as the BOEI, some significant information may have been picked up before these companies' integrity issues became the subject of international news. For example, one question asks employees if they see their organization as honest. As a point of comparison, 59% of employees we've surveyed feel their organization operates with integrity. A surprisingly high number, 18%, do not see their employers as operating with integrity.

This organization consistently operates on principles of integrity		
Disagree	Neutral	Agree
18%	23%	59%

In a recent article in the *Wall Street Journal*:

Top executives first have to take steps to assure employees that they are achieving profits honestly. "If you end up with employees who don't have any trust for their top leaders, you're not going to have productive, really committed employees," says Jeffrey Immelt, chief executive of General Electric.[16]

The article goes on to cite a study by Arthur Brief, a professor at Tulane University's Freeman School of Business who found:

In a 1996 study, for example, [Brief] was surprised to find that 47% of about 400 executives surveyed were willing to commit fraud by understating write-offs that cut into their companies' profits. "People in subordinate roles will comply with their superiors even when that includes wrongdoing that goes against their individual moral code," says Mr. Brief. "I thought they would stick with their values, but most organizations are structured to produce obedience."[17]

The article also makes this point:

Honesty in the workplace can't be regulated. It has to be encouraged by leaders who themselves are honest and willing to admit their failures. Warren Buffett, chief executive of Berkshire Hathaway, did this in his annual report in 2000, when he said that the company hadn't performed very well that year and that it was his fault.[18]

Significant research on integrity in executives has been carried out by psychologist Robert Hare, an internationally recognized expert in the area of psychopathology, and Paul Babiak, an industrial organizational psychologist. They have documented cases of what can go wrong when the wrong people climb the corporate ladder. Specifically, they have developed a screening measure called the B-SCAN that can be used to get a quick impression of an executive's integrity. The measure focuses on four areas found to be important:

Personal Style: reflects on how an individual sees himself or herself and his own attitudes towards others. It can influence how others will react, support, and follow direction.

Emotional Style: involves the understanding of one's own feelings and emotions, those of others, and the way in which the individual uses this understanding in the business environment.

Organizational Effectiveness: involves an understanding of what it takes to be a contributing member of an organization and to be able to use this understanding to moderate personal behavior and to enhance the overall ability of the group to achieve common goals.

Social Responsibility: determines how effectively an individual interacts with others as a member of the organization, both in one-on-one situations, or as a member of a team. Social responsibility is critical for the smooth operation of an organization.[19]

How can you increase optimism and integrity in your organization?

There are a number of key strategies that organizations can carry out to make employees feel that they are making a worthwhile contribution to the company and to underscore that ethical behavior is expected from all levels.

- Develop a sense of accomplishment within the organization. This can be done by setting clear organizational goals and objectives. Publicize the organizational goals. Chart the progress of these goals in public places, in a manner that is clear and easy for everyone to understand.

- Develop a positive sense of competition, in a way that promotes team spirit. This can be between departments, against sales targets, or towards any of the organizational goals.

- Set goals that are SMART: specific, measurable, attainable, realistic, and tangible.

- Develop a sense of optimism among leaders and managers. Managers need to learn how to focus on the positive. Communication with staff, especially in public, should focus more on what is going well in the organization. Problems should be dealt with in individual or small-group meetings where the focus should be on solutions as opposed to analysis-paralysis and blaming. Ideally, the preparations for setbacks and contingencies are an integral part of the strategic and operational planning processes.

- Avoid spending time exclusively in deep analysis of problems and concerns of the past. Determine the cause, take corrective action, and move forward, focusing on future behaviors and challenges.

- Stay aware of competitors. While your behavior should not be determined by competitors, at least be prepared for the directions they may take. Always use your own strategies to deal with changes in the marketplace and competitive advances.

- Take an active role in celebrating organizational achievements. Whether it involves meeting sales goals, gaining new customers or contracts, successfully meeting certain challenges, or dealing with difficult customers, build in opportunities to recognize the staff members involved. Make public their successes in these situations.

Social Responsibility

How socially responsible do employees see their workplace? We found that 61% of employees feel their workplace is socially and environmentally conscious. On the other hand, 17% report that their employer is not socially responsible.

This organization can be described as being socially and environmentally conscious		
Disagree	Neutral	Agree
17%	22%	61%

Business Ethics Magazine compiles a list of the best 100 corporate citizens each year. The most recent list was led by Green Mountain Coffee Roasters. Describing their ascent to the top of the list, they write:

Since its founding in 1981, the company has been socially and environmentally active, "but it wasn't all that extensive or organized at first," recalls CEO Bob Stiller. Green Mountain upped the ante in 1989 when it formed an environmental committee and created a rainforest nut coffee to support the Rainforest Alliance, a non-profit dedicated to protecting ecosystems. The company has grown increasingly active in the countries where coffee is grown and has been a pioneer in the fair trade movement, which pays coffee growers stable, fair prices. But the biggest change came in the early 1990s when the company began sending its employees on trips to see where the coffee is grown. Many employees "said it changed their lives," Stiller adds.[20]

Some of the specific programs Green Mountain developed include:

Green Mountain, with 600 employees, saw 2005 revenue of $161.5 million with net income of $9 million, a 15 percent increase over the year prior. Since 1988, it has donated more than $500,000 to Coffee Kids, an international nonprofit seeking to improve the quality of life for children and families in coffee-growing communities. Through the Coffee Kids program, the company supports a microlending facility in Huatusco, Mexico and a sustainable sanitation system in Cosaulan, Mexico. It also has provided financial support to the FomCafe cooperative's quality-control training program, which helps farmers earn higher profits for coffee.[21]

Another noticeable company on the list was Timberland. Their rise was described as follows:

> One of the most impressive advances on the list was made by Timberland, which jumped from No. 74 last year to No. 6 this year. Timberland has one of the strongest employee volunteer programs in the country, with its decade-old "Path of Service" program giving employees 40 hours of paid time to contribute to the community during working hours. Now the Stratham, N.H., footwear and apparel company, with $1.6 billion in sales, is placing greater emphasis on environmental programs. In early 2006 Timberland announced a new shoebox "nutritional label," detailing where the product was made, how it was produced, and its impact on the environment and communities. "We thought about how closely consumers read nutritional labels on food products and thought, why doesn't this happen in our space?" recalls Dave Aznavorian, a senior global brand manager at Timberland.[22]

What effect does working in a socially responsible organization have on its employees? At the University of Michigan, Adam Grant has been conducting an interesting series of studies looking at this issue. In one study he looked at three groups of students who volunteered to collect money from university alumni. The work itself was essentially quite boring as it included making repetitive phone calls, reading from a standardized script, and enduring frequent rejections.

The money was being collected to provide student scholarships for students who could otherwise not afford to attend university. Usually, callers do not meet the recipients of those who benefit from their solicitations. In this study, all groups received basic training in how to make phone calls and solicit funds. After two weeks, a meeting was set up for each of the groups. The first group met with their manager to discuss the job and how it was going.

In the second group's meeting, the callers read a letter from a student who was benefiting from the scholarship. The letter talked about how the scholarship enhanced the recipient's life. Then, in small groups, the callers and their manager had a five-minute discussion about the contents of the letter.

In the third group, the callers read the same letter as in the second group. However, this time following their reading of the letter, the student beneficiary was brought into the room. The manager then engaged the recipient in a brief question-and-answer period about his experience. This allowed for an interpersonal experience with an actual scholarship recipient.

All callers continued to be monitored for their performance over the next weeks. Grant looked at the callers' persistence—the amount of time they spent on the phone—and their job performance—the actual amount of money collected. The first group, who had a discussion with their manager, and the second group, who received the letter and discussed it, showed no change in their persistence or performance. Amazingly, the third group did significantly better after experiencing the interpersonal contact from a recipient. They spent 142% more time on the phone and collected 171% more donation money in a single week alone.[23]

Imagine the effect if we could have employees get more direct experience with the beneficiaries of their work. Changing the design of jobs so that this component could be built in could help to significantly increase worker motivation.

Organizational Courage and Adaptability

The company had to decide whether to introduce a new cleaning solution. Their main product, a disinfectant for medical instruments, was the market leader. Now they saw an opportunity to expand their product line with a new sanitizing spray for sports bags and equipment.

The CEO was excited about the opportunity to enter a new market. He felt their strong brand name could carry them into the new area. The marketing team, however, saw the transition as expensive and distracting. They were facing increasing competition in their leading products. There was word of another company breaking into the sports bag disinfectant business with a multi-million-dollar launch campaign and several sports celebrity endorsements.

Production was concerned about the distraction the new product would have from improvements they were making to their bestselling product. Meetings had been going on for several months without a decision. Their indecision was getting costly in terms of people's time. There was one more meeting called to come to a final decision.

Brad from the marketing department presented his report. "I've tried the numbers every which way. I don't think it's a good time for us to go into a new launch. As you can see from my projections, it's not likely that we could make back our investment for at least five years out. And that's if our competitors don't take the market lead."

"Well, I think we can beat them to the punch if we gear up our marketing campaign for the spring," replied Jean, from sales.

"How do you think we can get the formula perfected by then?" asked George, from production.

Jerome, the operations manager, stepped in. "Look, we've really got to make a decision here. This has been dragging on for months. It's using marketing and production time that could be better spent on preparing for the launch of the new formula for our bestselling disinfectant."

The discussion went on for another hour. Nobody seemed to take charge or be willing to make the decision one way or another.

How do employees generally see the decision-making process in their organization? In our survey, we found that 43% of employees feel their organization is too slow in making decisions. Only one-third of employees believed their organization was responsive to decision making quickly enough.

This organization is too slow in making decisions		
Disagree	Neutral	Agree
33%	24%	43%

What are the effects of slow decisions? They can be costly. Delaying major decisions can use up valuable resources, allow competitors to speed ahead, and frustrate all the employees who are dependent on decisions with clear outcomes.

What about making changes?

Today's workplace is all about change. Products and markets no longer stand still for long periods of time. How well do organizations adapt to change?

We found that 40% of employees feel their organization is too slow to make changes while another 40% believed their organization was good at change.

This organization is too slow to make needed changes		
Disagree	Neutral	Agree
40%	20%	40%

When we talk about courage in organizations, one aspect is the organization's ability to meet new challenges head on. The majority of employees (63%) believe their organization has the courage to take on new challenges. A sizeable number (17%) feels that their organization lacks courage for challenge.

In a study looking at emotional intelligence and attitudes towards organizational change, Maria Vakola and her colleagues evaluated 137 professionals who completed self-report inventories assessing emotional intelligence, personality traits, and attitudes towards organizational change. She found a relationship between personality traits and employees' attitudes towards change. Additionally, those employees with higher emotional intelligence had better attitudes to change.[24]

Another study looking at the characteristics of managers and their response to change across several different countries was carried out by Timothy Judge and his associates. Data was collected from 514 managers across six organizations. They looked at two characteristics: positive self-concept and risk tolerance.

Both of these factors significantly predicted self-report and independent assessments of coping with change. The ability to cope with organizational change was also related to extrinsic factors, such as salary, job level, plateauing (reaching the top of your job category), and job performance—as well as intrinsic factors, such as organizational commitment and job satisfaction.[25]

This organization meets new challenges head on		
Disagree	Neutral	Agree
17%	20%	63%

Making tough decisions is another aspect of courage. We find that 62% of employees feel their organization has the courage to make tough decisions. A surprising 14% did not agree that their organization dealt courageously with difficult decisions.

This organization has the courage to make tough decisions		
Disagree	Neutral	Agree
14%	24%	62%

Along the same lines, we asked if their organization confronts difficult issues or prefers to avoid dealing with these issues. We found that 59% of employees felt that their organization had the courage to confront difficult issues. There were 18% who rated their organization as lacking in courage.

This organization has the courage to confront difficult issues		
Disagree	Neutral	Agree
18%	23%	59%

The September 2004 issue of *Fast Company* was dedicated to the issue of courage. There were a number of stories and quotations from people in business and government providing examples of courage. One of the definitions of courage was given by Warren Bennis: "Courage is the capacity to wait until you've learned as much as you can and then take action. You're never sure of the results until you do it. You're still not going to know everything. You have to take gambles and learn more."[26]

He goes on to state: "Leaders articulate ... goals and incarnate the behavior through symbolic conduct to get people to follow. When Cicero spoke, people marveled; when Caesar spoke, people marched. Getting people to march behind your ideas takes courage."[27]

Merom Klein and Rod Napier defined five factors that characterize how courage is displayed in business. The first is candor. This includes the ability to speak and hear the truth. Second, they describe purpose as the courage to pursue lofty and audacious goals. Third, they include rigor, the courage to create disciplines and make them stick. Fourth, they talk about risk. This is the courage to empower, trust, and invest in relationships. Finally, they include will. This includes the courage to inspire optimism, spirit, and promise.[28]

Increasing Courage and Adaptability

Here are some suggestions to increase courage and adaptability in your organization:

- The organization may be seen as too reactive and not proactive enough. Look for opportunities in which the organization can take charge and set the direction.

- Anticipate trends and future directions. Environmental scanning makes use of many resources, including the internet, professional and industrial associations, publications, and analysis of market trends. Use these resources as part of your planning and decision-making process.

- When problem solving, generate a number of alternative solutions before making decisions. Get input from relevant people.

- Is there a formal business planning process in place? Is a plan developed, monitored and adhered to, or is it developed and then filed?

- It is important for leadership to be decisive in action. Difficult decisions should not be put off for too long. There has to be a willingness to execute difficult as well as simple decisions.

- In order for the organization to move forward, it must take risks. Innovation is largely about risks. Try new things, and vary your approach to situations. It's okay to make mistakes as long as people learn from their mistakes.

- Beware of organizational rigidity towards change, often evidenced by the "not invented here" attitude. Low levels of organizational adaptability can lead to stagnation and are a threat to organizational growth and survival.

What about the top management leadership?

Jose was the head of operations for a large manufacturing company. He loved to look over the reams of printouts of performance reports from the shop floor. He would constantly analyze and come up with theories on the increasing or decreasing rate of production each week.

Jose had four direct reports that oversaw the operation. He would meet weekly with his reports and feed back the data and his interpretation. Whatever instruction he had as a result of his analysis he would pass on to his subordinates to carry out.

The employees on the shop floor never saw Jose. Although he came in early in the morning and left late at night, he seemed to have no time to wander around and speak to anybody. There were workers who had been employed there for more than a year who had no idea of what Jose even looked like.

How sensitive would Jose's recommendations be to the average worker at the plant? How well would he know the employees' needs, requests, or motivators? It's not likely that he would have a full grasp of the operation without spending some time being seen and talking to the employees.

How well do organizational leaders know their employees? In our survey we found that almost half (45%) of employees feel their senior managers are too isolated from them. Only 37% of employees rated their leaders as involved in their issues. This is a critical area of winning the hearts and minds of employees. Being isolated from the people you are in charge of puts you in the position of being the "faceless bureaucrat." It creates the "us" versus "them" mentality that most leaders want to avoid.

Senior management seems isolated from the issues of the average employee		
Disagree	Neutral	Agree
37%	18%	45%

Part of being a good leader involves taking action and making good decisions. How are leaders' decisions perceived by the workforce? We found that 46% (again, almost half) of employees are unimpressed by the decisions their senior managers make. Only 31% of employees have confidence in their leaders' decisions.

This lack of confidence is often not due to the decision itself. I find that it's the communication—or lack of communication—about the decision, how it was reached, and how it will be implemented that causes the most problems. Leaders have to take the time to go over the reasons why certain actions are taking place. While it may be time consuming or costly, there is more to be lost in ignoring input and thrusting initiatives out there without having them understood by the people who will be directly affected.

Senior management's decisions seldom inspire my confidence and trust		
Disagree	Neutral	Agree
31%	23%	46%

Part of the communication expected of leaders is to let employees know where they are going. People want to have confidence in their leaders. One of the ways they become confident is by knowing that the leader has a strong vision of where she or he wants to go.

We found that just over half (53%) of employees feel their leaders have a clear vision of where they're going. However, 27% were seen as not communicating a clear vision.

Senior management communicates a clear vision of where we are going		
Disagree	Neutral	Agree
27%	20%	53%

Top Leadership and Emotional Intelligence

A number of studies have linked the importance of emotional intelligence to top leadership. One study that I carried out looked at the relationship between emotional intelligence and a number of factors among 76 CEOs of fast-growing companies. Overall, the group scored slightly higher than average in their total emotional intelligence score. Their scores were highest on independence, assertiveness, optimism, self-actualization, and self-regard.

Below-average scores were obtained in two factors: interpersonal relationships and impulse control. Female CEOs scored significantly higher than their male counterparts on the interpersonal scale. I broke the group into two, those whose companies were the most profitable and those that were least profitable. High-performing CEOs were found to differ from the rest of the group with higher scores on empathy, self-regard, and assertiveness.[29]

In a related study I tested the emotional intelligence of members of the Young Presidents' Organization (YPO) and found their emotional intelligence to be higher than the population at large. Specific strengths included flexibility, self-regard, and independence.[30]

There have been a number of studies looking at what is known as trans-formational and transactional leadership. Transactional leadership requires strong interpersonal skills as it involves telling employees what is expected of them and how tasks are to be completed. Transformational leadership, on the other hand, offers employees an overall vision and motivates them to excel beyond their expectations.

One study looking at these two leadership styles was carried out by Crystal Hoyt and Jim Blascovitch. Looking at both physical and virtual settings, they found that transformational leadership was associated with decreases in quantitative performance but increases in qualitative performance, leadership satisfaction, and group cohesiveness. They also found that group members preferred meeting with their leader face to face.[31]

In another study, Dong Jung and John Sosik examined 47 groups from Korean firms found that transformational leadership was positively related to empowerment, group cohesiveness, and group effectiveness. Empowerment was positively related to collective efficacy, which in turn was positively related to how group members perceived overall group effectiveness.[32]

In a study looking at social and emotional communication skills in leader effectiveness, Ronald Riggio and his associates found that, in a fire protection service organization, employees were more satisfied with leaders who scored higher on social skills and, in some cases, this led to higher performance.[33] Taking this one step further, Stephanie Halverson and her associates found that socially skilled leaders performed better both under stressful and non-stressful conditions.[34]

In a study looking at what makes a good global leader, Manfred Kets De Vries and Elizabeth Florent-Treacy interviewed 500 senior executives. The key factors they found included the ability to forge a group identity across the organization by speaking to the collective imagination of the workforce and ensuring that there was a match between what motivated the followers (employees) and the needs of the organization.[35]

Increasing Top Management Leadership

Often a lack of organizational responsiveness can lead to high turnover rates. Even a quick analysis of the costs of turnover will help clarify the importance of management. Such costs include temporary help, overtime related to staff shortfall, training time of other staff and managers, sick leave, absenteeism related to overwork and frustration felt by employees left to do the work, and costs associated with recruiting.

To address these problems, consider the following:

- Look into having 360-degree assessments of the organization's top leaders. This is a valuable way to learn more about the leaders' strengths and weaknesses.

- Determine how much time leaders spend communicating with people throughout the organization and the quality of those communications. Leaders may have a vision for the organization but are not getting it through to others. Has a clear and understandable vision been articulated?

- Is there a consensus-based leadership style or a more autocratically functioning leadership? Leaders who build a consensus have been found to be more successful in achieving organizational goals.

- Well-grounded leaders (leaders who can manage their emotions) are perceived as better leaders by people in organizations. Determine to what degree top leaders have a balanced, well-grounded style.

- Poor interpersonal skills have been found to be related to the derailment of top leaders. Interpersonal skills should be investigated as part of any leadership assessment.

- Consider how the organization helps its people when they are in need. Are there situations where special consideration has been made for individuals suffering from personal misfortune, illness, or family problems? What does the organization do for people who have had to put in considerable extra time to meet critical deadlines? Are they recognized or rewarded in any way?

- How visible is leadership, particularly senior leadership, in the workplace? Where possible, the "manage by walking around" approach done routinely provides employees access to leaders, and gives leaders "eyes and ears" to know what's going on with their organization and with their people.

In my research I find that organizational responsiveness accounts for the largest amount of variance in an organization's emotional intelligence.

Organizational responsiveness provides the heart of the organization. It demonstrates that the organization really cares, in an honest way, about its people, its customers, and society. It provides the learning environment employees need and want to be innovative. It's the optimism about the future of the organization, which is built on a solid foundation of integrity. The organization demonstrates by its deeds that it has the courage and adaptability to deal with change. And, of course, the top leadership is credible and competently guides the organization and its people forward.

Building an organization's responsiveness in these areas is the most significant step towards creating the great workplace. This is the strategic aspect that takes all the tactical steps to the next level.

CHAPTER 14

Putting It All Together —Organizationally, That Is

"Nothing energizes an individual or a company more than clear goals and a grand purpose. Nothing demoralizes more than confusion and lack of content."

Tony O'Reilly, CEO of H. J. Heinz & Co. from 1979 to 1998

"There are countless ways of achieving greatness, but any road to achieving one's maximum potential must be built on a bedrock of respect for the individual, a commitment to excellence, and a rejection of mediocrity."

Buck Rodgers, player, coach, and manager in
Major League Baseball

"Leadership is practiced not so much in words as in attitude and in actions."

Harold Geneen, founder of International Telephone and
Telegraph (ITT)

Throughout this book I have provided and explored seven key factors that are important in making organizations great. I base this on research carried out by our group at MHS using a standardized survey of thousands of working people. A number of examples and research studies have been provided to support the importance of these keys. In this chapter I would like to look at organizations that have been identified independently as great companies and see how these keys stack up against the world's best organizations.

Building Meaning

One of the most well-known ratings of "best" companies is the *Fortune* 100 Best Companies to Work For. According to Robert Levering, co-author of the list, the issue of *Fortune* magazine announcing this list is their most popular of the year.[1] Companies are selected based on two factors. First they evaluate policies and culture of the company through the attitude and behavior of their management. They stress the importance of how the management relates to its employees. Second, they seek the opinions of a minimum of 350 employees on issues that include their attitudes towards management, job satisfaction, and camaraderie.[2]

According to Levering, a comparison was made of a hypothetical portfolio of stocks from the first *Fortune* 100 Best Companies to Work For list in 1997. Their financial results were matched with a portfolio from Standard & Poor's 500 (an established stock market index) and followed for six years. The "100 Best" portfolio returned almost three times more than the S&P portfolio over the same time period. He reports that if an investor replaced the approximately 20 companies per year that drop off the list with the new 20, the return would have been more than five times the S&P group.

The best workplaces have higher productivity and profitability as well as better customer satisfaction. Staff turnover rates are much lower in these workplaces, meaning lower costs associated with recruiting new staff, training them, and waiting until they are up to speed in their new positions. And, as previously stated in earlier chapters, companies with great reputations attract great talent. The better the talent in an organization, the better their performance.[3]

In 2006, the number-one company on the *Fortune* 100 Best Companies to Work For list was Genentech, a biotechnology company. Among the products that Genentech develops are new treatments for cancer. What were some of the key factors in this company's selection among the "best"? First, they reported on the comments of employees about the company. These included comments like: "We love what we do because we know that our job has meaning ..." and "the culture of this company fosters such a warm and diverse environment where everyone is treated equally. You can just as easily talk to our CEO, Art, as you can with any other employee."[4]

A second major reason had to do with the company's human resource policies and practices. Among many innovative programs related to fairness in pay, social impact, and training, the company goes to great lengths to provide communication channels among managers and employees. These include an intranet site called gWiz, webcasting meetings, Town Halls, and "Art's Quarterly E-mail Surveys" where the CEO "typically responds to about 800 ideas, suggestions and complaints from employees."[5]

Finally, another one of Genentech's strengths is its ability to fit a myriad of programs together systematically. Rather than offer a hodgepodge of initiatives that are barely tied together or cohesive, Genentech has carefully thought through all these programs, from family initiatives to staff recognition programs, and created a unified and cohesive mechanism for delivering on these programs and more.

By the description given, Genentech represents a good example of what I have been discussing as a values-based organization. By focusing on values, companies like this win the hearts and minds of their employees. It's important for great companies to stand back, look at themselves, and define what they stand for in terms of values that have meaning to their employees and clients.

The Rules of Engagement

Another well-publicized list of great companies is the "London *Sunday Times* 100 Best Companies to Work For in the United Kingdom." Their selection is based on ratings of more than 86,500 employees across more than 500 companies.[6] One criterion used to select their winners is the degree of employee engagement—that is, the quality and strength of the relationship between employees and management. As they report, "everyone benefits when employees become fully engaged with their company. Staff get job satisfaction and bosses see business boom."[7]

The *Times* describes the conditions for engagement to be high when there is strong leadership, opportunities for personal development, good management, decent pay and benefits, a reasonable work/life balance, fun activities to help build close-knit teams, and staff believing the firm to be ethical. They describe an engaged employee as someone who really cares about the business. They not only do their job, but they "go the extra mile" and use their own initiative to innovate and generate success.

Tower Homes was the number-one company on the *Times* small-company list. It had the highest engagement score with 100% of its employees engaged. Its chief executive officer described how he saw different levels of engagement at work:

> Companies can have fantastic people (As), quite good people (Bs) and rubbish people (Cs). Your As are all stars, Bs could be As but need quite a lot of training and motivating and Cs are the people who are never going to buy in, they will always do nine-to-five and will have the wrong attitude. They can be malevolent or completely useless and have to go.[8]

The *Times* used eight items to measure engagement on their survey. The most highly related items were being excited about where your organization is going, believing the leader is doing a great job, and getting a buzz from your team. The item with the lowest correlation was "fair deal," which measures pay and benefits. They conclude that you can't fool people into being engaged, but rather that it has to come from inside them. As one of the winning company CEOs, Ruth Spellman of Investors in People UK, puts it, "money is not always the way to employees' hearts."[9]

Communication Is Key

The Society for Human Resource Management (SHRM) produces its own list of the "Best Small & Medium Companies to Work For in America." Their top list goes beyond selecting companies with fat paychecks and big benefits packages. More emphasis is placed on communicating clearly with employees and encouraging staff to voice their opinions.

The best medium-size company for three years in a row was Analytical Graphics, an information technology company. Among their activities they hold annual business review meetings for all employees, quarterly Town Hall meetings, and weekly Story Time meetings, in which departments share information about what's happening around the company. They also provide an on-site gym and free meals to make employees' lives easier.[10]

Healthier Workplaces

The American Psychological Association (APA) sponsors a Psychologically Healthy Workplace Awards competition. The program is designed to recognize employers that distinguish themselves in their efforts to take care of employees. It follows up on selections made by state and provincial psychological associations in which 200 companies in 35 states, provinces, and territories have been recognized.[11]

The APA national program recognizes organizations that excel in five categories of a psychologically healthy workplace: employee involvement, work/life balance, employee growth and development, health and safety, and employee recognition. The awards favor workplace practices such as "employee participation in decision making, skills training and leadership development, flexible schedules and benefits plans, easy access to mental health and substance abuse services, programs to prevent and manage workplace stress, programs that promote healthy lifestyle and behavior choices, and recognition of individual and team performance."[12]

The APA cites the American Institute of Stress statistics that U.S. companies lose nearly $300 billion per year, or $7,500 per worker, in employee absenteeism, decreased productivity, employee turnover, and direct medical, legal, and insurance fees related to workplace stress.

One of the awards for small for-profit companies was presented to Versant Inc., a marketing communications firm based in Milwaukee. They strongly believe in helping each employee reach his or her potential. As part of their corporate culture they allow employees to make important decisions, contribute to the company's success, and assume responsibility for the results. Continuous learning and employee development is strongly encouraged through coaching and mentoring, roundtable discussions, funded memberships in trade organizations and on- and off-site education. The results have been impressive. Between 2001 and 2006, Versant experienced a 36% increase in productivity, and fees billed per full-time worker have increased by 31%.[13]

Computerworld magazine surveys 27,108 information technology (IT) workers in order to select their pick of the "100 Best Places to Work in IT."

Participating companies, which include both private and public, are required to have (in 2005) revenue of $250 million or greater and employ a minimum of 500 total employees and a minimum of 75 IT employees in the United States.

A contact person in the participating organization completes a 100-item questionnaire asking about average salaries, bonus increases, percentage of IT employee promotions, training and development opportunities, and diversity of staff. More information is collected about how staff are rewarded, employee retention programs, various benefits such as eldercare, childcare, flextime, tuition reimbursement and so on.

Participating companies then agree to have some of their staff surveyed. Topics of the survey included satisfaction with training and development programs, base salary, bonuses, health benefits, and work/life balance. They were also asked to rate morale in their IT departments and the importance of various benefits. Career growth opportunities and management's fair and equal treatment of employees were also polled.[14]

The number-one company on *Computerworld*'s list was Quicken Loans, an online mortgage lender. They were ranked fourth for retention, third for benefits, and have an annual training budget of $2,500 for each IT employee. Thirty-two percent of the company's IT managers are women.

What were some of the comments made by employees about this great company? Workers value their ability to take ownership of ideas and projects. They appreciate the flexible environment that helps them balance home and work. They also report enjoying the collaborative atmosphere. As one employee states, "We have a company culture that's very strong and rich and entrepreneurial. Culturally, people take ownership and have the ability to make an impact."[15]

Fostering Social Responsibility

Another list of great places to work is "Canada's Top 100 Employers" compiled annually by Mediacorp Canada Inc. and published in *Maclean's* magazine. They invite 6,000 of the fastest growing Canadian employers to complete an extensive application process. Approximately 1,000 companies completed the process. Organizations are graded in eight areas, including physical workplace, work and social atmosphere, and health, financial, and family benefits.

The company chosen in 2004 as the best place to work in Canada was VanCity Confidential, a Vancouver credit union. They describe this company as giving employees autonomy, good pay, and "smart perks." It also provides workers with fun and—because it is driven by being socially responsible—a clear conscience.

VanCity is Canada's largest credit union, with 41 branches in Vancouver, the Lower Mainland of British Columbia, and Victoria. Customers with Van-City Visa cards can donate the points they accumulate to charity. The company itself donates $1 million per year to a local non-profit chosen by its clients. In 2003, it gave out $5.2 million in community donations, which amounts to 13.5% of earnings. This compares with average donations of 1% of earnings by Canada's eight largest banks.

One of the issues some companies struggle with today is the strategy behind their philanthropic and social responsibility focus. Some organizations give employees increasing input into or control over how these activities are run; for example, giving employees company time to dedicate to causes they select. Other companies place more emphasis on corporate social responsibility that ties into their broader strategic vision—having a few specific causes that the company supports as a whole. While there is no data yet on which of these approaches is more effective, I suspect that organizations that have adopted a strategic cause that fits their mission and rallies its people around it are positioned for the greatest success.

The list of benefits and perks offered to VanCity employees include three weeks' vacation in the first year, plus an option to trade unused benefits for more days off; low-interest loans, mortgages and credit lines; tuition subsidies; and transit subsidies for Vancouver's light-rail transit system. Their head office has meditation and lactation rooms, an employee-run library and subsidized parking for those who carpool. They also pay the full cost of a flexible benefits plan. As a result of their reputation, they receive 12,000 applications per year.

The corporate culture is described as a big family. The company hosts numerous employee events that include "recognition nights," family picnics and winter skating, an annual gala and themed costume parties (one of which included the CEO dressed as Alice Cooper), as well as softball, dragon boat, and kayak teams.[16]

Top Leadership Style

INC. magazine each year selects the "*INC. 500*" companies, based on revenue growth over four years. The minimum revenue of participating companies in the base year is $500,000. Similar to the testing of emotional intelligence that I did with the Innovators Alliance group of CEOs, Keith McFarland tested 250 former and current leaders of Inc. 500 companies with the Test of Attentional and Interpersonal Style, or TAIS.[17] The TAIS has been used by the U.S. military, corporate leaders, and Olympic athletes. It measures three basic building blocks: leadership, emotional control, and performance under pressure.

What did McFarland find in his testing of these entrepreneurial leaders? Are they risk takers? Well, they score quite high—in the 83rd percentile—in "performance under pressure." McFarland concludes that fast-growth CEOs actually enjoy facing adversity, but more of them also manage and mitigate their risk.

One would expect these CEOs to be control freaks. According to McFarland these CEOs scored quite high—91st percentile—in their need to control things. This is similar to other chief executives. But where they scored higher than other CEOs is in "focus over time"—the willingness to make sacrifices in order to achieve a goal. Here they are more similar to military commanders and athletes than with other business leaders.

It's often assumed that entrepreneurial leaders are poor at setting and executing strategy. On the TAIS this is assessed through attentional style, which looks at how one sees the world, processes information, and comes up with new ideas and solutions to problems. Scoring high in "awareness" means that you read people well and respond based on intuition. Being high in "analysis" means that you see the world as a series of problems to be solved, and think strategically. People who are high in "action" focus will narrow in on getting things done.

While you would expect these CEOs to fall in the "action" category, they are, in fact, mainly "analytical," falling in the 92nd percentile in this area. They also score higher than the normative sample of CEOs in "awareness" and higher than most people on decision-making speed.

One common perception of leaders in fast-growing companies is that they are prone to intimidating others to push the company forward. Are these fast-growth CEOs bullies? According to McFarland they score higher than 82% of the population in their ability to express support and encouragement—higher than any other group, with the exception of high-performing salespeople.[18]

Best-Managed Companies

Another awards program is Canada's 50 Best Managed Companies sponsored by Deloitte and Touche LLP, CIBC Commercial Banking, the *National Post*, and the Queen's University School of Business. To be considered for this program, a company's revenues must be greater than $10 million (Cdn), it must show superior results over the previous three years (e.g., profitability, growth), and it must be a Canadian-owned private or public company. After an initial screening, candidates are selected for a much more detailed assessment through a specially selected screening panel.

One of the winning companies of this award, National Leasing based in Winnipeg, Manitoba, focuses on attracting the best talent to build an exceptional culture. However, one of the unusual aspects of this mission is that new employees are encouraged to build their resumes for their next job, starting from their initial orientation. Their welcome message to new recruits is "Welcome aboard. Be prepared to leave."

The CEO, Nick Logan, believes that his employees want challenges and progress in their careers. Once they stop seeing progress at National Leasing, he believes it's time to start thinking of taking their skills elsewhere. On the other hand, he feels the company also has a responsibility to offer employees the opportunity for challenges. He strives to make their working lives fulfilling and full of opportunities for growth. While he admits he wants his employees to stay, he also wants them to be challenged and to be there because they really want to be there. He states that his goal is to make his employees a headhunter's dream.[19]

Logan is a strong believer in corporate culture and he believes that most companies and business academics have neglected the importance of an organization's culture. He states:

> Research makes it clear that even during an economic downturn, companies with strong adaptive cultures perform significantly better, financially, than those with a weak or poorly defined culture.
>
> Culture drives the organization and its actions. It's akin to the operating system of the organization. It guides how employees think, act, and feel. It is dynamic and fluid, and never static. A culture may be effective at one time under a given set of circumstances and ineffective at another time. There is no generically "good" culture.[20]

Focus Means Profitability

"The Profit 100: Canada's Fastest Growing Companies" is a program developed by the Canadian magazine called *Profit*. My company, Multi-Health Systems, is a three-time winner of the Profit 100 list of companies. This list is compiled after hundreds of companies provide financial data and are ranked by five-year revenue growth. Qualifying companies' revenue is verified through financial statements and the chief executive officers are interviewed by *Profit*.[21]

Only one entrepreneur has made the *Profit* 100 list twice, while heading up two different companies. That CEO is Don Schafer, who most recently got on the list with his company, Brahma Compression Ltd. Schafer has some interesting advice on management style: "I'm a huge believer in surrounding myself with good people and then letting those individuals do their jobs. I have the right people in place, have the controls and systems that we need to have, set very detailed targets or budgets for everybody and then let them go and do their jobs."[22]

According to Schafer the single most important factor in making any good company successful is: "Staying focused on what your business model is. It takes a tremendous amount of discipline to do that. We challenge ourselves weekly not to step out of the box, instead staying focused on what our business plan says and what our business model is."[23]

Getting a Return on Your Survey Investment: A Case Study

Perhaps the most efficient, honest, and cost-effective way to get at an organization's culture is through surveying employees. Why would you want to understand an organization's culture? Senior leaders are always interested in improving performance. Many leaders know that a benchmark of where people are at is a good starting point. Consultants who work with organizations need a quick way to get to know the organization in order to diagnose any problems.

I will present an example of a small company where an organizational survey was helpful in understanding their current status and then implementing a change process. The company had the assistance of a consultant whom I'll call Gail. Gail implemented the initial survey, and the follow-up survey about a year after the interventions began.

The company, a software developer, was interested in measuring the commitment and motivation of its staff and management and its readiness for anticipated growth over the next couple of years. The leadership was concerned about the engagement of their employees.

The makeup of the employees who completed the survey is presented in Figure 14:1. As can be seen, the breakdown was 6% senior managers, 15% supervisor/managers and 79% line staff.

Figure 14:1
Staff Composition of Software Company

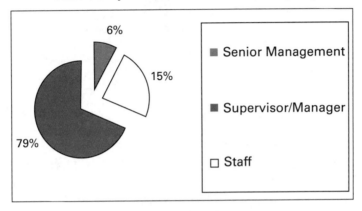

Reprinted with permission of Multi-Health Systems Inc (2006).

The data was also broken down by length of service as seen in Figure 14:2. As you can see, nearly one-third of the company had been there for a year or less. Just over 10% of employees had been there for more than 10 years. Seventy-two percent of the employees had been there for five years or less.

Figure 14:2
Employee Length of Service

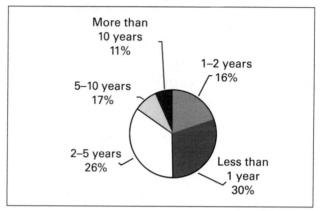

Reprinted with permission of Multi-Health Systems Inc. (2006)

Initial Benchmarking

In Figure 14:3, you can see the results of the initial administration of the Benchmark of Organizational Emotional Intelligence (BOEI). The area of greatest strength for this organization is its work/life balance. Employees report a higher-than-average level of satisfaction in this area. This organization helps reduce employee stress by having a fair degree of flexibility on work times. Employees can take time when needed to deal with child, parent, or personal needs. There's also flexibility for employees in their choice of holidays and days off.

The second highest area of strength for this company is in stress management. The atmosphere in this organization is fairly laid back. People also have the tools and resources they need to do their work. Timelines are realistic and employees do not feel under any excessive stress or pressure from work.

Third, this company is strong in co-worker relationships. That means that people in the organization get along, trust each other, and can depend on one another for support. Indications are that the teams in this company work well together. High scores in this area point to employees having trust in each other, good morale, complementary skills, group pride, ability to communicate, and good productivity.

On the other hand, there were several scales that were lower for this organization. The lowest area was in organizational courage and adaptability. Employees felt that this organization does not systematically solve problems. Rather, it lets problem issues fester and refuses to take the action required to get past them. Employees generally felt that the organization was too slow in making decisions. As a small company with several layers of management, decisions were going through too many checks and balances and the process was inefficient. Employees also felt the company failed to anticipate difficult decisions and prepare for them. Finally, the company was reported as slow in making needed changes. Organizational courage and adaptability problems are transformational in nature. That means they require some major organizational changes in order to deal with them.

Figure 14:3
Initial BOEI Profile of Software Development Company

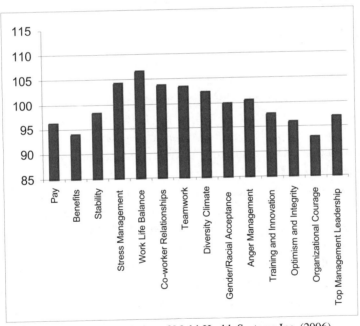

Used with permission of Multi-Health Systems Inc. (2006)

The second-lowest score for this organization was in the area of benefits. Employees reported feeling the benefit package of the company was inadequate. The package was reported as inflexible as it offered too little choice for employees.

Third, the category of optimism and integrity was reported as the next lowest area. When items in this scale were examined, it was found that employees were lower than expected in feeling the organization's positive atmosphere as energizing. Front-line staff responded 55% positively to this item. Supervisors and managers responded with only 33% in agreement and 33% neutral. Senior management, always the most positive, responded with 66% in agreement. Many employees also seemed to feel that the company did not have a strong winning attitude.

Finally, concerns about pay were identified. Employees felt their pay was not consistent with industry standards for their job. As well, their pay system did not seem to provide an incentive to work harder. They reported that the opportunity for pay increases were not acceptable.

The Analysis Stage

Gail reviewed the report and the many employee comments that were included with it. She knew how important it was to take action quickly once surveys such as this are administered. She met with the senior management team to review the results. Based on her experience with feeding back results to senior managers, she knew the best approach was to give them a sheet with a blank graph and all of the scales labeled. She then asked them to predict the scores for the organization. She had been in too many situations in which managers saw the results and immediately claimed that it was just as they expected. Often, that serves as an excuse for doing nothing about the findings.

Interestingly, the team was all over the map. The financial officer had identified pay and benefits as the main issues of concern. The human resource manager believed that training and innovation would be most problematic. The sales and marketing manager felt that co-worker relationships might be problematic due to some comments from some of his reports. The CEO had everything rated quite high, no real problems, except of course that everyone would want to be paid more. Well, as seen in Figure 14:3, they were all somewhat off. Asking them to predict the results definitely got their attention when Gail presented the feedback.

The CEO decided that a Town Hall meeting would be called for all employees. The initial feedback on the survey would be presented by Gail. At the meeting she presented an overview of the results. She described how the company overall compared to other companies, based on the data provided in the BOEI manual. One advantage of a standardized survey is that it allows you to compare results with other organizations.

She went on to describe a process that would unfold in order to deal with the results. Each employee would receive a personalized printout comparing their results to the organization as a whole, as well as to their own department. The survey was administered anonymously, but employees had the option of recording the certificate number that appeared at the end of their survey. It was their responsibility to write down or remember the certificate number in order to get their results, since nobody else would know it.

Employees were instructed to carefully review their personalized report. They would find, for example, that either they were in agreement with other employees on the scales, or they were in disagreement. Those who felt worse than most others about the company were encouraged to play a constructive role in making the organization better. For a few individuals, the results helped to confirm in their minds that the company was not the right place for them to be.

Several employees wanted to go over their reports individually with Gail. They found this quite useful in helping them understand how they fit in with others in the organization as well as giving them an opportunity to express their feelings about the company in more detail. Surveys like this provide an excellent opportunity for employees to be heard. At the same time it helps them validate their feelings against what others have reported. It's important to allow for this process of individual feedback to occur. The survey administrator needs to budget time and resources for this part of the process.

Next, Gail arranged to be at meetings set up by the manager of each department in the company. At those meetings the results of the company as a whole were compared to the results for the department. Areas of strengths and weaknesses were discussed. In some cases, Gail held meetings with employees in a department without the manager being present. This gave individuals with serious grievances an opportunity to be heard without fear of repercussions.

Interventions

Over the course of several months a number of initiatives were undertaken. The first and most immediate need that was attended to was the issue of pay. A task force was pulled together involving employees from throughout the company and the human resource manager. They surveyed various sources in the business community to determine equivalent pay scales for jobs relevant to those in the company. They also looked at various incentive plans and how they could apply to the organization.

Then, the company's benefits provider was called in to meet with the human resource manager and Gail. Based on comments from Gail's meetings with staff, a number of specific concerns were brought to the attention of the provider. Significant changes were requested in the benefits package that would make it more flexible.

As noted in the optimism and integrity area, the concerns were most notable among the supervisors and managers. Gail met with this group and discovered a number of issues that needed to be dealt with. The major concern had to do with the inexperience of most of those in management positions. The good news was that the company was promoting people from within. This gave confidence and hope to many front-line staff about future prospects with the company. However, supervisors and managers were not being well prepared for their new roles. Gail brought in an experienced management trainer she had worked with in the past, and arranged a customized management training program for these supervisors consisting of individual testing (with a 360-degree measure) and coaching provided.

Another area uncovered during this process had to do with training and innovation. There were a number of initiatives that were identified that the company could do to improve this area. One involved increased training sessions being conducted within the company. Another was increased funding available for employees to use for educational purposes. As well, managers were instructed to help employees put together career development plans.

Finally, Gail worked with the senior leadership team around issues that had to do with the seemingly slow nature of making decisions and dealing with change. A weekend retreat was arranged for the senior team where they would explore this among other issues. In addition, members of the senior team agreed to take a 360-degree rating measure. These results would be discussed by way of individual meetings at the retreat.

One of the issues that arose at the retreat was the CEO's insistence on being involved in what he considered all "major" decisions of the company. The CEO, a company founder, had difficulty letting go of responsibilities as the company grew and needed a more professional and corporate management style. There were clearly personal issues that had to be worked on with the CEO.

The retreat also helped the senior team become more cohesive and gave them a safe environment in which to air a number of their grievances. Some of the departments had worked more as "silos," with little contact and communication among them. Turf wars were not uncommon. The senior team was presented with the benefits of cross-functional teams and the importance of working towards organizational goals, which became more clearly defined.

None of these interventions was simple or one-shot events. The people in this organization were committed to making the necessary changes over time to put the company in a more secure position for growth. Some of the changes, which were transformational in nature, required significant modification of the organization.

Follow-up Results

Approximately a year and a half later, the BOEI was administered again. Figure 14:4 shows the results of the first and second administrations, plotted together.

Figure 14:4
BOEI Scores in 2004 and 2006

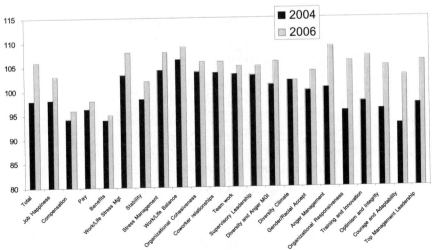

Used with permission of Multi-Health Systems Inc. (2006)

You can see that some significant changes in the organization occurred. First of all, the total score of the BOEI was significantly aincreased in the 2006 administration. The specific areas that showed significant change were job happiness and organizational responsiveness. The areas of organizational responsiveness that were significantly increased were training and innovation, optimism and integrity, courage and adaptability, and top management leadership.

The highest score was still in the area of work/life balance. Employees still report feeling good about their workloads, and the fact that their job demands did not significantly impact their personal or family life.

The second-highest area is now diversity and anger management. This indicates that behaviors in the organization are not motivated by anger. This scale, when low, acts as a warning sign of tension and bad feelings in the organization.

Third, stress management was high. This indicates, as before, that people have the tools and resources they need and project timelines are realistic. Employees are not experiencing significant work stress.

There are a number of other interesting results. Teamwork has increased over the previous survey. People reported feeling they were supported by and could rely on co-workers. There were significant differences in other areas as well. Employees reported higher satisfaction with learning and innovation, with 87% now agreeing it is encouraged. Now, 62% of employees agree that the company has a well-developed career path program.

Changes were noted in optimism and integrity. Seventy-three percent of employees now agree that the organization's positive atmosphere is energizing. Ninety-four percent of employees now agree that the company takes seriously the comments and needs of customers and 91% of employees agree the organization has a winning attitude. Finally, 63% reports that the company is at or near the top of their industry.

This time around, benefits ranked the lowest on the survey. Unfortunately, the benefits provider was slow to come up with and begin the implementation of a revised benefit package. This area, as a result of the second survey, rose up to higher priority among the senior leaders. As well, the restructuring of the pay system had not yet been fully implemented by the time of the second survey. The increases in the other areas of the BOEI at least provide comfort that employees trust that the process is proceeding in good faith.

The areas that achieved statistically significant higher scores in the second survey were job happiness, compensation, work/life balance and stability, organizational cohesiveness (teamwork), and organizational responsiveness (training and innovation, optimism and integrity, courage and adaptability, and top leadership). This indicates that Gail's work led to important changes in the organization that were felt by employees throughout the company.

In addition, employees were asked on the survey to suggest what areas were most important for the future success of the company and what areas were most in need of improvement. Areas important for success that were indicated by employees included:

- Professional development and teamwork
- Retaining talent
- Customer satisfaction and loyalty
- Marketing and web initiatives
- Product innovation and adaptability
- Communication among departments
- Focus and vision

Areas that staff reported as needing improvement included:

- Communication, especially of vision
- Focus
- Career path, employee recognition
- Pay, bonus structure and incentives
- Web presence
- Negative thinking

An Ongoing Process

A number of action steps were taken as a result of the second survey. First, once again, results were to be shared with staff, first in a Town Hall meeting, then in each of the departments. The purpose would be to validate the feedback and get a deeper understanding of the results from the employees. Then action plans would be developed for each of the specific areas of improvement. Increased communication processes would be developed. Finally, employee involvement in all of these initiatives would be encouraged.

Return on Emotion

What were the bottom-line effects of these interventions? While creating a better workplace has its benefits, it's fair to ask about any additional benefits. At the time of the second survey company sales had increased by approximately 20%. The senior team felt that the financial success had some direct links to changes made in the organization.

Just as it is possible to measure and increase one's individual emotional intelligence, it is possible to measure and increase the emotional intelligence of a company or organization. The financial investment in a survey is relatively small compared to the investment required to act upon the results, which in turn can be minuscule compared to the cost of not doing anything. Is your organization losing time and money by funneling funds into the wrong perks? Benchmarking organizational emotional intelligence can be a powerful first step in fostering a top organization.

So what can we conclude about great workplaces? I've presented seven keys and a rationale for why I believe that paying attention to these keys can positively impact the bottom line of any organization. People are the key to success in today's workplace. Measuring, intervening, and then measuring again will help your organization along the path to greatness. I believe that few organizations systematically follow that path today. By learning from today's great workplaces we can develop our own strategic path to greatness for companies, employees, clients, and society. I look forward to many more workplaces achieving greatness in the future.

Reference Notes

Introduction

1. S. J. Stein and H. E. Book, *The EQ Edge: Emotional Intelligence and Your Success*. Toronto: Wiley/Jossey-Bass, 2006.
2. Jim Collins, *Good to Great: Why some companies make the leap… and others don't*. New York: HarperCollins, 2001.
3. S. J. Stein, *The Benchmark of Organizational Emotional Intelligence Technical Manual*. Toronto: Multi-Health Systems Inc., 2005.

Chapter 1: Changes in Society and Their Impact on Work

1. When Work Works. Families and Work Institute, http://familiesand work.org/3w/
2. Ibid.
3. Amy Harmon, "On the Office PC, Bosses Opt for All Work, and No Play." *New York Times*, Sept. 22, 1997, pp. A1 and C11.
4. "Internet Use Tops Workplace Time-Wasting Tasks," SmartPros. Dulles, VA, and Needham, MA, Jul. 13, 2005, http://accounting smartpros.com/x48929.xml

5. Ibid.
6. For a more complete discussion, see G. P. Latham and M. Budworth, "The study of work motivation in the 20th century," in L. Koppes (Ed.), *The History of Industrial and Organizational Psychology.* Hillside, NJ: Laurence Erlbaum Associates, 2006.
7. H. Munsterberg, *Psychology of Industrial Efficiency.* Boston & New York: Houghton Mifflin, 1913.
8. S. P. Robbins and N. Langton, *Organizational Behavior, Concepts, Controversies, Applications.* Scarborough, ON: Prentice Hall, 1999.
9. C. C. Pinder, *Work Motivation: Theory, Issues, and Applications.* Glenview: Scott, Forseman and Co., 1997: p. 71. See also G. P. Latham, T. R. Mitchell, and D. L. Dorset, "The importance of participative goal setting and anticipated rewards on goal difficulty and job performance," *Journal of Applied Psychology* 63, 1978: pp. 163-171; as well as G. P. Latham, M. Erez, and E. A. Locke, "Resolving scientific disputes by the joint design of crucial experiments by the antagonists: Application of the Erez-Latham dispute regarding participation in goal setting," *Journal of Applied Psychology Monograph* 73, 1988: pp. 753-772; and C. Lee and P. C. Earley, "Comparative peer evaluations of organizational behavior theories," *Organizational Development Journal* 10, 1992: pp. 37-42.
10. Adapted from "Excelling as a first time manager or supervisor," SkillPath Seminars, 1997.
11. L. Duxbury, presentation at the Wisdom Exchange, Innovators Alliance, Toronto, May 23, 2006.
12. D. Sirota, L. A. Mischkind, and M. I. Meltzer, *The Enthusiastic Employee: How companies profit by giving workers what they want.* Upper Saddle River, NJ: Wharton School Publishing, 2005.
13. Ibid.

Chapter 2: What Keeps CEOs Up at Night?

1. R. Bar-On, *Bar-On Emotional Quotient Inventory (EQ-i®) Technical Manual.* Toronto: Multi-Health Systems Inc., 1997.
2. Patricia Buhler, "Managing in the new millennium: Building a high-performance organization: Ten tips for managers." *Supervision,* June 2002.

3. "Managing People." Audit Commission, Audit Commission Publications. www.audit-commission.gov.uk

4. Dan Tomas, "Staff retention and talent management are top HR challenges for 2006." Personneltoday.com, Mar. 21, 2006.

5. "Report of the Business NZ Skills and Training Survey," Business NZ and Industry and the Industry Training Federation of New Zealand for the Department of Labour, June 2003.

6. Lee Iacocca, "Henry Ford." *Time* (*Time 100*) 153(23), Dec. 7, 1998.

7. Bill Gates, http://www.microsoft.com/billgates/speeches/

8. David Gelertner, "Bill Gates." *Time* (*Time 100*) 153(23), Dec. 7, 1998.

9. Omar El Akkad, "Boot Camp teaches lesson in managing change." *Globe and Mail*, Update, May 8, 2006. http://www.theglobeandmail.com/servlet/story/RTGAM.20060508.gtcoculture08/BNStory/Business/

10. Ibid.

11. Accenture and the Conference Board: The CEO Challenge Survey, http://www.accenture.com/Global/Research_and_Insights/By_Role/CEO/AccentureSurvery.htm

12. Ibid.

13. The Leading CEOs: Technology Fast 500 Asia Pacific 2004 CEO Survey, Deloitte, Touche, Tohmatsu, Dec. 2004, www.deloitte.com

14. Flying High: 2006 Global Survey of CEOs in the Deloitte Technology Fast 500. Deloitte, Touche, Tohmatsu, 2006.

15. Ibid, p. 5.

16. Ibid, p. 3.

17. Website, The Body Shop, www.thebodyshopinternational.com/web/tbsgl/about_where.jsp#seventies

18. Website, Timberland, www.timberland.com/corp/index.jsp?clickid=topnav_corp_txt

Chapter 3: What Do We *Really* Know About Job Satisfaction and Productivity?

1. H. M. Parsons, "What happened at Hawthorne?" *Science* 183, 1974: pp. 922-932.

2. Gina Kolata, "Scientific Myths that Are Too Good to Die," *New York*

Times, Dec. 6, 1998, http://query.nytimes.com/gst/fullpage.html?sec =health&res=9B06E1DB1E3BF935A35751C1A96E958260

3. Elton Mayo, *The Human Problems of an Industrialised Civilisation.* New York: MacMillan, 1933, ch. 3.

4. A. H. Brayfield and W. H. Crockett, "Employee attitudes and employee performance." *Psychological Bulletin* 52, 1955: pp. 396-424.

5. See T. A. Judge, C. J. Thoresen, J. E. Bono, and G. K. Patton, "The job satisfaction-job performance relationship: A qualitative and quantitative review." *Psychological Bulletin* 127(3), 2001: pp. 376-407.

6. Ibid.

7. Keith H. Hammonds, "How Google Grows...and Grows...and Grows." *Fast Company*, Mar. 2003, p. 74.

8. Ibid.

9. Ibid.

10. Ibid.

11. Julie Mack, "Success breeds more success: Black girls at K-Central greatly improve academic performance." *Kalamazoo Gazette*, May 28, 2006.

12. Ibid.

13. Judge, Thoresen, Bono, and Patton, p. 22.

14. Melanie Johnson, "In Focus 1: Mood Swings and Job Performance." *Small Business Monthly,* July 2004, http://www.kcsmallbiz.com/july-2004/in-focus-1-mood-swings-and-job-performance.html

15. "Mood Fluctuations Can Affect Work." *USA Today* magazine (Published by the Society for the Advancement of Education), April 2000.

16. Cynthia D. Fisher, "Mood and emotions while working: missing pieces of job satisfaction?" *Journal of Organizational Behavior* 21, 2000: pp. 185-202.

Chapter 4: Emotional Intelligence and Organizational Culture: A New Relationship

1. Daniel Goleman, *Emotional Intelligence: Why It Can Matter More than IQ.* New York: Bantam, 1995.

2. R. Bar-On, *Bar-On Emotional Quotient Inventory (EQ-i®) Technical Manual.* Toronto: Multi-Health Systems Inc., 1997.

3. P. Salovey and J. D. Mayer, "Emotional Intelligence." *Imagination, Cognition and Personality* 9, 1990: pp. 185-211.

4. J. D. Mayer, P. Salovey, and D. Caruso, *Mayer-Salovey-Caruso Emotional Intelligence Test (MSCEIT) User's Manual.* Toronto: Multi-Health Systems Inc., 2002.

5. R. Bar-On, *The Development of a Concept of Psychological Well-Being,* draft copy of an unpublished doctoral dissertation presented in 1985 (Rhodes University, South Africa, 1988). See also R. Bar-On, *The Development of a Concept and Test of Emotional Intelligence,* unpublished manuscript, 1992 (published as part of the *Bar-On Emotional Quotient Inventory (EQ-i®) Technical Manual,* Toronto: Multi-Health Systems Inc., 1997).

6. Bar-On, *Bar-On Emotional Quotient Inventory (EQ-i®) Technical Manual.*

7. S. J. Stein, and H. E. Book, *The EQ Edge: Emotional Intelligence and Your Success.* Toronto: Wiley/Jossey-Bass, 2006.

8. H. Book, "One Big Happy Family: The Emotionally Intelligent Organization." *Ivey Business Journal*, Sept./Oct. 2000, pp. 44-47. http://www.iveybusinessjournal.com/article.asp?intArticle_ID=259

9. T. E. Deal and A. Kennedy, *Corporate Cultures: The Rites and Rituals of Corporate Life.* New York: Perseus Books, 1982.

10. Ibid, p. 4.

11. Ibid, p. 5.

12. Zhang Zhen, Ma Li, and Ma Wenjing, "The relationship between organizational climate and employee involvement: An empirical study on companies in the Chinese context." *Acta Psychologica Sinica* 34(3), May 2002: pp. 312-318.

Chapter 5: Selecting the Right People: Round Pegs in Round Holes

1. Jim Collins, *Good to Great: Why some companies make the leap... and others don't.* New York: HarperCollins, 2001.

2. Lynn A. McFarland, Anne Marie Ryan, Joshua M. Sacco, and S. David Kriska, "Examination of Structured Interview Ratings Across Time: The Effects of Applicant Race, Rater Race, and Panel Composition." *Journal of Management* 30(4), 2004: pp. 435-452.

3. Caren B. Goldberg, "Relational Demography and Similarity-Attraction in Interview Assessments and Subsequent Offer Decisions: Are We Missing Something?" *Group & Organization Management* 30(6), Dec. 2005: pp. 597-624.

4. Joey George and Kent Marett, "The Truth About Lies." *SHRM* magazine, Society for Human Resource Management Online. May 2004, Vol. 49, No. 5

5. Limiting employment reference risks, CCH Business Owner's Toolkit, 2006, http://www.toolkit.cch.com/text/P05_8670.asp

6. The Standards for Educational and Psychological Testing, developed jointly by: American Educational Research Association (AERA), American Psychological Association (APA), and National Council on Measurement in Education (NCME). Washington, DC: American Psychological Association, 1999.

7. Society for Industrial Organizational Psychology (SIOP) web page, http://www.siop.org/workplace/employment%20testing/employment_testing_toc.aspx

8. Richard K. Wagner, "Intelligence, training, and employment." *American Psychologist* 52(10), Oct. 1997: pp. 1059-1069. This review article points out that the average observed validity coefficient or correlation between cognitive ability test scores and job performance is between .20 and .30, which amounts to between 4% and 9% of the variance. That leaves somewhere between 91% to 96% of job performance due to other factors.

9. See R. Bar-On, *Bar-On Emotional Quotient Inventory Technical Manual.* Toronto: Multi-Health Systems Inc., 1997. D. Goleman, *Working with Emotional Intelligence.* New York: Bantam Books, 1998. S. J. Stein and H. E. Book, *The EQ Edge: Emotional Intelligence and Your Success*, 2006.

10. J. D. Mayer, P. Salovey, and D. Caruso, *Mayer-Salovey-Caruso Emotional Intelligence Test (MSCEIT) User's Manual.* Toronto: Multi-Health Systems Inc., 2002.

Chapter 6: Taking the Organization's Temperature

1. Gary G. Peacock, "Profiting through personality? It's true! Decatur Memorial Hospital is transforming its organizational culture to drive high performance and quality," Healthcare Financial Management, May 2005.

2. A. C. Higgs and S. D. Ashworth, "Organizational surveys: Tools for assessment and research," in A. I. Kraut (Ed.), *Organizational surveys: Tools for assessment and change*. San Francisco, CA: Jossey-Bass, 1996, pp. 19-40.

3. Charlotte Garvey, "Connecting the organizational pulse to the bottom line: employee survey results get morphed into actionable items in business goals," *HR Magazine*, June, 2004 http://www.findarticles.com/p/articles/mi_m3495/is_6_49/ai_n6099201

4. Lisa L. Roberts, Lee J. Konczak, and Therese Hoff Macan, "Effects of Data Collection Method on Organizational Climate Survey Results." *Applied H.R.M. Research* 9(1), 2004: pp. 13-26.

5. Garvey.

6. Ibid.

7. Ibid.

8. S. J. Stein and MHS Staff, *Benchmark of Organizational Emotional Intelligence (BOEI™) Technical Manual*. Toronto: Multi-Health Systems Inc, 2005.

9. Marcia Hughes, personal communication.

Chapter 7: Job Happiness: Don't Worry, Be Happy

1. Scott Edward Schneider, "Organizational commitment, job satisfaction and job characteristics of managers: Examining the relationships across selected demographic variables." *Dissertation Abstracts International Section A: Humanities and Social Sciences*, 64(4-A), 2003: p. 1331.

2. Jane Hager Paradowski, "Positive affectivity, negative affectivity, and job satisfaction: A meta-analysis." *Dissertation Abstracts International: Section B: Sciences and Engineering*, 61(12-B), 2001: p. 6749.

3. Benjamin Schneider, Paul J. Hanges, D. Brent Smith, and Amy Nicole Salvaggio, "Which comes first: Employee attitudes or organizational

financial and market performance?" *Journal of Applied Psychology*, 88(5), Oct. 2003: pp. 836-851.

4. Daniel R. Denison, *Corporate Culture and Organizational Effectiveness*. Oxford, England: John Wiley & Sons, 1990: p. xvii.

5. See C. Ostroff, "The relationship between satisfaction, attitudes, and performance: An organizational level analysis," *Journal of Applied Psychology* 77, 1992: pp. 963-974; and A. M. Ryan, M. J. Schmitt and R. Johnson, "Attitudes and effectiveness: Examining relations at an organizational level," *Personnel Psychology* 49, 1996: pp. 853-882.

6. Schneider et al, p. 849.

7. Jane von Bergen, "Happiness equals productivity: That's the prevailing wisdom at Analytical Graphics Inc. in Exton, named the top small U.S. company to work for." *Philadelphia Inquirer*, July 7, 2004.

8. J. A. Ritter and R. Anker, "Good jobs, bad jobs: Workers' evaluations in five countries." *International Labour Review* 141 (4), (2002): pp. 331-358.

9. Peter Cappelli and Monika Hamori, "The New Steps to Career Advancement." Harvard Business School's *Working Knowledge* (website), Apr. 4, 2005. Excerpted with permission from "The New Road to the Top," *Harvard Business Review* 83(1), Jan. 2005.

10. Linda Hill, "How New Managers Become Great Managers." Harvard Business School's *Working Knowledge* (website), Aug. 18, 2003.

11. "Career advancement: Build a plan," from mayoclinic.com. Special to CNN, Oct. 15, 2004.

12. "Career advancement: Build a plan that limits stress," from mayoclinic.com, October 16, 2006: http://www.mayoclinic.com/health/stress/WL00052

13. Mary Brandel, "Special Report: 100 Best places to work in IT 2006." *Computerworld*, June 19, 2006.

Chapter 8: Compensation: Show Me the Money

1. Sirota, "Gap Between Management's and Non-Management's Satisfaction with Their Pay Grows by 45%," media release, http://www.sirota.com/pressrelease/PAYSATISFACTIONJOBSECURITY927.pdf

2. JobQuality.ca is managed by the Work Network of Canadian Policy Research Networks (www.cprn.org, ©2006 Canadian Policy Research Networks), http://jobquality.ca/indicator_e/pay004.stm

3. Steven Currall, Annette Towler, Timothy Judge, and Laura Kohn, "Want a successful company? Pay your employees well." Research@ Rice, Oct. 15, 2005.

4. Kathryn Bartol, "Pay Levels and Pay Raises," Research@Smith 6(3), Fall 2005. This research has also been published as "Is it pay levels or pay rises that matter to fairness and turnover?" by Amanuel G. Tekleab, Kathryn M. Bartol, and Wei Liu in *Journal of Organizational Behavior* 26(8), Dec. 2005: pp. 899-921.

5. Sunny C. L. Fong and Margaret A. Shaffer, "The Dimensionality and Determinants of Pay Satisfaction: A Cross-Cultural Investigation of a Firm's Group Incentive Plan." Paper presented at the Micro-Organizational Behavior and Human Resources Management Track of the Competitive Paper Sessions of AIB 2001 Annual Meeting.

6. Ibid.

7. Bartol et al.

8. Hay Group/MLA 2005 Compensation and Benefits Survey. http://www.mlanet.org/publications/hay_mla_05ss.html#1

9. Bartol et al.

10. JobQuality.ca.

11. Frederick P. Morgeson, Michael A. Campion, and Carl P. Maertz, "Understanding pay satisfaction: The limits of a compensation system implementation." *Journal of Business and Psychology* 16(1), Fall 2001: pp. 133-149.

12. Gordon D. A. Brown, Jonathan Gardner, Andrew Oswald, and Jing Qian, "Rank Dependence in Pay Satisfaction." Paper presented at the Warwick-Brookings conference in Washington, D.C., June 5 and 6, 2003.

13. Jeff Grabmeier, "Link Between Worker Pay and Satisfaction Not Simple, Study Shows," *Research News*, Ohio State University http://researchnews.osu.edu/archive/workpay.htm.

14. Ibid.

15. Ibid.

16. Mary Jo Ducharme and Parbudyal Singh, "Exploring the Links Between Performance Appraisals and Pay Satisfaction," *Compensation & Benefits Review* 37(5), 2005: pp. 46-52.

17. Hay Group/MLA (2005).

18. John M. Ivancevich, "The performance to satisfaction relationship: A causal analysis of stimulating and nonstimulating jobs." *Organizational Behavior and Human Performance* 22(3), Dec. 1978: pp. 350-365. See also John M. Ivancevich, "High and low task-simulation jobs: A causal analysis of performance-satisfaction relationships." *Academy of Management Journal* 22, 1979: pp. 206-232.

19. Nico W. Van Yperen, "The perceived profile of goal orientation within firms: Differences between employees working for successful and unsuccessful firms employing either performance-based pay or job-based pay." *European Journal of Work and Organizational Psychology* 12(3), Sept. 2003: pp. 229-243.

20. Alexander D. Stajkovic and Fred Luthans, "Differential effects of incentive motivators on work performance." *Academy of Management Journal* 44(3), 2001: pp. 580-590.

21. Christopher M. Lowery, N. A. Beadles II, and Thomas J. Krilowicz, "Note on the relationships among job satisfaction, organizational commitment, and organizational citizenship behavior." *Psychological Reports* 91(2), Oct. 2002: pp. 607-617.

22. Sridhar N.Ramaswami and Jagdip Singh, "Antecedents and consequences of merit pay fairness for industrial salespeople." *Journal of Marketing* 67(4), Oct. 2003: pp. 46-66.

23. Jerald Greenberg, "Creating unfairness by mandating fair procedures: The hidden hazards of a pay-for-performance plan." *Human Resource Management Review* 13(1), Spring 2003: pp. 41-57.

24. Neil M. Ford, Orville C. Walker and Gilbert A. Churchill, "Differences in the attractiveness of alternative rewards among industrial salespeople: Additional evidence." *Journal of Business Research* 13(2), Apr. 1985: pp. 123-138.

25. Lawrence B. Chonko, John F. Tanner and William Weeks, "Selling and sales management in action: reward preferences of salespeople." *Journal of Personal Selling and Sales Management* 12(3), 1992: pp. 67-75.

26. Ibid.
27. Lawrence B. Chonko, "Pay satisfaction and sales force turnover: the impact of different facets of pay on pay satisfaction and its implications for sales force management." *Journal of Managerial Issues:* Summer, 1996 issue.
28. Jerald Greenberg, "Creating unfairness by mandating fair procedures: The hidden hazards of a pay-for-performance plan." *Human Resource Management Review* 13(1), 2003: pp. 41-57
29. E. E. Jones and K. E. Davis, "From acts to dispositions: the attribution process in social psychology," in L. Berkowitz (Ed.), *Advances in Experimental Social Psychology* (vol. 2). New York: Academic Press, 1965: pp. 219-266.
30. Chonko.
31. S. P. Robbins and N. Langton, *Organizational Behaviour: Concepts, Controversies, Applications.* Scarborough, ON: Prentice Hall, 1999.
32. Simone Kauffeld, Eva Jonas, and Dieter Frey, "Effects of a flexible work-time design on employee- and company-related aims." *European Journal of Work and Organizational Psychology* 13(1), Mar. 2004: pp. 79-100.
33. Natalie J. Allen and John P. Meyer, "The measurement and antecedents of affective, continuance and normative commitment to the organization." *Journal of Occupational Psychology* 63(1), Mar. 1990: pp. 1-18. See also M. P. Micheli and M. C. Lane, "Antecedents of pay satisfaction: A review and extension" in K. Rowland and G. Ferris (Eds.), *Research in personnel and human resource management* (vol. 9). Greenwich, CT: JAI Press, 1991.
34. Robbins and Langton.
35. E. E. Lawler, "Human resource productivity in the 80s." *New Management* 1, 1983: pp. 46-49.
36. Barton L. Weathington and Lois E. Tetrick, "Compensation or right: An analysis of employee 'fringe' benefit perception." *Employee Responsibilities and Rights Journal* 12(3), Sept. 2000: pp. 141-162.
37. B. Gros, "Communication is king when it comes to employees valuing remuneration." *Canadian HR Reporter* 17, 2004: p. 19.
38. Expedia.com surveys conducted by Harris Interactive and Ipsos-Reid, 2006.

39. salary.com, "New Salary.com Survey Finds Growing Number of Workers Value Personal Time Over Money," http://www.salary.com/aboutcompany/layoutscripts/abcl_display.asp?tab=abc&cat=Cat27&ser=Ser341&part=Par513, 2005.

Chapter 9: Work/Life Stress Management: I've Been Workin' Overtime

1. Adapted from Ron Verzuh, "It's time to declare Workplace Freedom Day," http://cupe.ca/WorkloadStories/4073, Feb. 7, 2001.
2. Christina Maslach and Michael P. Leiter, "Teacher burnout: A research agenda," in Roland Vandenberghe and Michael A. Huberman (Eds), *Understanding and Preventing Teacher Burnout: A Sourcebook of International Research and Practice*. Cambridge: Cambridge University Press, 1999: pp. 295-303.
3. Canadian Policy Research Networks, JobQuality.ca, http://www.jobquality.ca/indicator_e/dem001.stm, 2006.
4. J. T. Bond, E. Galinsky, and J. E. Swanberg, "The 1997 national study of the changing workforce." New York: Families and Work Institute, 1998.
5. Ibid.
6. Diane F. Halpern, "Psychology at the Intersection of Work and Family: Recommendations for Employers, Working Families, and Policymakers." *American Psychologist* 60(5), Jul.-Aug. 2005: pp. 397-409. See also Diane F. Halpern, "How time-flexible work policies can reduce stress, improve health, and save money." *Stress and Health: Journal of the International Society for the Investigation of Stress* 21(3), Aug. 2005: pp. 157-168.
7. E. Galinsky, J. T. Bond, S. S. Kim, L. Backon, E. Brownfield, and K. Sakai, "Overwork in America: When the way we work becomes too much." New York: Families and Work Institute, 2005.
8. American Institute for Stress website http://www.stress.org/job.htm, 2005.
9. Dirk Enzmann, Wilmar B. Schaufeli, Peter Janssen, and Alfred Rozeman, "Dimensionality and validity of the Burnout Measure." *Journal of Occupational and Organizational Psychology* 71(4), Dec. 1998:

pp. 331-351. See also Joan E. Van Horn, Wilmar B. Schaufeli, and Dirk Enzmann, "Teacher burnout and lack of reciprocity." *Journal of Applied Social Psychology* 29(1), Jan. 1999: pp. 91-108.

10. Reported in Boston College Center for Work and Family, Executive Briefing Series http://www.bc.edu/centers/cwf/news/ See also E. Galinsky et al., "Overwork in America."

11. Canadian Union of Public Employees, Workload and Patient Care Survey: Highlights, May 8, 2001, http://cupe.ca/Workload Surveys/4091

12. Wendy MacDonald, "The impact of job demands and workload on stress and fatigue," *Australian Psychologist* 38(2), 2003: pp. 102-117.

13. Verzuh.

14. Reported in the Los Angeles Times, Sept. 8, 2006. Article appears in October issue of American Heart Association journal, Hypertension.

15. Verzuh.

16. D. Elisburg, "Workplace stress: legal developments, economic pressures, and violence," in J. F. Burton (Ed.), *1995 Workers' Compensation Year Book*. Horsham, PA: LRP Publications, 1995: pp. 1217-I222.

17. Verzuh.

18. Ibid.

19. E. Galinsky, S. S. Kim, and J. T. Bond, "Feeling overworked: When work becomes too much," New York: Families and Work Institute, 2001. www.familiesandwork.org

20. Reported in Boston College Center for Work and Family, Executive Briefing Series, WFD Consulting, 2005.

21. Galinsky et al., "Overwork in America."

22. Reported in Boston College Center for Work and Family, Executive Briefing Series.

23. "Stress at work," National Institute for Occupational Safety and Health (NIOSH), Department of Health and Human Services, Publication No. 99-101. www.cdc.gov/niosh

24. Northwestern National Life Insurance Company (now ReliaStar Financial Corporation), "Employee burnout: America's newest epidemic." Minneapolis, MN: Northwestern National Life Insurance Company, 1991.

25. "Labor day survey: state of workers. Princeton, NJ: Princeton Survey Research Associates, 1997.

26. St. Paul Fire and Marine Insurance Company, "American workers under pressure: Technical Report." St. Paul, MN: St. Paul Fire and Marine Insurance Company, 1992.

27. L. R. Murphy and S. L. Sauter, "The USA perspective: Current issues and trends in the management of work stress." *Australian Psychologist* 38(2), Jul. 2003: pp. 151-157.

28. T. Raymond and Blake E. Ashforth, "A meta-analytic examination of the correlates of the three dimensions of job burnout." *Journal of Applied Psychology* 81(2), 1996: pp. 123-133.

29. R. Cropanzana, D. Rupp, and Z. S. Byrne, "The relationship of emotional exhaustion to work attitudes, job performance, and organizational citizenship behaviors." *Journal of Applied Psychology* 88(1), 2003: pp. 160-169.

30. Oi-ling Siu, "Job stress and job performance among employees in Hong Kong: The role of Chinese work values and organizational commitment." *International Journal of Psychology* 38(6), 2003: pp. 337-347.

31. Oi-ling Siu, Chang-Qin Lu, and K. H. C. Cheng, "Job stress and work well-being in Hong Kong and Beijing: The direct and moderating effects of organizational commitment and Chinese work values." *Journal of Psychology in Chinese Societies* 4(1), 2003: pp. 7-28.

32. W. R. Boswell, J. B. Olson-Buchanan, and M. A. LePine, "Relations between stress and work outcomes: The role of felt challenge, job control, and psychological strain." *Journal of Vocational Behavior* 64(1), 2004: pp. 165-181.

33. V. Dulewicz, M. Higgs, and M. Slaski, "Measuring emotional intelligence: Content, construct and criterion-related validity." *Journal of Managerial Psychology* 18(5), 2003: pp. 405-420.

34. M. Slaski and S. Cartwright, "Emotional intelligence training and its implications for stress, health and performance." *Stress and Health: Journal of the International Society for the Investigation of Stress* 19(4), 2003: pp. 233-239.

35. S. Zivnuska, C. Kiewitz, W. A. Hochwarter, and K. L. Zellars, "What is too much or too little? The curvilinear effects of job tension on

turnover intent, value attainment and job satisfaction." *Journal of Applied Social Psychology* 32(7), 2002: pp. 1344-1360.

36. L. Van Dyne, K. A. Jehn, and A. Cummings, "Differential effects of strain on two forms of work performance: Individual employee sales and creativity." *Journal of Organizational Behavior* 23(1), 2002: pp. 57-74.

37. Murphy and Sauter.

38. UK National Stress Network, www.workstress.net

39. See report http://www.allbusiness.com/news/daily_news.asp?ID= 2975941#2975940

40. S. L. Sauter, L. R. Murphy, and J. J. Hurrell, "Prevention of work-related psychological disorders: A national strategy proposed by the National Institute for Occupational Safety and Health (NIOSH)." *American Psychologist* 45(10), Oct. 1990: pp. 1146-1158. See also Murphy and Sauter, "The USA perspective."

41. Linda Duxbury and Chris Higgins, "Work-Life Balance in the New Millennium: Where Are We? Where Do We Need to Go?" CPRN Discussion Paper Wl12, Ottawa: Canadian Policy Research Networks, 2001. Available at http://www.cprn.org

42. Abraham Carmeli, "The relationship between emotional intelligence and work attitudes, behavior and outcomes: An examination among senior managers." *Journal of Managerial Psychology* 18(8), 2003: pp. 788-813.

43. Toni Schindler Zimmerman, Shelley A. Haddock, Lisa R. Current, and Scott Ziemba, "Intimate partnership: Foundation to the successful balance of family and work." *American Journal of Family Therapy* 31(2), Jan.-Feb. 2003: pp. 107-124.

44. Duxbury and Higgins.

45. Ibid.

46. Ibid.

47. Ibid.

48. Ibid.

49. Reported in Boston College Center for Work and Family, Executive Briefing Series.

50. Steve Harvey, E. Kevin Kelloway, and Leslie Duncan-Leiper, "Trust in management as a buffer of the relationships between overload and

strain." *Journal of Occupational Health Psychology* 8(4), Oct. 2003: pp. 306-315.

51. Reported in Boston College Center for Work and Family, Executive Briefing Series.

52. Ibid.

53. Reported in Boston College Center for Work and Family, Executive Briefing Series, Business or Busyness: Strategies for Managing Workload. http://www.bc.edu/centers/cwf/news/ (Some of this was compiled from Katcher, 2003, as cited in Bates, 2003; Galinsky et al., 2005; Maslach & Murphy, 2005, as cited in Diane F. Halpern and Susan Elaine Murphy (Eds.), *From Work-Family Balance to Work-Family Interaction: Changing the Metaphor*, Lawrence Erlbaum Associates, 2005; and Galinsky et al., "Overwork in America.")

Chapter 10: Organizational Cohesiveness: We're All in This Together

1. Peter J. Jordan, Neal M. Ashkanasy, and Charmine E. J. Härtel, "The case for emotional intelligence in organizational research." *Academy of Management Review* 28(2), Apr. 2003: pp. 195-197.

2. Lawrence D. Fredendall and Charles R. Emery, "Productivity increases due to the use of teams in service garages." *Journal of Managerial Issues* 15(2), Sum. 2003: pp. 221-242.

3. Craig L. Pearce and Michael D. Ensley, "A reciprocal and longitudinal investigation of the innovation process: The central role of shared vision in product and process innovation teams (PPITs)." *Journal of Organizational Behavior* 25(2), Mar. 2004: pp. 259-278.

4. Phillip A. Chansler, Paul M. Swamidass and Cortlandt Cammann, "Self-managing work teams: An empirical study of group cohesiveness in 'natural work groups' at a Harley-Davidson Motor Company plant." *Small Group Research* 34(1), Feb. 2003: pp. 101-120.

5. Sandra A. Kiffin-Petersen and John L. Cordery, "Trust, individualism and job characteristics as predictors of employee preference for teamwork." *International Journal of Human Resource Management* 14(1), Feb. 2003: pp. 93-116.

6. Peg Thoms, Jeffrey K. Pinto, Diane H. Parente, Vaness Urch Druskat, "Adaptation to self-managing work teams." *Small Group Research* 33(1), Feb. 2002: pp. 3-31.

7. David F. Caldwell and Charles A. O'Reilly III, "The determinants of team-based innovation in organizations: The role of social influence." *Small Group Research* 34(4), Aug. 2003: pp. 497-517.

8. Flavia Cavazotte, "Diversity, efficacy beliefs and cooperation in small work groups: Exploring the role of identification and emotional competence." *Dissertation Abstracts International, Section A: Humanities and Social Sciences* 63(10-A), 2003: pp. 3630.

Chapter 11: Supervisory Leadership: You're Not The Boss of Me

1. Leslie Meyers, "Still wearing the 'kick me' sign." *APA Monitor* 37(7), 2006: pp. 68-70.

2. Ibid.

3. Sadie F. Dingfelder, "Banishing bullying." *APA Monitor* 37(7), 2006: pp. 76-78.

4. M. N. Ruderman, K. Hannum, J. B. Leslie, and J. L. Steed, "Leadership skills and emotional intelligence," unpublished manuscript (Greensboro, NC: Center for Creative Leadership), presented at the Applying Emotional Intelligence to Business Solutions & Success Conference, Toronto, Aug. 9-10, 2001.

5. R. Bar-On, *EQ-i® Leadership User's Guide*. Toronto: Multi-Health Systems Inc.: 2006.

6. Abraham Carmeli, "The relationship between emotional intelligence and work attitudes, behavior and outcomes: An examination among senior managers." *Journal of Managerial Psychology* 18(8), 2003: pp. 788-813.

7. Thomas Sy, Susanna Tram and Linda O'Hara, "Relation of employee and manager emotional intelligence to job satisfaction and performance." *Journal of Vocational Behavior* 68(3), June 2006: pp. 461-473.

8. Kim Soonhee, "Participative management and job satisfaction: Lessons for management leadership." *Public Administration Review* 62(2), Mar.-Apr. 2002: pp. 231-241.

9. Esther Mok and Betty Au-Yeung, "Relationship between organizational climate and empowerment of nurses in Hong Kong." *Journal of Nursing Management* 10(3), May 2002: pp. 129-137.

10. Zhang Zhen, Ma Li, and Ma Wenjing, "The relationship between organizational climate and employee involvement: An empirical study on companies in the Chinese context." *Acta Psychologica Sinica* 34(3), May 2002: pp. 312-318.

11. "Corporate Leaders: It's what you don't know." *Training* Jan. 2003, p. 19.

Chapter 12: Diversity and Anger Management: It's a Wide, Wide World – Take This Job and Shove It

1. Susannah B. F. Paletz, Kaiping Peng, Miriam Erez, and Christina Maslach, "Ethnic Composition and Its Differential Impact on Group Processes in Diverse Teams." *Small Group Research* 35(2), Apr. 2004: pp. 128-157.

2. Warren E. Watson, Lynn Johnson, and George D. Zgourides, "The influence of ethnic diversity on leadership, group process, and performance: An examination of learning teams." *International Journal of Intercultural Relations* 26(1), Feb. 2002: pp. 1-16.

3. F. J. Panzer, "The influence of gender and ethnic diversity on team effectiveness." *Dissertation Abstracts International: Section B: The Sciences and Engineering* 64(3-B), 2003: p. 1534.

4. K. A. Rand, "The measurement of valuing diversity: Construction and use of a new scale for work groups." *Dissertation Abstracts International: Section B: The Sciences and Engineering* 59(5-B), 1998: p. 2470.

5. Vergil Leonard Metts, "Work team diversity and team effectiveness: A correlational field study." *Dissertation Abstracts International: Section B: The Sciences and Engineering* 56(8-B), Feb. 1996: p. 4623.

6. Jeffrey T. Polzer, Laurie P. Milton, William B. Swann, Jr. "Capitalizing on diversity: Interpersonal congruence in small work groups." *Administrative Science Quarterly* 47(2), June 2002: pp. 296-324.

7. Robert T. Keller, "Cross-functional project groups in research and new product development: Diversity, communications, job stress, and outcomes." *Academy of Management Journal* 44(3), June 2001: pp. 547-559.

8. U.S. Merit Systems Protection Board, "Sexual harassment in the federal workplace: Trends, progress and conflicting challenges." Washington, DC: U.S. Government Printing Office, 1994.

9. Adam B. Malamut and Lynn R. Offerman, "Coping with sexual harassment: Personal, environmental, and cognitive determinants," *Journal of Applied Psychology* 80(6), 2001: pp. 1152-1166.

10. L. F. Fitzgerald, S. Shullman, N. Baily, M. Richards, J. Swecker, A. Gold, A. J. Ormerod, and L. Weitzman, "The incidence and dimensions of sexual harassment in academia and the workplace." *Journal of Vocational Behavior* 32, 1988: pp. 152-175.

11. Sandy Lim and Lilia M. Cortina, "Interpersonal mistreatment in the workplace: The interface and impact of general incivility and sexual harassment." *Journal of Applied Psychology* 90(3), 2005: pp. 483-496.

12. See Barry Roberts and Richard Mann, *Sexual Harassment in the Workplace: A Primer.* http://www3.uakron.edu/lawrev/robert1.html

13. Steve Bates, "Hispanics see discrimination in the workplace" (Executive Briefing). *HRMagazine*: Feb, 2003.

14. Nolo.com, "Avoiding Discrimination Based on Race and National Origin: You may not make job decisions based on an employee's race, ethnicity, or national origin." http://www.nolo.com/article.cfm/pg/1/objectId/7A07A84A-481B-48BB-92A7F3BB6531720B/catId/DE34C24C-9CBE-42EF-917012F2F6758F92/111/259/283/ART/

15. Deborah Prussel, "Discrimination in the Workplace." http://www.sfsu.edu/~career/Handouts_Forms/DiscriminationAtWork.pdf

16. Diane Cadrain, "Equality's latest frontier: more companies are knocking down barriers pertaining to employees with nontraditional gender identities—and for good business reasons." (Diversity). *HRMagazine*: Mar. 2003.

17. Marcus Robinson, Charles Pfeffer, and Joan Buccigrossi, "Business case for diversity with inclusion." Rochester, NY: wetWare, Inc., 2003, pp. 2.10-2.16. http://www.rochesterdiversitycouncil.com/docs/Business_Case_3.pdf

18. Charles Fishman, "The War for Talent," *Fast Company*, Issue 16, Aug. 1998, p. 104.

19. Robinson et. al., pp. 2-14.

20. Ibid.

21. Ray Novaco, "Remediating anger and aggression with violent offenders." *Legal and Criminological Psychology* 2, 1997: pp. 77-88.

22. Robert A. Baron, Joel H. Neuman, "Workplace violence and workplace aggression: Evidence on their relative frequency and potential causes." *Aggressive Behavior* 22(3), 1996: pp. 161-173.

23. Raymond DiGiueseppe and Raymond Chip Tafrate, *Anger Disorders Scale Technical Manual.* Toronto: Multi-Health Systems, Inc., 2004.

24. Alicia A. Grandey, Anita P. Tam, and Annalea L. Brauburger, "Affective states and traits in the workplace: Diary and survey data from young workers." *Motivation and Emotion* 26(1), Mar. 2002: pp. 31-55.

25. Caren Baruch, "Organizational factors, anger-related variables, and demographics associated with productivity among NYC DOT traffic enforcement agents." *Dissertation Abstracts International: Section B: The Sciences and Engineering* 58(8-B), Feb. 1998: p. 4497.

26. DiGiuseppe and Tafrate, p. 2.

27. Bureau of Justice Statistics, "National crime victimization survey report, 1993-1999." Washington, D.C.: Author, 2001.

28. Bureau of Labor Statistics, "Survey of occupational injuries and illnesses, 1999." Washington, D.C.: Author, 2000.

29. Bureau of Labor Statistics, U.S. Department of Labor (1995, August 3). National cases of fatal occupational injuries, 1994 [news release]. Washington, DC: Author. See also Northwestern National Life, Employee Benefits Division (1993). Fear and violence in the workplace: A survey documenting the experience of American workers. Minneapolis, MN: Author.

30. See Joel H. Neuman and Robert A. Baron, "Workplace violence and workplace aggression: Evidence concerning specific forms, potential causes, and preferred targets." *Journal of Management* 24(3), 1998: pp. 391-419. See also Robert A. Baron, Joel H. Neuman, and Deanna Geddes, "Social and personal determinants of workplace aggression: Evidence for the impact of perceived injustice and the Type A behavior pattern," *Aggressive Behavior* 25(4), 1999: pp. 281-296; Theresa M. Glomb, "Workplace anger and aggression: Informing conceptual models with data from specific encounters," *Journal of Occupational Health Psychology* 7(1), Jan. 2002: pp. 20-36; and Liane Greenberg and Julian Barling, "Predicting employee aggression against coworkers, subordinates and supervisors: The roles of person behaviors and

perceived workplace factors," *Journal of Organizational Behavior* 20(6), Nov. 1999: pp. 897-913.

31. Theresa M. Glomb, "Workplace anger and aggression: Informing conceptual models with data from specific encounters." *Journal of Occupational Health Psychology* 7(1), Jan. 2002: pp. 20-36.

32. Kirk R. Calabrese, "Interpersonal conflict and sarcasm in the workplace." *Genetic, Social, and General Psychology Monographs* 126(4), Nov. 2000: pp. 459-494.

33. Irene Gianakos, "Issues of anger in the workplace: Do gender and gender role matter?" *Career Development Quarterly* 51(2), Dec. 2002: pp. 155-171.

34. Scott C. Douglas and Mark J. Martinko, "Exploring the role of individual differences in the prediction of workplace aggression." *Journal of Applied Psychology* 86(4), Aug. 2001: pp. 547-559. See also Robert A. Baron, Joel H. Neuman, and Deanna Geddes, "Social and personal determinants of workplace aggression: Evidence for the impact of perceived injustice and the Type A behavior pattern," *Aggressive Behavior* 25(4), 1999: pp. 281-296; Mark J. Martinko, Michael J. Gundlach, and Scott C. Douglas, "Toward an integrative theory of counterproductive workplace behavior: A causal reasoning perspective." *International Journal of Selection and Assessment* 10(1-2), Mar. 2002: pp. 36-50; and Mark J. Martinko, Scott C. Douglas, and Paul Harvey, "Understanding and Managing Workplace Aggression." *Organizational Dynamics* 35(2), 2006: pp. 117-130.

35. Willie Hepworth and Annette Towler, "The Effects of Individual Differences and Charismatic Leadership on Workplace Aggression." *Journal of Occupational Health Psychology* 9(2), Apr. 2004: pp. 176-185.

36. Daniel P. Skarlicki and Robert Folger, "Retaliation in the workplace: The roles of distributive, procedural, and interactional justice." *Journal of Applied Psychology* 82(3), June 1997: pp. 434-443.

37. Melissa M. Sloan, "The Effects of Occupational Characteristics on the Experience and Expression of Anger in the Workplace." *Work and Occupations* 31(1), Feb. 2004: pp. 38-72.

38. John D. Mayer and Peter Salovey, "The intelligence of emotional intelligence." *Intelligence* 17(4), Oct.-Dec. 1993: pp. 433-442.

39. R. P. Thomlinson, "Emotional intelligence, dispositional affectivity, and workplace aggression: An exploratory study." Retrieved Feb. 12, 2004, from http://www.apa.org.

Chapter 13: Organizational Responsiveness: Big Brother Is Looking Out For You

1. Canadian Policy Research Network, www.cprn.com. see also http://www.trainingreport.ca/articles/story.cfm?StoryID=359
2. ASTD Releases New Data in its 2005 State of the Industry Report. Includes expenditures and trends in employee learning. News release, Dec. 6, 2005, http://www.astd.org/NR/rdonlyres/E4406810 -8C04-4796-AB0E-B34851C6238C/8201/ASTD2005StateoftheIn dustryReportpressrelease.pdf
3. Ibid.
4. Report of the Business NZ Skills and Training Survey 2003. Findings of research conducted by Business NZ and the Industry Training Federation of NZ for the Future of Work Research Programme, Department of Labour, June 2003.
5. P. M. Senge, *The Fifth Discipline: The Art and Practice of the Learning Organization.* New York: Doubleday, 1990: p. 3.
6. Ibid, p. 4.
7. Ibid, p. 8.
8. Ibid, p. 9.
9. Nancy Da Silva, Lois E. Tetrick, Kelley J. Slack, Jason M. Etchegaray, Jean Kantambu Latting, Mary H. Beck, and Allan P. Jones, "Is there a relationship between employee perceptions of organizational learning practices and employee performance?" *Psychologist-Manager Journal* 6(1), 2003: pp. 104-116.
10. Senge, p. 203.
11. Ibid, pp. 273-286.
12. Ibid, pp. 287-301.
13. Wesley M. Cohen, Daniel A. Levinthal, "Absorptive Capacity: A New Perspective on Learning and Innovation." *Administrative Science Quarterly* 35, 1990.
14. Canadian Policy Research Network, see also http://www.trainingreport.ca/articles/story.cfm?StoryID=250

15. Graham Lowe, "A Good Job is Hard to Find." *Alberta Views*, May/June 2000.
16. Carol Hymowitz, "Managers Must Counter New Honesty Concerns," *The Wall Street Journal Online*, http://www.careerjournal.com/columnists/inthelead/20020220-inthelead.html
17. Ibid.
18. Ibid.
19. P. Babiak and R. D. Hare, Business Scan (B-SCAN™), Unpublished paper, Toronto: Multi-Health Systems Inc., 2006. See also P. Babiuk, "Psychopathic manipulation at work," in Carl B. Gacono (Ed.), *The Clinical and Forensic Assessment of Psychopathy: A Practitioner's Guide*, Mahwah, NJ: Lawrence Erlbaum, 2000; and P. Babiak and R. D. Hare, *Snakes in Suits: When Psychopaths Go to Work*, New York: Regan Books, 2006.
20. 100 Best Corporate Citizens for 2006: Celebrating companies that excel at serving a variety of stakeholders well. Project Director Marjorie Kelly; article by David Raths; statistical analysis designed by Sandra Waddock and Samuel Graves, Boston College; social data from KLD Research & Analytics.
21. Ibid.
22. Ibid.
23. Adam Grant, "Prosocial Impact Coping: How making a difference makes a difference." Paper presented at the American Psychological Association annual meeting in Washington, D.C., 2005.
24. Maria Vakola, Ioannis Tsaousis, and Ioannis Nikolaou, "The role of emotional intelligence and personality variables on attitudes toward organisational change." *Journal of Managerial Psychology* 19(2), 2004: pp. 88-110.
25. T. A. Judge, C. J. Thoresen, V. Pucik and T. M. Welbourne, "Managerial coping with organizational change: a dispositional perspective." *Journal of Applied Psychology* 84, 1999: pp. 107-22.
26. Warren Bennis, Michael Feiner, John Kotter, Marion Krauskoff, Jeffrey Sonnenfeld, Noel Tichy, and Michael Useem, "Everything you always wanted to know about courage but were afraid to ask." *Fast Company* 88, Sept. 2004: pp. 97-104.
27. Ibid.

28. Merom Klein and Rod Napier, *The Courage to Act: 5 Factors of Courage to Transform Business.* Mountain View, CA: Davies-Black Publishing, 2003.

29. S. J. Stein, "Emotional Intelligence and Performance of CEOs of High Growth Companies." Paper presented at the Society for Industrial Organizational Psychologists (SIOP), Chicago, 2005.

30. S. J. Stein and H. E. Book, *The EQ Edge: Emotional Intelligence and Your Success.* Toronto: Wiley/Jossey-Bass, 2006.

31. Crystal L. Hoyt and Jim Blascovich, "Transformational and transactional leadership in virtual and physical environments." *Small Group Research* 34(6), Dec. 2003: pp. 678-715.

32. Dong I. Jung and John J. Sosik, "Transformational leadership in work groups: The role of empowerment, cohesiveness, and collective-efficacy on perceived group performance." *Small Group Research* 33(3), June 2002: pp. 313-336.

33. Ronald E. Riggio, Heidi R. Riggio, Charles Salinas, and Emmet J. Cole, "The role of social and emotional communication skills in leader emergence and effectiveness." *Group Dynamics: Theory, Research, and Practice* 7(2), June 2003: pp. 83-103.

34. Stefanie K. Halverson, Susan Elaine Murphy, and Ronald E. Riggio, "Charismatic leadership in crisis situations: A laboratory investigation of stress and crisis." *Small Group Research* 35(5), Oct. 2004: pp. 495-514.

35. Manfred F. R. Kets De Vries and Elizabeth Florent-Treacy, "Global leadership from A to Z: Creating high commitment organizations." *Organizational Dynamics* 30(4), 2002: pp. 295-309.

Chapter 14: Putting It All Together—Organizationally, That Is

1. Robert Levering, Creating a Great Place to Work®. *Corrections Today*, Aug. 2004.

2. Robert Levering, "How we pick the 100 best." *Fortune*, Jan. 24, 2005.

3. Levering, 2004.

4. Robert Levering and Milton Moskowitz, "What it takes to be #1: Genentech tops the 2006 100 Best Companies to Work For® in America list." www.greatplacetowork.com

5. Ibid.

6. Richard Caseby, "The *Sunday Times* 100 Best Companies to Work For: A benchmark for excellence." Timesonline, Mar. 5, 2006. www.timesonline.co.uk

7. Pete Bradon and Zoe Thomas, "The *Sunday Times* 100 Best Companies to Work For: Falling in love with your job." Timesonline, Mar. 5, 2006. www.timesonline.co.uk.

8. Ibid.

9. Ibid.

10. Jessica Seid, "Best small companies to work for." CNNMoney.com, June 26, 2006.

11. Zak Stambor, "Employees: A company's best asset: APA honors companies for fostering psychologically healthy workplaces." *Monitor on Psychology* 37(3), Mar. 2006: pp. 28-31.

12. Russ Newman, "Shining a light on psychologically healthy workplaces." *Monitor on Psychology* 37(3), Mar. 2006: pp. 31- 33.

13. Stambor.

14. Mari Keefe and Ellen Fanning, "How they were chosen." *Computerworld*, June 19, 2006: p. 50.

15. Mary K. Pratt, "Inside the Top 5: No. 1 Quicken Loans." *Computerworld*, June 19, 2006: pp. 34-35.

16. Katherine Macklem, "Canada's top 100 employers: No. 1 VanCity Confidential," *Maclean's*, Oct. 11, 2004: pp. 22-36.

17. Robert M. Nideffer, Test of Attentional and Interpersonal Style (TAIS). For information contact www.mhs.com or 1-800-345-6006 (US) or 1-800-268-6011 (Canada) or 1-416-492-2627 for more information.

18. Keith McFarland, "The psychology of success." *INC.*, Nov. 2005: p. 158.

19. Anthony Grnak, John Hughes, and Douglas Hunter, *Building the Best: Lessons from Inside Canada's Best-managed Companies.* Toronto: Viking, 2006.

20. Ibid, pp. 211-233.

21. Jennifer Myers, "Ready for the world." *Profit*, June 2006: pp. 30-40.

22. Kim Shiffman, "Twice upon a time." *Profit*, June 2006: p. 101.

23. Ibid.

The Benchmark of Organizational Emotional Intelligence (BOEI)

The Benchmark of Organizational Emotional Intelligence (BOEI), published by MHS, is a powerful organizational survey designed to measure the level of emotional intelligence (EI) in an organization as a whole, as well as across and among its divisions, departments, and units. Identifying areas for improvement and developing emotional intelligence within your organization will enable your company to:

- promote communication
- improve productivity
- enable employee empowerment, and
- increase job satisfaction.

While there are several definitions of emotional intelligence, they all share basic themes. Organizational emotional intelligence involves people's feelings and thoughts about the work they do, their co-workers, supervisor, top leadership, and the organization itself.

Organizational emotional intelligence can be more formally defined as "an organization's ability to successfully and efficiently cope with change and accomplish its goals, while being responsible and sensitive to its people, customers, suppliers, networks, and society."

The BOEI, a scientifically developed tool, is based on cutting-edge research surveys of more than 2,000 people working in a variety of organizations that include financial services, military, publishing, engineering, high tech, sales, professional services, and others. Factors have been identified that significantly contribute to organizational morale and overall success. The key areas measured are:

- Job Happiness
- Compensation
- Work/Life Stress Management
- Organizational Cohesiveness
- Supervisory Leadership
- Diversity and Anger Management, and
- Organizational Responsiveness.

The BOEI can help build an organization from within by identifying key areas for growth, making BOEI results integral to an organization's strategic plan. The BOEI pinpoints areas of facilitation for management consultants and coaches.

Reports provide results on a) performance of the overall organization, and b) department/unit comparisons. All reports provide practical interventions for the top three and bottom three factors.

The BOEI assessment comprises factors that range from workplace necessities to company ideals. These scales provide feedback on specific areas that impact company performance, allowing organizations and their departments to have a clear picture of where high and low points lie. The BOEI assessment indicates which weaknesses should be targeted and which strengths can be enhanced for the best results.

Total BOEI Score (TB)

The Total BOEI score is the degree to which the organization as a whole is seen to be meeting the basic-, intermediate-, and high-level needs of the people within the organization. This is also the degree to which the organization is able to cope with change and accomplish its goals while being responsible and sensitive to its people, customers, suppliers, networks, and society. The Total score breaks into the following factors and subfactors.

Job Happiness (JH)

This scale measures the degree to which people are challenged and fulfilled by their job. It includes job satisfaction and enjoyment of the workplace.

Compensation (CO)

This scale measures how satisfied people are with their basic pay, bonuses, commissions, vacations, and benefits. It contains two subscales: Pay and Benefits.

Pay

This subscale focuses on people's satisfaction with their pay and the degree to which they believe remuneration keeps them committed to the organization. It includes their feelings about pay as an incentive, fairness of assignment of pay increases, and openness of the organization in sharing financial successes.

Benefits

This subscale evaluates employees' perceptions of the organization's benefit package, specifically its competitiveness, flexibility, and importance in retention.

Work/Life Stress Management (WL)

This scale measures how stable employees perceive the work environment to be, how well they report managing stress, and how balanced they feel their work and home life is. It contains three subscales: Stability, Stress Management, and Work/Life Balance.

Stability

This subscale measures the degree to which the nature and amount of work has remained consistent over the past six months.

Stress Management

This subscale measures how well people report coping with work stressors.

Work/Life Balance

This subscale measures people's success in maintaining a comfortable balance in which job demands do not interfere with home and social activities.

Organizational Cohesiveness (OC)

This scale measures the ability of co-workers to get along and work in cohesive teams. It contains two subscales: Co-worker Relationships and Teamwork.

Co-worker Relationships

This subscale measures the degree to which people in the organization feel they get along, trust each other, and can depend on one another for support.

Teamwork

This subscale measures the degree to which members of a team work well together. It includes trust, morale, complementary skills, group pride, communication, and productivity.

Supervisory Leadership (SL)

This scale evaluates the effectiveness of supervisors as seen by the people they supervise. It measures people's general satisfaction with their immediate supervisors, and specifically examines their perceptions of the supervisor's willingness to share information and involve others in decision making, as well as the supervisor's ability to coach, provide feedback, and mediate conflicts. It also measures perception of the supervisor's trustworthiness, confidence, and self-awareness.

Diversity and Anger Management (DA)

This scale measures the degree to which the organization is open to employee diversity and is free from employee anger and frustration. It contains three subscales: Diversity Climate, Gender/Racial Acceptance, and Anger Management.

Diversity Climate

This subscale measures the degree to which people within the organization are treated fairly, regardless of age, race, gender, culture, physical limitation, or disability.

Gender/Racial Acceptance

This subscale measures the degree to which people are not harassed or discriminated against due to race or gender.

Anger Management

This subscale measures the degree to which the organization has been low in internal conflicts over the previous six months. It deals with verbal and physical aggression as well as attempts at getting even with others or with the organization.

Organizational Responsiveness (OR)

This scale measures the degree to which the organization meets the needs of its people by offering training, encouraging innovation, having an optimistic attitude, promoting honesty and integrity, dealing with difficult issues, solving problems, taking appropriate risks, and providing support in order to meet needs and gain trust. It contains four subscales: Training and Innovation, Optimism and Integrity, Courage and Adaptability, and Top Management Leadership.

Training and Innovation

This subscale measures the degree to which employees feel that training and innovation are valued by the organization. It includes the individualization of training as well as the availability of a career path program within the organization.

Optimism and Integrity

This subscale measures the degree to which employees view the organization as optimistic and honest in terms of what it stands for. It includes perceptions of whether the organization's actions reflect the organization's mission, the degree to which the organization listens to its customers or clients, and whether the organization is socially and environmentally conscious.

Courage and Adaptability

This subscale measures the degree to which employees feel the organization handles challenges head on. It includes the ability to confront difficult issues, solve problems systematically, make decisions efficiently, act on its decisions, and address mistakes when they occur. It also includes taking appropriate risks and organizational flexibility.

Top Management Leadership

This subscale measures the degree to which people see top management as supportive of their ideas and initiatives, committed to earning the trust and confidence of its employees, and devoted to leading with a clear vision that is communicated to the employees.

Validity Scales

One of the unique components of the BOEI is that it contains validity scales. We have found that some employees are overly and unrealistically positive about their workplace. They tend to skew the average score artificially high. Alternatively, some people are overly and unrealistically negative about their workplace. It's important to have the option to filter out those respondents when looking at the organization or department ratings. This provides a more accurate view of the workplace.

Positive Impression (PI)

This scale measures the degree to which people present an overly positive view of the organization.

Negative Impression (NI)

This scale measures the degree to which people present an overly negative view of the organization.

Want to learn more about the BOEI?

To learn more about the BOEI and how it's used in organizations, or to find a consultant who uses the BOEI, visit www.7KeysToGreatWorkplace.com. See the next page for more on how to contact me or find a consultant.

Index

How to Get in Touch with the Author

If you are interested in information regarding the Benchmark of Organizational Emotional Intelligence (BOEI), please call, 1-800-456-3003 (U.S.) or 1-800-268-6011 (Canada) or + 1-416-492-2627 (International). Or you can email makeyourworkplacegreat@mhs.com or visit www.makeyourworkplacegreat.com.

Does your workplace do something creative or extraordinary in one of the seven key areas of workplace emotional intelligence? If so, send it to me for consideration in one of my next books. Please get in touch with me and describe how one or more of the 7 keys I've written about in this book are related to some extraordinary achievement. Stories should reveal how the innovation has made a difference in your workplace.

If you can share such a story with us and our readers, please send it to:

Dr. Steven Stein

e-mail: 7KeysToGreatWorkplace@mhs.com

Please include a return email, fax number, or address. Due to the anticipated volume of responses, we may not be able to reply to everyone who contacts us, but we would like to thank you in advance for your participation.